THE COMPLETE IDIOT'S GUIDE® TO

Critical Reading

by Amy Wall and Regina Wall

ALPHA

A member of Penguin Group (USA) Inc.

We would like to dedicate this book to the newest readers in our family: Joe and Matthew Côté, Tara O'Brien, and Madeline Wall. We wish them a lifetime of wonderful reading experiences and newfound knowledge.

ALPHA BOOKS

Published by the Penguin Group

Penguin Group (USA) Inc., 375 Hudson Street, New York, New York 10014, U.S.A.

Penguin Group (Canada), 10 Alcorn Avenue, Toronto, Ontario, Canada M4V 3B2 (a division of Pearson Penguin Canada Inc.)

Penguin Books Ltd, 80 Strand, London WC2R 0RL, England

Penguin Ireland, 25 St Stephen's Green, Dublin 2, Ireland (a division of Penguin Books Ltd)

Penguin Group (Australia), 250 Camberwell Road, Camberwell, Victoria 3124, Australia (a division of Pearson Australia Group Pty Ltd)

Penguin Books India Pvt Ltd, 11 Community Centre, Panchsheel Park, New Delhi—110 017, India

Penguin Group (NZ), cnr Airborne and Rosedale Roads, Albany, Auckland 1310, New Zealand (a division of Pearson New Zealand Ltd)

Penguin Books (South Africa) (Pty) Ltd, 24 Sturdee Avenue, Rosebank, Johannesburg 2196, South Africa

Penguin Books Ltd, Registered Offices: 80 Strand, London WC2R 0RL, England

International Standard Book Number: 1-59257-340-1
Library of Congress Catalog Card Number: 2005920506

07 06 05   8 7 6 5 4 3 2 1

Interpretation of the printing code: The rightmost number of the first series of numbers is the year of the book's printing; the rightmost number of the second series of numbers is the number of the book's printing. For example, a printing code of 05-1 shows that the first printing occurred in 2005.

Printed in the United States of America

Note: This publication contains the opinions and ideas of its authors. It is intended to provide helpful and informative material on the subject matter covered. It is sold with the understanding that the authors and publisher are not engaged in rendering professional services in the book. If the reader requires personal assistance or advice, a competent professional should be consulted.

The authors and publisher specifically disclaim any responsibility for any liability, loss, or risk, personal or otherwise, which is incurred as a consequence, directly or indirectly, of the use and application of any of the contents of this book.

Most Alpha books are available at special quantity discounts for bulk purchases for sales promotions, premiums, fund-raising, or educational use. Special books, or book excerpts, can also be created to fit specific needs.

For details, write: Special Markets, Alpha Books, 375 Hudson Street, New York, NY 10014.

Publisher: *Marie Butler-Knight*
Product Manager: *Phil Kitchel*
Senior Managing Editor: *Jennifer Bowles*
Senior Acquisitions Editor: *Randy Ladenheim-Gil*
Development Editor: *Lynn Northrup*
Production Editor: *Janette Lynn*

Copy Editor: *Keith Cline*
Cartoonist: *Richard King*
Cover/Book Designer: *Trina Wurst*
Indexer: *Heather McNeil*
Layout: *Ayanna Lacey*
Proofreading: *John Etchison*

Contents at a Glance

Contents

15 Reading Philosophy Books — 185

16 Essays and Memoirs — 195

Foreword

Because Composition is a required course in most colleges, the majority of my students are not English majors. They are studying biology, accounting, psychology, and computer science. While they may feel right at home in the laboratory or at a computer terminal, many admittedly feel uncomfortable turning the pages of a novel.

However, even those students who arrive in class professing a love of the English language and literature—the ones who devour short stories, breeze through essays, actually enjoy poetry—are often surprisingly as deficient in critical reading skills as the students who haven't picked up a book since they were required to read *Of Mice and Men* in high school.

And can you blame them? We live in a fast-paced world, where text-messages and e-mails are the preferred methods of communication. We glance at the headlines over breakfast, take in the latest-breaking news story on the banner scrolling past on the bottom of our TV screens. Is it any wonder that, as an instructor, my first order of business is to convince my students they will have to *slow down* before they can begin to make anything meaningful out of the texts they encounter?

After that, just like dissecting a frog or analyzing numerical data, learning to read critically is a matter of identifying significant parts and examining how those parts are related to each other to make a whole. That's where *The Complete Idiot's Guide to Critical Reading* becomes an invaluable resource for students, or just about anyone seeking to get more out of just about everything they read.

Authors Amy Wall and Regina Wall encourage readers to rely on their natural curiosity to ask relevant questions about what they read—in other words, to become active rather than passive readers. Each discipline has its specialized vocabulary, and early in this guide terms such as simile and metaphor, irony and imagery, and the narrative voice are not only defined but explained. With this knowledge, students are empowered to think, talk, and write about what they are reading.

There are sections devoted to fiction and nonfiction, including poetry, plays, essays, even historical and scientific writing, all written in a clear, engaging style. As an English instructor, I was delighted to find a wealth of excerpts from actual texts used as examples—a poem by Emily Dickinson, part of a short story by Sherwood Anderson—as well as interesting biographical notes about the authors scattered throughout the book, providing a useful context for readers. There are even appendixes with a model for note-taking, a helpful glossary, and a suggested booklist for those inspired by their newly learned skills to begin reading on their own.

Reading critically is about taking the time to make connections—connections that have the power to increase knowledge, experience, and insight. With this book as a companion, anyone—accounting and biology majors included—can master this life-enriching skill.

Jessica Anderson

Jessica Anderson holds a B.A. in English and a Masters of Fine Arts in Fiction Writing from Columbia University. She teaches composition and creative writing at Queens College and Nassau Community College, and is the editor of a local Long Island newspaper. Her short story "Dreams" was recently published in *Carve Magazine*.

Introduction

One of the greatest gifts my parents gave to me is the love of reading. Books were everywhere when I was growing up, and I read whatever I could get my hands on. I can barely remember a time when I didn't know how to read. In fact, it feels like I was born reciting the alphabet.

My parents did not come from families of big readers, it was something they developed themselves as they grew up. It was sometimes hard for them to get their hands on certain books because of their strict Catholic educations—certain books were acceptable, whereas others were not. Well, we all know what happens when you tell curious children not to do something; they do it anyway. So my parents lapped up every book they could get their hands on and went on to be educators themselves: my father a historian, my mother a literature professor (and now a psychotherapist). You should see their unbelievable collection of books that now lines the walls of my mother's home (and her garage!). I have rarely had to go to a library in recent years. I just go to my mother's house.

My parents read to me and my four siblings every night: Books such as *Winnie the Pooh, The Little Prince, Charlotte's Web,* and *Stuart Little* were mainstay favorites. As we got older and discovered that books do not need pictures, we discovered the miracle of being able to read these books for ourselves. Later, you could spot my entire family, every summer, lounging beside a cold mountain lake … reading. We traded books with each other, wearing them down with countless turns of each page.

Despite the amount of reading we all did, that is not what made us good readers. It helped that we all loved books, but what made us really love reading was the ability to talk to each other about the books, argue about them, laugh about them, and admire them. Through sharing books and ideas, we learned automatically to build arguments and back them up with other reading experiences as well as with our own interpretations and ideas. In other words, we learned to make connections between ways of thinking at a very early age.

Our love of books outside of school made us all rather good students in our English classes, which carried over to our history reading and our outside interests in arts and sciences of all kinds. Through the love of words, we learned, on our own, to connect the dots between not only the various books we read but between ideas, complex concepts, as well as abstract and concrete thinking.

Not everyone had the upbringing I did—I consider myself lucky. But everyone has the ability to learn how to read and read well. It starts with a love of books, grows with the desire to learn, and ends with your ability to make connections between ideas and draw conclusions on your own. The whole point of reading is to learn and is completely dependent on your desire to grow as a person.

My mother, Regina, and I took great pleasure in collaborating on this book, and we hope, with all our hearts, that this book helps you discover everything you ever wanted to know about reading beyond the ability just to make sense of the words or even simply the enjoyment of a story. We hope you learn how to make connections and grow your mind. No matter how well read you are, we hope that this book opens a whole new world of ideas for you.

What You'll Find in This Book

Part 1, "Getting Started: Understanding and Inspection," introduces you to the concept of critical reading, or simply put, how to become a better reader. Learn to recognize specific author techniques and find out what gives a book staying power.

Part 2, "All About Fiction," tells you what you can expect from different genres of fiction. Learn what it takes to read and absorb fiction and gain a deeper knowledge of how the material is written. All of this information will help you understand why it is so important to read fiction—and read it well.

Part 3, "Reading Nonfiction," covers every aspect of the nonfiction genres. Learn why it is so important to read history, philosophy, science, and biographical literature. Understand what it means to your personal growth as you learn about the world around you.

Part 4, "The Final Analysis," gives you an overview of what you have read and tells you how to make connections between various pieces of literature. Find out why it's important to connect the dots of understanding to make you not only a better reader, but a more well-rounded individual.

We also include three helpful appendixes. Take a look at the suggested reading list and see how much you have read so far, what books you would like to add to your reading inventory, and even what books you might want to reread now that you know so much more! The glossary is a handy tool to guide you not only through this book, but other works of literature you pick up on your reading journey. Finally, we provide a fill-in-the-blanks template that you can photocopy and keep as your reading diary. Keep a log of what you've read, what you've understood from the reading, and most of all, how the piece of literature made you feel.

Extras

Bookmarks

Check these boxes for tips that may be helpful to you as you become a critical reader.

Look It Up

In these boxes you'll find definitions of specific literary terms and ideas.

Between the Lines

These boxes contain little-known facts that are both fun and informative, as well as helpful related information.

Take Note!

These boxes alert you to things to watch for in your reading.

Acknowledgments

I would like to thank my mother, Regina Wall, for all her enthusiasm and love, and for her expertise, input, and long, hard, late-night writing hours. It was wonderful to share this experience with her. I would also like to thank Jacky Sach of Bookends for her friendship and professionalism. Many thanks to Shelley Hagan for finding the time to edit this book at the last minute, and to Alpha Books for giving me the opportunity to write about the subject we love most—literature.

Finally I would like to thank Grigoriy Lerman for his patience and excellent proof-reading skills—but mostly for his undying love and support. Thank you, honey.

Trademarks

All terms mentioned in this book that are known to be or are suspected of being trademarks or service marks have been appropriately capitalized. Alpha Books and Penguin Group (USA) Inc. cannot attest to the accuracy of this information. Use of a term in this book should not be regarded as affecting the validity of any trademark or service mark.

Part 1

Getting Started: Understanding and Inspection

In this part, we introduce you to the art of reading. What does it mean, exactly, to be a good reader? What's the difference between being well read and reading well? We introduce you to the concept and breakdown of literary genres and give you an overview of each. Begin this section with your eyes wide open because it will give you a strong foundation for the more detailed explanations in the next parts.

You will also learn literary terminology that will help you in any discussions you have about books and assist you with your own writing about literature. You will learn how to identify literary techniques that will boost your overall understanding of one particular book or even an entire literary genre.

Let's Get Critical

In This Chapter

- Curiosity and the reader

- Growing as a person and as a reader

- The importance of objectivity and subjectivity

- Active versus passive reading

- Analytical reading: getting the most from the material

- Understanding the author-reader relationship

> Reading furnishes the mind only with the materials of knowledge; it is thinking that makes what we read ours.
>
> —John Locke (1632–1704), English philosopher

It may be hard to imagine that after several years of education and a pretty good reading list under your belt that you need to pick up a book on how to read. Well, just because you know how to read the words on a page does not necessarily mean you know how to digest the material.

Ask yourself why you picked up this book in the first place. Chances are you probably feel you're not getting as much out of your reading experiences as you would like to. Or perhaps you're looking to become a better reader and don't know where to start. Well, you've come to the right place!

In this chapter, you'll learn that no matter what your experience has been with reading up until this point, you can get more out of the books you read by reading texts with a critical eye.

What Is Critical Reading?

Critical reading begins with one simple thing: curiosity. You were curious enough about this book when you picked it up, weren't you? That's the first step. You've just made your first move toward learning how to read with a critical eye.

When referring to *criticism* in terms of literature, we don't mean "to find fault." Literary criticism is the ability to judge the quality and/or meaning of a piece of writing. Critical reading is a way of reading that will allow you to take a deeper look at literature. It's an acquired skill that you will develop with some knowledge and experience.

Look It Up

Critical reading is a way of looking at a book and analyzing what the author is saying and the methods the author is using to communicate a message or idea. Your analysis is complete when you have formed your own interpretations of the author's intentions.

You may hear certain people referred to as being "well read," which implies that they have read many different books and other forms of literature. But there's a difference between being well read and knowing how to read well. In other words, it's not quantity but quality that counts.

To read critically means to read analytically, which means to question and to think about the written material in front of you. When you question something, it usually leads to finding answers. Keep in mind that there are no *right* answers when you read—there are only the author's intentions and your interpretations.

Insight and Perspective

Consider this book your ticket to understanding literature from new perspectives. In your hands you hold your very own private literary instructor. When you are finished reading this book, you will have a better understanding of what it means to read. (May you never leave a reading group with nothing more than a recipe again!)

But there's a catch! Understanding literature can be taught, but it helps if you have a good understanding of yourself to begin with. What do you believe in? What kind of a person are you? What are your principles? Why are you on this voyage of self-discovery? Why do you need to ask all these questions? Because it identifies what kinds of questions you should be asking yourself. It's simple. The more you understand about yourself, the better you will be at interpreting other points of view, including those you encounter in your reading. In other words, you may agree or disagree with an idea, or you may simply identify with what is being said in a book; if you don't know enough about yourself to begin with, however, you won't know where to start with an analysis of what you're reading.

Growing as a Reader

You may be frustrated to realize that you aren't the reader you hoped you would be when you graduated from high school. Some people realize this when they get to college and are surrounded by classmates who seem to be gleaning invisible information from their textbooks. Other people may realize it when they join a book club and are surrounded by fellow book lovers who seem to be using a decoder ring to crack the secrets of metaphor and meaning in a book. Where are these students and book club members getting this stuff from?

You've always considered yourself a competent reader. You've plowed through Dickens, the Brontë sisters, and Dostoevsky. You've read everything you were supposed to read in school and then some—so why are you the one who always seems to miss what everyone else has grasped in a certain text? You understood the book, you learned from it, and you were even entertained by it, but it's the same old thing every time: No matter how many books you read, you feel you aren't able to absorb them in a way that feels complete and fulfilling.

It's never too late to learn to read with a critical eye. Whether you're looking to score an *A* next semester in your English Lit class, or you want to wow other members at the next book club meeting, you've already grown as a reader, just by realizing that there are some things about this subject you don't know. (But you will know them, and soon!)

Between the Lines

Charles Dickens was a British nineteenth-century author renown for several works of fiction, including *David Copperfield* and *Oliver Twist*. The Brontë sisters (Charlotte, Emily, and Anne) were early-nineteenth-century British authors famed for many works of fiction, including *Jane Eyre, Wuthering Heights,* and *Agnes Grey,* respectively. Fyodor Dostoevsky, a nineteenth-century Russian author, has many books to his credit, including *Crime and Punishment.*

Making the Grade

Many of us realize relatively late in our reading lives that we are not quite the readers we thought we were. The co-author of this book, Amy, has been devouring books since she was old enough to turn pages for herself, but it wasn't until she saw a big letter *B* written in red ink at the top of a paper she wrote for an advanced college literature class that she realized she was missing something.

Amy had construed a rather challenging argument by comparing the two main characters of Henry James's *Portrait of a Lady* and Edith Wharton's *House of Mirth.* Amy called her paper "The Observation of the American Girl." She was very excited about her discoveries as she read the books and decided to base her thesis on the two characters.

Isabel Archer in *Portrait of a Lady* is a poor American girl with wealthy European relatives who finds herself the heiress to a tremendous fortune. A cousin arranges the fortune because he wants to see what will become of this interesting woman if she actually has the means to do all of the exciting things in life he presumed she wanted to do. Lily Bart in *The House of Mirth* is not necessarily as interesting a character as Isabel Archer, but she is very beautiful and manages to survive for quite some time amid her high-society friends thanks to her looks and charm. Both of these literary women were scrutinized by their respective societies and met with very different, although both unhappy, ends.

Take Note!

Summarizing a plot is a big no-no in writing a paper for a class. It works for book reports when you're in grade school, but as a more developed student you're expected to use your analytical abilities to define and defend your argument with facts to validate your point of view.

The way these women are scrutinized by their peers has a great deal to do with their sad outcomes, and that is precisely the argument Amy made in her paper. Unfortunately, what Amy turned out was one gigantic plot summary comparing the two books. Despite the good grades she had received in most of her previous literature classes, this paper was a good idea but had an outcome almost as disappointing as those of Isabel Archer and Lily Bart combined.

Amy did what any good daughter of a literary scholar would do. She called her mom (who happens to be co-author of this book). Regina helped Amy see where she needed to reveal her argument and how to back it up without simply giving a plot summary. Amy's critical eye had been on the right track; she just needed to fine-tune her vision—and the communication of her ideas—a bit.

You may be having the same sort of experiences in your academic career. You think you get it, and then you realize you don't. There's hope for you and your grades. It's just a matter of learning to piece together your reading and your interpretations, and that can only start by taking a closer look at what's been going wrong, either in your reading or in your interpretations.

The Reading-Group Experience

Other people seem to recognize their somewhat cloudy critical-eye vision when they join book groups. Why do you feel speechless in the group? Why didn't you see what *that* person saw? Why can't you answer some of the review questions presented by the group's organizer? You might feel as uninspired by the group setting as you do by your own reading experience. So out of the reading-group experience, you wind up with nothing more than a good recipe for the gooey chocolate fudge that your neighbor brought along. The night isn't a total loss (because, after all, everyone loves fudge), but it's not exactly what you had in mind.

How can you turn this around and get the most out of the book that the group will discuss next month? You guessed it: by learning to read with a critical eye.

> **Between the Lines**
>
> Reading groups have been given new life by TV talk show host Oprah Winfrey. She began a television book club that not only gave authors a mass venue for their work, but also brought reading into the spotlight. You will find many books today stamped with Oprah's seal of approval spawning a new pseudo-genre of literature referred to as "Oprah books."

The Plot Thickens

Knowing the basic structure of literature certainly serves a purpose in your ability as a good reader, and is a crucial building block to understanding the greater meaning in many texts. We explore the following elements in greater detail throughout the book. For now, however, here's a summary of the elements of the basic structure of fiction:

- **Plot.** The action that makes up the story.

- **Theme.** The overall meaning of the story.

- **Character analysis and development.** Who are the characters in the story and what changes do they undergo (if any)? Who are the protagonists? Who are the antagonists?

- **Rising action.** The action that builds to the climax of the story.

- **Climax.** The peak of the story that builds from the rising action and is the turning point of the story.

- **Falling action or denouement.** The build-down of the story that leads to the summation of the plot.

- **Conclusion.** The end of the story, which should include the result of the changes that occur in the characters and lead the reader to a complete understanding of the theme. These are the bricks of a story. You can't just throw them together willy-nilly; otherwise, they'll end up in a pile having formed nothing except a mess. When they're stacked just right, however, you'll see that the whole thing takes a familiar shape, and that you can even point out which elements are which as you read. (The climax, for example, should be easy to identify.)

Curiosity Is Key

Think about some of the books you've read. What made you choose one in particular? Was it the catchy title? The picture on the cover? Interest in the subject matter? The information on the flap of the book or about the author? A recommendation someone made to you? Whatever made you choose the book, chances are, unless you were a little bit curious about it—about the characters in a novel, about the scientist who wrote about his theory of atoms—you didn't get much out of it. Without the tiniest spark of curiosity, you might as well be reading a phone book (and not the oh-so-entertaining Yellow Pages, either).

Learning to read critically will not only start you on a journey to reading well, it will also help you understand all kinds of literature from newspapers to great works of fiction. It is also about you finding out more about your own process—who you are, who you are becoming, what makes you tick.

What does curiosity have to do with critical reading? Absolutely everything! Learning to read in depth, with comprehension, and being open to new ways of thinking and understanding can only start with an itch to want to know more, whether it's for your own personal knowledge or for a class.

Think of it this way: It's one thing to describe a mountain, and quite another to climb it. And to experience the mountain meadows, rock ledges, and paths into the forests is an adventure in itself, but it's even better to have a guide to help you understand the nature around you, making the adventure an even richer experience. And a guide on such an adventure can take you to places you may never have found on your own.

CAUTION Take Note!

Curiosity means that you have a desire to learn about anything and everything. Curiously enough, the word *curiosity* has taken on a folkloric negativity over the ages. *Curious George,* for example, is a children's story about a monkey who always gets into trouble by being curious. And consider the adage "curiosity killed the cat," implying that curiosity is dangerous—which couldn't be further from the truth!

Exploration and Discovery

When you read a book, the author invites you into her world with the use of different literary techniques. As your guide, it's the author's job to guide you through the text using descriptions and dialogue, or to linger in one spot of the story more than some others, all for the purpose of bringing you into her world. Your job is to be curious and to pay attention.

We discuss these at length in upcoming chapters, but for now, here are some definitions of literary techniques authors use to pull readers into a text:

◆ **Metaphor.** Using an imaginative reference (a word or phrase) to represent an object or action without being literally explicit. For example: *A seagull is a laughing jester of the air.*

◆ **Simile.** Using an imaginative reference (a word or phrase) as a description to compare one thing to another (usually using the words *like* or *as*). For example: *The seagull moves like a laughing jester in the air.*

◆ **Symbolism.** A word or phrase used to represent or recall something else like an idea, quality, function, or process. For example, when Snow White bites into a poisoned apple, it recalls the biblical reference of Eve biting into the forbidden fruit in the Garden of Eden. Snow White's experience can be considered symbolic of Eve's actions, while the apple itself can be considered symbolic of evil or wrongdoing. Symbolism is open to interpretation in most literary works.

When you are engaged in the story, the author has done his job. He has grabbed your attention, and now it's your job to intermittently evaluate your reading experience. Start asking yourself some basic critical reading questions:

◆ What kinds of feelings are you having while reading this book?

◆ What do you think and feel about the world the author has created?

◆ Are you noticing a certain style of writing or the use of symbols?

◆ How and why is the author trying to hook you?

Let these feelings be your inner compass. Trust yourself. If you're experiencing some kind of reaction to the book (and you're not being bored to tears—not *that* kind of reaction!), the author has at least done his job well. If you think you're catching on to what the author is saying, you're doing your job. Remember, the depth of your interpretation depends on your level of curiosity.

When you're up for an even more involved look at your response to the book, start asking yourself more questions: What is it about the writing that has grabbed you and taken you along for this ride? Is it a particular character that captivates you? Is it a description of a person, place, or situation that reminds you of someone in your past, or of someone currently in your life? Is it the tone of the book? Is it the story or subject matter that you can relate to? Can you relax into it, the way you can into a comfy chair?

Although the desire to read begins with curiosity, the act of reading is deeply entwined with your process of self-exploration. As with any learning process, you have to take your time. Be patient with yourself and with the written material. When you look at literature carefully, you open yourself up to new understanding and awareness—skills that can carry over into real life, by the way—you did not have before you picked up that book.

The Importance of Subjectivity and Objectivity

Everyone is *subjective*. If you are alive, breathing, thinking, and feeling, you are a subjective individual. In your life experiences, you have feelings and thoughts that shape your perceptions. It is inevitable, therefore, that you will bring that subjectivity to your reading. That is one reason that you will pick out aspects of a book that are important to you. It is the reason you might choose a book that someone else might not choose. It doesn't mean that you are right and someone else is wrong. All it means is that you and that other person are looking at the same book from different perspectives.

Look It Up

Subjectivity is the ability to think from your own point of view with your own ideas, thoughts, and feelings without being literal or impartial.

Seeing the Big Picture

Recently, Regina was at a book-group gathering. The book under discussion was Graham Greene's *The Quiet American*. Different people offered their interpretations of the novel, providing us with a case study in subjective reading.

One person, a movie buff, talked about how vivid the book was in its delineation of character and places, so much so that it lent itself easily to becoming a movie, which, of course, it later was. She experienced the book as scenes and pictures, bringing a more visual perception to the reading.

Someone else in the group remarked on the politics of the Vietnam conflict addressed in the novel, and how he felt some characters were used as symbols. He brought his love of politics and history to the reading of this book, and pointed out every political nuance in it.

Another member of the group noted that the narrator of the story was essentially a stand-in for Graham Greene and his opinions at the time. This man had also read a biography of Graham Greene, which helped him see the autobiographical aspect of the story.

Each person was coming from a different place in terms of what he or she took away from the reading of this book. No one person had gotten at all of it—but everyone got a piece of it. As a result, the group wound up with a greater interpretation of what the book was about through the eyes of its various readers who all came with their subjective viewpoints. If you were to see their opinions as right or wrong, you wouldn't learn from their perspectives; therefore, you wouldn't be able to add even more meaning and significance to your own understanding of it.

Keeping an Open Mind

Objective reading is very different from subjective reading. To read objectively, you have to apply yourself as a student who has something to learn. This can be a greater challenge than subjective reading because it means you have to shut down certain preconceptions or biases that you have as a human being. Objective reading requires you to go into the material with an open mind, which may be a very difficult task depending on how far the book varies from your own subjective thinking.

When you read objectively, you should be asking yourself one basic question from the get-go: What do I want to learn from this article or book? Then, as you continue reading, you should be able to formulate more questions for yourself:

- What does this mean?

- Do I really understand this?

- What am I supposed to be getting from this?

- What is this author trying to say?

- Am I paying attention to the author's prejudices and biases?

- Are my own prejudices and biases coming into play in my reading? If so, what are they?

- Do I agree or disagree with any of these points?

Look It Up

Objectivity is the ability to think with impartiality—that is, without the baggage of your own feelings, point of view, or biases.

And finally, perhaps the two most important questions you can ask yourself are these:

- Has the author proven his or her point?

- What did I get out of this book?

Although your reading experience needs to be as objective as you can possibly make it in order to get the most out of the book, your reaction will be subjective. Sure, you might be able to see the author's points from an objective standpoint, but ultimately what you take away from the book will have a great deal to do with your own feelings and opinions.

Active and Passive Reading

One of the best ways to imagine the difference between active and passive reading is to think of visual media as compared to written forms of media. Some people say that watching TV or movies, or listening to the radio, is a passive activity. You turn on the TV set and images and sounds and ideas are just pumped out at you to be readily absorbed by your brain. Unless you're matching wits with that game show host you love to hate or really busting a move to a song on the radio or taking notes during a movie, it's pretty fair to say that these are passive forms of entertainment.

Now for the flip side—entertainment that engages your mind. Consider the *Harry Potter* books by British author J. K. Rowling. The books came out before the movies and delighted children and adults all over the world. Before the movies were released, many children (and adults) were interviewed about what they thought about the potential of the movies. Surprisingly, many people said they didn't want to see the movies because they didn't want it to ruin their own imaginative interpretation of the books. This is the reason that 9 out of 10 people who have read a book and seen the big-screen rendition of it will say that the book was better. Although many movies are incredible spectacles of sight and sound, very few filmmakers have the ability to one-up a reader's active imagination.

In the most basic sense of the word, reading is an active experience. You pick up the book, open it, put your face in front of it, and move your eyes over the words on the page. When you put the words together and make sense out of them, you've moved the simple action of reading into the more internal action of interpretation. When we read we make up our own world through our imaginative process. Reading engages our minds in a way that visual media cannot.

Action and the Reader

Active reading, then, is the ability to be fully engaged with a book's content. You're affected by the material and conscious of how it's affecting you. You spend time making connections through images, dialogue, and descriptions. You're on a hunt to

Bookmarks

You can find book reviews in anthologies as well as in many local and national newspapers. *The New York Times* has an excellent book review section and also lists the bestsellers in fiction, nonfiction, hardcover, paperback, and children's books.

determine the author's intentions. You're also active in the desire to want to understand the material as well as you can. This means you may find yourself reading reviews of the book or delving into other books explaining literary criticism—or, especially in the case of nonfiction, exploring the bibliography, footnotes, introductions, prefaces, glossaries, table of contents, and notes on further reading—all so that you can understand why the writer wrote the book.

So, What Is Passive Reading?

We've already compared passive and active forms of entertainment. What you may not know is that it is also possible to read passively.

Passive reading is effortless reading. It's when you pick up a magazine or what we refer to as "light reading" (think beach books, "chick lit," romance novels, etc.). You want the words to be easy, and the action to be fast and exciting or relaxed and simple. You don't want to have to think too much. You just want to sit back, relax, and be entertained.

Between the Lines

Everyone has favorite passive reading material, but what is passive reading for some may actually be active reading for others. Although that might sound contradictory, for some people entertainment reading is their only form of reading material and is as active as they may know how to be in their reading experiences.

"Passive reading" is an expression more than anything. You are actively reading the material, but the deeper level of activity (such as looking for symbolism, or wondering what message the author is trying to convey to you) is not as intense as that of active reading. When you read passively, you may not be taking away new ideas or opinions, but you are being entertained.

Passive reading is really only as good as the material you choose to read. It would be very difficult to read Plato's *Republic* passively. If you even tried, you would find yourself digesting absolutely nothing.

Analytical Reading: Digging Up the Skeleton

At the root of every book, whether fiction or nonfiction, is a central idea based on an outline of intentions. Think of the basic structure of the book as the skeleton and the elements that make up the story (and/or the themes) as the organs that complete the body. The life that this body takes on is based on your interpretation. You may wonder why you need to dig up the skeleton at all. Isn't the book's structure inherent in its outcome? Not always. You may find new interpretations if you look more closely at the core of the book. What you think is true in the outcome may change if you look closer at certain elements that make up the book.

Analyzing a book involves the ability to ask questions. Analysis does not have to lead to conclusions, it need only lead you toward a deeper examination. When it does lead to answers, however, it makes for a more satisfying reading experience.

Starting Point: Asking Why, Who, and How

When looking for answers from any text, start by asking *why?* Why did the author need to tell this story? Why did the author need to reveal this particular argument? Why did the author choose this particular way of expressing himself or herself?

After you've exhausted *why*, move on to *who*. Who is this author? Is this the voice of a storyteller? A journalist? A dreamer? A poet? A political activist? Is the author trying to be funny? Is he or she trying to teach me something?

Now, move on to *how*. How did the author put together this piece of writing? As important as it is to be involved in your own process as a reader, you must also be involved in the writer's process. To expose a book's skeleton, you need to focus your interest on finding metaphors and symbols and how they connect with the author's message(s). Even more than that, you need to be interested in the creative process itself and how the author is attempting to communicate his or her message to you.

Don't be afraid to admit there are things you don't know, and don't feel frustrated if you can't answer these questions immediately. After all, you're playing the part of a literary archaeologist here. You're digging to reveal more about the text to yourself. As long as you're asking questions, you're on the right track!

Fiction's Frame

To highlight what it means to dig up the skeleton of a book, let's take a closer look at fiction. Asking yourself certain questions while reading a fictional story can help you to understand more about the story. Keep the following in mind while reading fiction:

♦ How is the plot developed?

♦ How does the author move the story along? Does the story move along, for that matter?

♦ Is there a switch in *narrative voice?* If so, why and how does it pertain to the meaning of the story?

♦ Why does the author repeat a particular phrase? What is he or she trying to emphasize by using that technique?

♦ Is there a historical context that needs to be understood?

Look It Up _____

The **narrative voice** is the style the author uses to tell the story (in the case of fiction). The author and the narrator are not necessarily one and the same. Sometimes the narrator is a character in the story; other times you don't know who the narrator is. But you need to be aware of how he or she is interpreting the action for the reader.

Let's say you're analyzing a Shakespeare play. In addition to researching the time Shakespeare was writing about, it's a good idea to research the times in which Shakespeare lived. How did the political influences of the time infiltrate Shakespeare's opinion of Henry V, for example? Digging deeper will help you understand where the author is coming from, which will reinforce your ability to be objective. That combined with your subjective viewpoint will lead you toward a more balanced conclusion of the literature.

To dig up the skeleton means to find out everything you can about a piece of writing. The more questions you ask, the more informed your conclusions will be.

Recruiting the Experts

Outside resources, such as articles and/or reviews concerning an author and/or story, are a huge help in critical reading. Although your interpretations of a text are important, there may be more you need to know to finalize your opinions and come to accurate conclusions about the material you've read. Utilizing outside sources and applying them to your reading takes some time and experience (mostly in learning how to do research). But remember, a huge part of being a good reader is wanting and needing to know everything you can about a particular subject. Or, in the absence of a burning need to know, good readers simply realize that there are some things they should look up to better understand a text—and then take the appropriate action.

The Author-Reader Relationship

The relationship between the author and the reader is a deeply personal one. How can that be? The author doesn't know the reader, and the reader doesn't know the author, at least not personally. The author is sharing a huge piece of himself—his work—with readers. Through his own feelings, experiences, and ideas, the writer is communicating some kind of message to a large audience—that means he is attempting to communicate with *you*. If the author can connect with a wide enough audience, it means he has successfully communicated a theme that many people can relate to. The author is successful because he has connected with you through the piece of writing. (You'll read more about the author-reader relationship in Chapter 6.)

What the Author Wants

All the author asks is for your time and attention so that he can tell you something. It's really that simple. You may discover that you don't relate at all to what the author is trying to say. You haven't learned anything new for yourself, and you weren't entertained in the slightest by the text. That happens, and it's okay. What matters is that you recognize the message. It is irrelevant whether you agree with it or relate to it at all. The author is asking for a chance from you, the reader; he's not demanding that you accept everything he is saying.

What the Reader Needs

You, as the reader, want to connect with what the author is trying to say. You want to gain more insight into yourself, to learn something you didn't know before, or to be entertained. That makes the author-reader relationship a unique partnership.

Do you want to feel connected to the author? Sometimes authors give lectures about the books they have written. Attending these lectures can give the reader a more

Bookmarks _____

If you're interested in meeting the author, a good way to find his public schedule is to check out his website. Also check the publisher's website or your local newspaper for information. Your local bookstore may offer upcoming author presentations or book signings.

personalized relationship to the writing and with the author. More often, though, the author remains rather anonymous to the reader. He is the mind behind the writing, but you have no idea who the person really is.

What a reader always has in terms of a connection to an author is the piece of literature that's been created for you. Ultimately, the relationship you have with the author will be based on how much time, attention, and effort you give to his or her book.

The Least You Need to Know

♦ Critical reading is the ability to take a more in-depth look at literature with the intention of formulating your own opinions and conclusions.

♦ Curiosity and critical reading go hand in hand. It's very difficult to analyze a text if you're not even a little bit interested in anything about it.

♦ It's important to understand the difference between subjective and objective reading and how and where to apply this skill.

♦ Active reading is the act of putting yourself into the book so that you can find more than what is on the surface. Passive reading is the act of reading for pleasure or entertainment.

♦ To know a book, you need to first have a grasp of its structure. To understand that book, you need to see how the book forms around the structure to give it depth and complexity.

♦ Get to know the author both through her writing and from outside sources such as reviews, book signings, or lectures.

Chapter 2

Types of Literature: Fiction

In This Chapter

- ◆ Why categorize literature into genres?
- ◆ Fiction genres and subgenres
- ◆ The origins, change, and growth of genres
- ◆ How critics have influenced the uses and meanings of genres
- ◆ What genre means to you, the reader

In life we tend to categorize things to make them easier to understand. We categorize jobs, art, news, and, unfortunately, sometimes even people. Literature is no different, and the study of literary categories (or genres) is an art in itself.

In this chapter, you will learn about different types of literary genres with a broad look at how you should approach them as a reader. After giving you an overview of genres, we'll focus on fiction in this chapter and cover nonfiction in Chapter 3.

Genres in General

As a reader, you may already know that there are several different categories of literature, but let's start from the beginning anyway.

Look It Up

Genre, a French word that means "kind" or "type," is used in literary criticism to signify a literary species or literary form. If you are referring to genre in the plural, you add an *s* to the end: genres. Genre as a singular noun does not have an *s* at the end.

Literature basically falls into two category types: fiction and nonfiction. Within the fiction and nonfiction categories are several other subcategories that help to define literature in terms of its type. These subcategories are called *genres*.

Fiction comprises the following genres and subgenres:

1. **Prose fiction.** Stories that are invented

   ♦ Novel

   ♦ Novella

   ♦ Short story

2. **Poetry.** The use of words that tell a story, create an image, or reveal an emotion

   ♦ Dramatic poetry

   ♦ Lyric poetry

   ♦ Epic poetry

   ♦ Prose poetry

   ♦ Haiku

3. **Drama (plays and film).** A performance on stage or in film using dialogue and/or scene setting to tell a story

   ♦ Comedy

   ♦ Romance

   ♦ History

   ♦ Tragedy

   ♦ Horror

Nonfiction comprises the following genres and subgenres:

1. **Autobiographies/biographies.** True stories about a real person's life either written by that person or by someone else

   ◆ Memoirs

   ◆ Diaries (or journals) and letters

2. **Essays.** Commentaries that build an argument or hold to an opinion about any topic (often found in academic journals)

   ◆ Social commentary

   ◆ Political commentary

   ◆ Philosophical essays

   ◆ Satiric essays

   ◆ Theological essays

   ◆ Literary criticism/reviews

3. **Journalism.** Current information about events and people in the world

   ◆ Newspapers

   ◆ Magazines

   ◆ Internet

All creative arts fall into specific categories—for example, painting, writing, music, and film. Each category is represented by a genre. Literature is classified into genres as a means of better understanding what to expect from the writing and a means by which to compare similar types of literary forms.

Why Bother with Genre?

There are many reasons for categorizing art forms, but let's start with the most basic. Think of it this way: A friend tells you there's a great new movie starring Nicole Kidman. You haven't heard of the movie so you ask what it's about. You're not asking for a detailed plot summary; what you really want to know is what genre of film it is.

When you're told the movie is about a woman who lives with her children in a haunted house, you say, "Thanks, but no thanks." You hate scary movies; they give you the willies. By placing the film into a horror genre, you know what to expect when you get there (and you'll make sure you aren't there, in this case). Let's turn to categorizing literature. Your sister happens to know that you enjoy history and you love a good romance, so she recommends a historical romance that she has recently read. If it were just history or just romance, maybe it wouldn't interest you as much, but put the two together and it's a slam-dunk must-read for you.

You and Your Great Expectations

Let's say you've read the poems of William Wordsworth (1770–1850) and Samuel Taylor Coleridge (1772–1834)—British poets who are often compared to each other by literary scholars. In fact, most romantic poetry classes spend some time focusing on and comparing these two poets. The question is: What do they have in common?

Wordsworth and Coleridge were both poets of the romantic era—a time when nature, love, and life were introspectively reflected as intertwining entities. Nature is love; nature is life; life is nature and love, and so on. The romantic poets not only personalized romantic ideals, but translated them into a form that their readers could relate to.

Although Wordsworth and Coleridge wrote quite differently from each other, they basically wrote in the same genre—not just as romantic poets but as lyric poets as well. Coleridge is best known for epic poems such as *The Rime of the Ancient Mariner* and *Kubla Khan*. Wordsworth is best known for his *Ode: Intimations of Immortality from Recollections of Early Childhood*. Together they published *Lyrical Ballads* in 1798— a combination of their work.

They were contemporaries—friends who often wrote together and influenced each other's work, ideas, and styles. But they shouldn't be pigeonholed as lyric romantic poets. They were known to cross genres as well.

Although it's important to recognize the uniqueness of each writer in terms of his or her style and artistry, it's also important to realize how genre can affect writing styles as well as evoke further expectations of the reader. Pick up a Stephen King book and you're ready to have your wits scared right out of you, but King is also responsible for the short story that went on to become the movie *Stand By Me*. Because it's not gruesome or terrifying, many people have no idea that the master of the horror novel penned this story as well. They just don't expect such a tame tale from him.

Between the Lines

Samuel Coleridge's epic poems have become legendary and even part of our daily language. Ever hear the expression that someone has "an albatross around his or her neck"? That actually comes from Coleridge's epic poem *The Rime of the Ancient Mariner*:

Ah! well a-day! what evil looks
Had I from old and young!
Instead of the cross, the Albatross
About my neck was hung.

The Origins of Genre

In *A Glossary of Literary Terms* (1957), M. H. Abrams describes genre as follows: "The genres into which literary works have been classified are numerous, and the criteria for classification have been highly variable; but the most common names still are such ancient ones as tragedy, comedy, epic, satire, lyric, plus some relative newcomers, like novel, essay and biography."

Not much has changed since the 1950s. Categorizing literature into specific genres has always been a useful tool for writers, readers, reviewers, critics, and scholars.

In the Olden Days

We can take the concept of genre back even further. Plato and Aristotle placed literary works into three different genres: lyric, drama, and epic. Believe it or not, these genres, which are well over 2,000 years old, are still useful today. What makes them different from each other, according to Plato and Aristotle, is the way they are presented in terms of action and characterization:

◆ **Lyric.** Poetry usually written in the first person (using I) with the "I" being either the author or another character telling the story.

◆ **Drama.** A play with different characters who have separate identities from the author. Their dialogue reflects their respective personalities, and the author is invisible except in stage direction.

◆ **Epic.** Poetry written as a long narrative in the third person with the poet occasionally making his or her presence known through using first person references.

Keep in mind that there were not as many styles of writing in ancient times as we have now. They had poetry, plays, and nonfiction writing (usually philosophy). Now we have short stories, novels, novellas, autobiographies, memoirs, prose poetry, and so on. Within each of those literary forms are a host of genres and subgenres. We take a closer look at each of these types of classifications in upcoming chapters.

The Bard and His Genres

If you've ever studied the writing of William Shakespeare, you may know that he is one of the most heavily categorized writers in history, not only because he has been so intensively studied, but because he crossed so many genres in his writing. Shakespeare's plays generally fall into four main genres: history, tragedy, comedy, or romance.

Teachers often find that categorizing Shakespeare's work is a helpful way to introduce students to his plays, which are heavily laden with unfamiliar words, antiquated expressions, and archaic theatrical conventions. As a result, educators often have their students begin with one of the lightest Shakespeare genres as an introduction—the comedy (maybe *Twelfth Night* or *A Midsummer Night's Dream*). These plays tend to focus on comical errors and are even fun to read, which makes diving into sixteenth-century England all the more appealing. Teachers then move on to his tragedies such as *Romeo and Juliet* or *Hamlet*. Finally, students are ready to begin reading the "heavies"— histories such as *Richard III* or *Henry V.* If you decide to take your Shakespearian studies even further, you will probably find yourself reading the romances like *Pericles*, *The Tempest*, or *Cymbeline*.

Bookmarks

If you're reading Shakespeare outside of an academic setting, try classifying his works on your own to further familiarize yourself with the concept of genre.

Genres and the Critics

Critics have employed the genre approach to literature in a number of ways over the centuries. From the Renaissance through most of the eighteenth century, for example, they often attempted to judge a text according to what they thought of as the fixed "laws of kind," insisting upon purity—meaning staying loyal to a type of writing. In other words, there was a tendency to pigeonhole various types of writing. So the placement of comic episodes in otherwise serious works was frowned upon, and hybrid types of genres such as tragicomedy were dismissed.

There was also a tendency to rank the genres in a hierarchy, usually with epic or tragedy at the top and shorter forms such as the lyric at the bottom.

Over the ages, literary genres have taken on many forms from the logical to the ridiculous. When Shakespeare was alive, he used to poke fun at some of the critics who categorized, sub-categorized and even sub-subcategorized his plays. For some scholars, this kind of categorization helped them understand not only the writing, but the writer himself. But try telling that to Shakespeare!

> **Between the Lines**
>
> Shakespeare's epitaph reminds us not only of his incredible creative talent, but his sense of humor as well:
>
> *Good friend, for Jesus' sake forbeare*
> *To dig the dust enclosed here.*
> *Blessed be the man that spares these stones,*
> *And cursed be he that moves my bones.*

Genres Through the Ages

Genres cannot be set in stone. Wouldn't it be easy—and boring!—if you could put things in their place and leave them there? Easy, because you would have a clear-cut idea about where it belonged and how to understand it, and boring for the same reasons. If things could be so easily grouped and labeled, there would be no room for growth and exploration.

When studying genres, it's tempting to look for a theory that will hold fast. But it's just not possible. The whole point of reading is to be able to change and grow as a person. If new ideas don't emerge, and genres don't intersect, there will be no room for new interpretations.

Time marches on, people change, writing develops, readers grow, and new critics come into the picture bearing new ideas. This automatically forces genres to shift and to change as well. Writing styles and themes have taken on different forms over the ages, and so the way we classify literature has changed, too.

A Great Leap Forward

In the latter part of the eighteenth century, a drastic alteration took place in the ranking of genres in English literature when the short lyric poem came into existence, which shifted critical theories about genres.

The theory of the big three genres of ancient Greece—lyric, epic, and drama—suddenly shifted when the English romantic poets such as William Wordsworth and Lord Byron came on the scene. Suddenly they were writing introspectively with new ideas and themes—and keeping it brief. Their intention in the short-form lyric style was not to tell an epic tale, but to take a snapshot of a smaller piece of life and give it a philosophical or emotional perspective. They spoke to the everyday persons in terms that they could relate to.

Here is an example of a short lyric poem of the romantic era. It is titled *O Do not Love too Long:*

> SWEETHEART, do not love too long:
> I loved long and long,
> And grew to be out of fashion
> Like an old song.
> All through the years of our youth
> Neither could have known
> Their own thought from the other's,
> We were so much at one.
> But O, in a minute she changed
> O do not love too long,
> Or you will grow out of fashion
> Like an old song.
>
> —William Butler Yeats (1865–1939)

This romantic era of writing changed the concept of genres for eternity. Since then, genres have become arbitrary and convenient ways to classify works of literature.

Look It Up

A **coming of age** novel falls into the literary category of *Bildungsroman* which, when translated from German, means "a novel of formation." A *Bildungsroman* is a novel that tells the story of an individual's growth, usually from childhood to adulthood.

Crisscrossing Genres

As you saw with William Shakespeare, genres are not always so cut and dry. Sometimes a novel (or a movie, or a poem, or any work of art) can fall into a couple of different subgenres. For example, let's return to the *Harry Potter* series, written by J. K. Rowling.

Harry Potter is an unusual *coming-of-age* story. A boy who discovers he is actually a wizard (and perhaps one of the greatest wizards of all time) and learns the hardship, joy, and responsibility that go along with it. Although it's highly unlikely that any adult or child will relate to this specific revelation, that's not what makes people read the books. It's a story that almost anyone can identify with: The aches and pains of growing up, the sadness of loss, the joys of friendship, dealing with bullies and unfavorable teachers—all are depicted in a realm of magical imagination.

Within the stories, Harry and his friends usually encounter some horrifying evil that they must conquer to save themselves and sometimes the rest of the world. There is also often some secret that is disclosed in the book that helps Harry understand more about himself and where he comes from.

So how many fiction genres does this series of novels fall into?

♦ Coming of age

♦ Horror

♦ Mystery

♦ Fantasy

You can look at the books from each of these perspectives. The books crisscross genres, making them more interesting to evaluate as works of literature.

> **Between the Lines**
>
> Did you know that the *Harry Potter* books are so popular they have been translated into more than 55 languages? In 2004, *Forbes* magazine estimated that J. K. Rowling was a billionaire, making her the first writer ever to make that much money off her work. She is said to be richer than the queen of England herself.

What It Means to You

Think about some of the books you've read in your life and try to categorize them. Why? Well, aside from it being a fun exercise, it's a way for you to really grasp the concept of genre.

If you can understand the classification of books, you will be a much better critical reader. For example, if I said the word *Frankenstein* to you, you would most likely conjure up images of a seven-foot monster with green skin, nodes on the side of his neck, walking without bending his legs, his arms outstretched, moaning as he totters from side to side on stiff legs.

But did you know that long before Frankenstein was a popular Halloween costume, Boris Karloff lookalike, or Herman Munster derivative, he was a character in a book, *Frankenstein*, by Mary Shelley, written in 1818?

Frankenstein wasn't even the monster, but the creator. Dr. Frankenstein decided to experiment and create a human being using body parts from cadavers. The result was a "monster" that the doctor immediately rejected out of horror at its hideous appearance. The creature was then left on his own to negotiate a world that didn't want him. Contrary to popular belief, the monster didn't choose victims arbitrarily. Dr. Frankenstein became the focus of the creature's revenge.

The Nature of the Beast

So you've picked up *Frankenstein* and started out with the wrong impression, thanks to pop culture. You have this image of a heartless, murdering giant, so immediately you may think you're picking up a horror novel. And you are, sort of. It's a tale of horror because of the gruesome descriptions of Dr. Frankenstein's work while creating his "monster." But when you read it, you might find that you have a different reaction to the story—one that makes you think the story fits another category as well, such as drama or tragedy.

You can even make the argument that the book is also a *Bildungsroman*, or novel of formation. *Frankenstein* begins with a creature who is given a brain and is able to think, learn, and feel strong emotions. When he is abandoned by his creator, he is like a sad orphaned child left to learn the hard, cruel ways of the world all alone. All he wants is to be loved by the man who made him. He is innocent when he begins his "human" existence, and by the end he is bitter and angry. His experiences, then, form him. It's possible that you will relate to the lost monster in some way. After all, many of us, at some point in our lives, have felt the same way.

In most horror stories, the author writes so that you sympathize with the victim and not the assailant. Shelley, however, makes us think beyond that. She takes a risk, as every good author should, to make us see the horror with more pathos. By allowing us to know the monster, by allowing us to hear his thoughts and experience his feelings, Shelley is allowing her readers to empathize with the creature and question the behavior of the creator. The reader is left wondering what the heck happened to their preconceptions about the book, and just who the heck the bad guy is in the story. That's an interesting twist on the traditional horror story, isn't it? This is a great example of how pigeonholing a book into a single genre can end up being a wildly inaccurate practice.

Bookmarks _____

If you're part of a book club, why not suggest reading *Frankenstein* for your next meeting? Introduce the idea of pathos in reference to the monster and see what reactions people have. Try to see the story from the monster's perspective and help others see it, too. If you can do that, you can reclassify the book for yourself and for others, and you just might start your book-club pals on the path to considering how other books are categorized (correctly and/or incorrectly).

In the Eye of the Creator

Isn't it amazing that you can empathize with a monster? Because of this newfound angle on the story, don't you want to find out more about Mary Shelley, the author of the book? Why did she take this approach? Was it intentional, to make you feel sorry for the monster, or did she want you to feel sorry for the doctor? Did she feel that she was like Dr. Frankenstein in that she was the creator, too, by virtue of being its author?

Scholars have surmised that the monster was actually Shelley herself. She ran away from home at the age of 16 to be with her future husband. As a result, she was cast out of society and shunned by her parents. Perhaps Shelley created the monster from her own painful real-life circumstances. Does this knowledge change what genre you think the book might fall into? Shelley may have written this book as a condemnation of the restrictive society she was a part of; maybe she wrote it as a way to purge her own demons, seeking her own kind of revenge on the family who abandoned her.

It might also be interesting to look at the book from a strictly historical perspective. How did the early-nineteenth-century readers view the book? Did they feel sorry for the monster, or is that a modern-day concept? Would nineteenth-century people feel sorry for the doctor the way you might have? Did they see any analogies to their political or social climate?

> ### Between the Lines
>
> Mary Shelley was born in 1797, and became a key literary figure in the British romantic era. She was the daughter of the famous feminist author Mary Wollstonecraft and philosopher and novelist William Godwin. Later she married poet Percy Bysshe Shelley. She died in 1851 of a brain tumor.

By knowing more about the author's life and intentions, you have a better shot at correctly categorizing any work of art. And when you understand genre, you will be able to define the book in so many different ways. Some books will remain in one genre, whereas others will span over several different ones—depending on your interpretation and your ability to build a case for your arguments.

The Least You Need to Know

- ◆ Categorizing books into genres means to find the type (or kind) of book it is.

- ◆ You will know what to expect from a book if you know what genres it fits into.

- ◆ The concept of the genre has its roots in ancient Greece.

- ◆ The standard for genres took a drastic turn in the eighteenth century with the introduction of the short lyric poem.

- ◆ Some books fit more than one genre.

Types of Literature: Nonfiction

In This Chapter

♦ Nonfiction genres and subgenres

♦ Practical and theoretical nonfiction

♦ Understanding biographical writing and essays

♦ Media as nonfiction

Like fiction, nonfiction is classified into genres, usually based on subject matter. Nonfiction subject matter falls into two main categories: practical (informative writing) and theoretical (experimental writing).

It is as important in nonfiction as it is in fiction to know which genre you are reading in order to gain a full appreciation of the reading experience. You will probably be able to classify your reading quite easily. In fact, the more nonfiction you read, the easier it will get.

In this chapter, in addition to learning how important genre is to non-fiction reading, you learn the differences in nonfiction genres and how to identify them.

Nonfiction Genres

Scholars and critics do not overly concern themselves with classifying nonfiction into genres because nonfiction literature is fairly cut and dry and doesn't cross boundaries quite as often as fiction tends to. Nonfiction shouldn't cross over into the fiction genres, whereas fiction often crosses over to nonfiction. (Confused? Keep reading!) For example, you can read a novel about a fictitious person who lives in the court of Queen Elizabeth I of England. The historical facts are authentic, but the main characters and the dialogue are not.

One incidence where nonfiction material can cross into the genre of fiction is when an author writes an autobiographical novel. The story may be based on certain truths from his life (for example, a character based on himself or someone else from his real life). Another example is when an author inserts his or her opinion into a work of fiction—something Mark Twain liked to do quite often. Twain regularly employed illogic, unreasonableness, and bizarre assumptions to make the reader laugh while simultaneously slipping his message between the lines, so to speak.

For example, in *The Adventures of Huckleberry Finn*, Twain paints a picture of Huck's guardian, Widow Douglas, as a harsh, judgmental Christian. Twain himself was not a fan of religion, and believed zealots such as Widow Douglas did more harm than good in the world. However, rather than say this straight out, Twain writes a humorous exchange in which the widow harasses Huck about his godlessness. The reader, of course, is on Huck's side, thinking that Huck's righteous guardian should give him a break. Who knows how many readers took that message with them, though, and carried it over into their lives?

Even though he uses humor, his purpose is a serious one, to alert and to teach the reader. But the only way to know what Mark Twain intended is to get to know Mark Twain as the man and the author and to become familiar with his intentions for his readers.

> **Between the Lines**
>
> Nonfiction is factual information written as truth—in both practical and theoretical ways. It differs from fiction in that fiction is intentionally invented and does not claim to be truthful in any way.

Practical Nonfiction

On the most basic level, nonfiction can be divided into two categories: *practical* and *theoretical.* Practical books (such as this one, for example) require you, as the reader, to take some kind of action. If you were to read this book as the theories of Amy and Regina Wall on critical reading, you wouldn't be required to do anything but peruse it and think about it. But the goal of this book is to teach you something. And for you to learn from it, you have to actually go do some of your own work—such as taking notes on what you've read, doing some further reading on literary criticism or about the author of a particular book, or talking with others about what you have read. This book is a starting point, a little kick in the pants. The rest is up to you as the student.

Different kinds of practical books include the following:

- Self-help books

- Instruction manuals, books, and guides

- Cookbooks

- Textbooks

- Travel guides

- Reference books such as dictionaries, encyclopedias, and thesauruses

Theoretical Nonfiction

The other type of nonfiction you will encounter is theoretical. Theoretical books don't require you to take any action except thinking. An author of a theoretical book chooses an idea and then tries to prove it to you by backing up his or her idea with facts.

For example, someone who writes a book on the decline of the Soviet Union will have a theory about why the Soviet system didn't work. Whereas one person might blame the decline on communist theory itself, others will insist that it was international pressure that made the system economically unsound. Then maybe someone else will determine that it was the internal politics that made the system collapse in the end.

Look It Up

Practical nonfiction is usually a teaching tool that requires you to take further action on your own after you've finished reading. **Theoretical** nonfiction reading is designed to help develop the way you think.

In theoretical nonfiction, it's the author's job to prove his theory to you, the reader. For any argument to be valid, the author must back it up with facts and sound ideas.

You are not required to do anything but read and decide for yourself whether the author has done his job.

Some categories of theoretical nonfiction include the following:

♦ Historical

♦ Philosophical

♦ Theological

♦ Scientific

Within each of these types of theoretical nonfiction categories are several more sub-categories. For example, books on mathematical theory or astronomical theory would fall under the scientific book category, whereas the study of Judaism or Christianity would fall under the theological category.

Reading About Someone's Life

Books about someone's life, whether written by that person or by someone else, would fall under the category of theoretical nonfiction. You might be wondering how this is possible if their lives are factual and not theoretical. Although you would expect an autobiography, memoir, or journal to be factual—because it is written by the person who lived the life—you just can't know for sure whether the story is true. Without having lived that life, you will never know; you can only trust that the author is being truthful. In fact, autobiographical nonfiction is really someone's own theory and perception of who he or she is.

Suppose, for example, that you have written an autobiography about what a great person you are and all of the wonderful things you have done for various charities. Someone else could write another book refuting your claims, saying that your generous contributions were actually tax write-offs, and you benefited more than anyone. There's no way any one of us, as readers, can really know the truth.

And ultimately, reading autobiographical nonfiction does not require you to do anything except read and think—another reason this type of nonfiction would be considered theoretical.

Biography Versus Autobiography

Although nonfiction cannot cross the boundary to the fiction genres, nonfiction can be written as though it were fiction. For example, the biography by Mitch Albom called *Tuesdays with Morrie* is a work of nonfiction. It's a story about the lessons a man learns from his dying college professor whom he hasn't seen in 20 years. Before he dies, Morrie teaches his former student, Mitch, how to live. You get to know these real people in the same way you would get to know the characters in a work of fiction.

Although this is a true story with real-life characters, it reads like a novel and even like a philosophical piece of nonfiction. And although *Tuesdays with Morrie* is technically a biographical tribute to Morrie, a reader could argue that it's also an autobiography, because after all, who is this book really about? Morrie or Mitch?

Biographies are theoretical nonfiction. The author of the biography can only theorize what that person's life was all about. To draw your own reasonable conclusions, it is best to read several biographies about that person.

Since not everyone is a writer, there are people who will hire someone to write about his or her life. An author will often write the biography based on a series of conversations or interviews. When the subject agrees to or approves of a book about his or her life, it means that the biography is authorized. An unauthorized biography is written by doing research about a person without the person's consent or approval.

Look It Up

Getting confused about what's what? Here's a handy summary:

- An **autobiography** is a life story about a person written by that person.
- A **biography** is a life story written about someone else's life.
- A **memoir** is a detailed, sometimes chronological telling of significant events in a person's life, written by that person, focusing on some sort of theme.
- A **journal** is a writer's observation of daily life and what it means.
- A **diary** is different from a journal in that it often only reflects day-to-day events without tying them to any greater meaning.

Autobiography Versus Memoir

Although it is quite clear that a biography is written by someone about someone else's life, what is an autobiography, or a memoir, for that matter?

Ask yourself why someone would write an autobiography. Most people do it because they feel they have gone through some kind of transformation in life that they want to share with others or because they've had a very interesting and/or unusual life, and they believe the particulars of their existence are interesting enough to share with others. (Many of you may be saying "Come on, it's for the money!" Well, that may be true—but only if the writer expects to sell millions of copies of his book.)

So how is an autobiography different from a memoir? An autobiography is a life story that shows the growth of an individual through his or her life experiences. It's an exploration of identity that often reflects a person's development from childhood to adulthood. Memoirs follow a certain theme, and the writer tries to make sense of what certain past events mean to his present-day life.

Most books that are marketed as memoirs aren't memoirs at all; they're high-priced, hardcover tabloids. A celebrity who writes a "memoir" detailing whom she regularly lunches with and how much she pays for shoes isn't really sticking to a theme, and she's probably not wondering how paying $600 for a pair of boots last year has affected her life. A book focusing on that same celebrity's struggle to overcome poverty during her childhood could be considered a memoir (and then she could even throw the shoe thing in there as a way of saying "I made it!").

Between the Lines
Autobiographies can really grab the reader's interest. Stores had a tough time keeping Bill Clinton's *My Life* in stock when it was first published in 2004. The primary reason people bought the book was probably to find out more about his affair with Monica Lewinsky and get the behind-the-scenes scoop on how his wife and daughter dealt with his very public infidelity. Another reason for the book's popularity, of course, is that Bill Clinton had been president of the United States. Would he share unclassified information that we may be interested in hearing in this post–9/11 world?

Journal or Diary Writing

One of the most famous diaries ever written is *The Diary of Anne Frank*. Anne Frank was born in Frankfurt, Germany, in 1929. The Frank family fled to the Netherlands in 1933 after Adolf Hitler was appointed chancellor of Germany. In 1942, the family and four friends went into hiding in Amsterdam. In 1944, the family was found by the Nazis and sent to various concentration camps. Anne later died in the Bergen-Belsen camp. She was only 15.

The Diary of Anne Frank is Anne's day-to-day recounting of her life. She shares the story of her time living in cramped quarters by writing everything down, at times writing to herself, at other times to an imaginary person whom she called "Kitty."

Anne Frank's diary cannot be called an autobiography because she wrote it day by day. Although there is room for some reflection on her past and present and ponderings about the future, there is no way she can reflect on her changing self because she is still developing. Also, autobiographies are most often intended to be the author's life story, presented to the masses. Anne did not begin writing her diary with the intention of having anyone read it.

When she began her writing, Anne had no idea her youthful interpretation of wartime events would be studied in schools and made into motion pictures and stage productions. She didn't intend for her writing to become a historical document and an inspiration to future generations. So although *The Diary of Anne Frank* is an inspiring true story, it doesn't fall into the category of a true autobiography.

The Essay

The essay also falls into the classification of theoretical nonfiction. An essay is a brief composition in prose that attempts to discuss a matter, express a point of view, or wants to persuade the reader to accept an idea. The essay is different from a treatise or dissertation because it doesn't pretend to be a complete explanation of anything. The essay is for a more generalized (rather than specialized) audience. A treatise or dissertation usually pertains to one particular subject such as *Media Scrutiny of the Presidency* or *Violence in the Art of Francis Bacon*. Dissertations are written for people specializing in a specific area. An essay, however, can be read and understood by pretty much anyone. An essay topic could be *Moving from the Big City to a Dairy Farm* or *My Trip to the Everglades*. That's not to say that an essayist in not knowledgeable, but he is writing for the general population.

Media as Literature

Journalism is a specialized field that serious and respected writers spend years perfecting as a craft. The object of American journalism is to report facts objectively as they occur in the world. The type of newspaper or magazine you choose to read will determine what kind of journalistic information you will be receiving.

Look It Up

Journalism is the reporting of current events, based on factual information, for public information and can be found in newspapers, magazines, on television, and on the radio.

It may seem strange to place media under the category of theoretical nonfiction, but in fact it is. In digesting media reports, you are not required to do anything but read (or listen), think, and draw your own conclusions. In fact, you can even subcategorize journalistic media into the history genre of nonfiction. Current events change with every passing day and eventually become our history. When you compare certain historical situations to current-day events, you will often come out with a theoretical concept. For example, there is no way you can understand why there is violence in Israel right now without understanding the history of that region and the struggles of the people who live there.

Newspapers and Magazines

The New York Times, *The Wall Street Journal*, *The Washington Post*, *The Chicago Tribune* and *The San Francisco Chronicle* are some of the most respected newspapers in the United States. This is because they make every effort to hire talented writers, editors, researchers, and fact checkers who do their best to be objective and stick to the art of their craft as unbiased journalists.

Of course, human beings have opinions, and one can spot biases in even the most respected print media. This is where it is critical for you to be a good reader. The more you read, the more you develop your own opinions, which will enable you to spot poor or slanted journalism and draw your own conclusions about what is being reported as "fact."

There are international, national, regional, and local newspapers, all of which provide different levels of information. It just depends on what you want to know.

There are many different genres of magazines as well. There are news magazines such as *Time*, *Newsweek*, and *US News and World Report*. These magazines are published weekly and often reflect upon current news stories or recently published medical studies. They give you longer, more in-depth looks at particular stories in the news.

There are countless magazines out there for your perusal, too: entertainment, travel, home decorating, cooking, society, and … well … lewd periodicals. Magazines tend to include specialized information about specific areas of interest.

> **Take Note!**
>
> This kind of media is renowned for inventing "news" or writing stories based on unreliable sources. That doesn't mean all tabloids are full of lies, but the content and the way they report their "news" should leave you questioning the truthfulness of any tabloid story.

Literature on the Internet

Many respected newspapers and magazines have websites where they publish articles in addition to printing their papers. This enables people to sit at home and read the same headlines they would in the daily paper without getting newsprint all over their hands. Television stations also publish transcripts of their programming so you can be sure you didn't miss anything.

But beware! Anyone can publish anything on the Internet. It's simple to get a domain address and create a web page. That means absolutely anyone can create articles that appear to be factual news stories. The sites look respectable, but you have no idea who is behind the writing. Many of these sites are referred to as blogs. Try to stick to websites of well-known and well-respected news organizations. If you don't, you will probably be reading more gossip than truth.

Now that you know everything about genres of literatures, you have more information to help you in the development of your reading skills. Knowing the genre will open your eyes in new ways to the literature in front of you.

The Least You Need to Know

- ◆ Practical nonfiction requires the reader to follow through with some kind of action. Theoretical fiction requires only reading.

- ◆ The more familiar you are with nonfiction genres, the easier it will be to know what you are reading.

- ◆ Nonfiction can be opinionated, so always keep your own ideas on hand as you read.

- Autobiographical nonfiction focuses on the retelling of the author's life.

- Media also has a place as a nonfiction genre.

- Don't always trust what you read as "news" or "fact" on the Internet.

Chapter 4

What's Between the Covers?

In This Chapter

- ◆ How the novel is structured
- ◆ Where to find clues about a book's content
- ◆ Examining nonfiction
- ◆ A close look at references and sources
- ◆ How a book "grabs" you and keeps you interested

How many times have you opened a book—any book—and skipped over the table of contents, the preface, and even the blurb on the back or on the inside dust-jacket flap? We all want to get right to the nitty-gritty, but it might pay to slow down a little and take your time with a book before you plunge in. Before you invest time and money in a book, it's important to know what you're about to read.

There are plenty of readers out there who have countless books on their bookshelves that sit unread because they weren't enjoying them after they brought them home. You should plan to check out the book thoroughly before you buy it to see whether it holds any interest for you. A good examination of a book can prevent this from happening to you and will even leave you some extra space on your bookshelf.

Inspecting Fiction

When you pick up a novel you have never read before, you really have no idea what to expect. But there are clues all over the book that can guide you. For example:

- Title and cover

- Table of contents

- Introduction and preface

- Structure and style

- Appendixes such as a bibliography, glossary, and footnotes or endnotes

When you're first examining a book, one of the first things you'll do is flip the book over and read the blurb on the back or open the book, in the case of most hardcover books, and read the inside flaps of the dust jacket. The back cover or inside flaps usually give you a quick summary of the book without giving the story away. They are written to pique a reader's interest. The back cover may also include a few lines from recent book reviews. But remember the reading material has to call out to you somehow. Reviewers and enticing blurbs aside, what you think is all that matters.

Bookmarks

Your local library is a great resource for book inspection because you can borrow several books at a time. This way you can look them over at your leisure without feeling any pressure to spend money.

In the following sections, we take a tour of the parts of a book. If you're going to become a good reader, it's best to get acquainted with the basics of what you'll find inside the book.

Let Me Introduce You

When someone introduces you to a friend at a party, he or she will often disclose a few details about the person that will help you grasp who it is you are talking to. For example, you might be introduced to someone thusly: "This is my friend Jill. We were roommates at the University of British Columbia when I studied in Canada for a semester."

This introduction tells you about the relationship between Jill and the other person. You know that they have maintained a relationship over the years and that Jill might be Canadian. So that information combined with what you already know gives you a starting point to launch a conversation. That's exactly what the introduction of a book can do for your reading experience. It can (and hopefully will) give you some of the information you need to decide whether you want to continue with the book.

Sometimes a book will be introduced by someone other than the author. If the book is in reprint, for example, or if the author is deceased, sometimes a scholar familiar with the writer or an editor who worked on the edition will write the introduction.

For a good analysis of the examination of a novel, let's take a look at some novels both old and new. You may have already read *The Scarlet Letter* by Nathaniel Hawthorne, in which case you're one step ahead, but let's take more introductory look at this classic nineteenth-century novel. Published in 1850, it's about a woman accused of adultery in seventeenth-century Boston. She is humiliated in front of her community by being forced to wear a scarlet letter *A* on her clothing.

The Scarlet Letter has one of the longest introductions of any piece of fiction, and it is extremely important that you read it to get a full understanding of the novel. Hawthorne explains what led him to write the novel in the first place. Hawthorne even gave the introduction a title, "The Custom House," which ties his introduction specifically to the content of the book.

> **Bookmarks** _____
>
> Although it's common and logical to read an introduction before beginning a book, in the case of *The Scarlet Letter*, it's a good idea to read this introduction *after* you've finished the book. Form your own opinions about the book first, then go back and read what Hawthorne had to say about his writing.

Title

As readers, we are always struck by the title of a book—which is often the first clue to what we'll find inside. Hawthorne chose a good title, as well as a very accurate one, because it is also symbolic of what the book is about. So the basics begin with the title. *The Scarlet Letter?* What could that possibly be about? The title is an attention grabber, which makes you want to know more.

Table of Contents

Part of inspecting a book is to read through the table of contents. This applies to fiction and nonfiction alike. (Not all novels contain chapter titles. Sometimes chapters are just numbered, so you will not always find a table of contents.) Authors and editors work very hard to make a table of contents as concise and relevant for the reader as possible. In a novel, the chapter titles offer clues as to what you will find inside as well. Take a look at the table of contents of this book. You'll see it is carefully constructed to let the reader know exactly what to expect from the text.

The Scarlet Letter has 24 relatively brief chapters. And this novel does contain a table of contents. If you look it over carefully you may find the chapter headings intriguing. The first four chapters and their titles are as follows:

Chapter I: "The Prison Door"

Chapter II: "The Market Place"

Chapter III: "The Recognition"

Chapter IV: "The Interview"

Every chapter name represents exactly what you can expect that chapter to be about. It was as if Hawthorne had no time to waste. He knew exactly what he wanted to say, and he said it. In fact, he had the whole book in mind before he ever sat down to write a word. He wrote it in a matter of weeks.

Opening Lines

As a child Trudi Montag thought everyone knew what went on inside others. That was before she understood the power of being different. The agony of being different. And the sin of ranting against an ineffective God. But before that—for years and years before that—she prayed to grow.

—Ursula Hegi, *Stones from the River* (1994)

Let's look at another way of checking out a book using a different book as an example. These words are the introductory words of a novel called *Stones from the River*, a book about a German girl who is physically different from the other people in her life and how she struggles with loneliness during the tumultuous times of World War II.

Different readers have different feelings about the opening lines of a novel. Amy happens to like it when an author grabs her in the first few sentences, or in the first paragraph. If the author doesn't do this, however, it's not a reason to stop. Other people enjoy a slow buildup to the story—a description of a place or a main character, for example. But the opening words of *Stones from the River*, combined with the blurb on the back cover, were more than enough for Amy to want to take this book home and stick with it through the next 525 pages.

The Blurb and the Dust Jacket

Here is what it says on the back cover of *Stones from the River*:

> Trudi Montag is a *Zwerg*—a dwarf—short, undesirable, different, the voice of anyone who has ever tried to fit in. Eventually she learns that being different is a secret that all humans share—from her mother who flees into madness, to her friend Georg whose parents pretend he's a girl, to the Jews Trudi harbors in her cellar.

If you are currently a reader, you know that it's instinct to flip the book over and read the back or, in the case of a hardcover, to open the book and read the inside flaps of the dust jacket, where the publisher will often provide a summary of the story. After the title and the cover, of course, the next thing you want to know is what it's all about. Some cover blurbs are better than others, but the blurb combined with the opening lines of a book will often be the elements that make you want to know more.

Sense of Style

If nothing really entices you to want to read the book, read the opening paragraph or even a few paragraphs from the middle of the book to get a sense of the author's style. Is the style something that appeals to your own reading sensibilities? Is the tone something you think you might relate to? Maybe the book is written in a completely different way than what you are familiar with and you feel you're up for a new challenge.

It's important to pay attention to the author's style and tone. This book could be with you for several weeks, and you want to get the most you can out of it. There's no point in reading something that you won't absorb or that will bore you to tears.

CAUTION

Take Note!

You don't have to like a book to stay with it, but the book itself has to offer you something that will keep you reading it, such as a new perspective or way of looking at an issue. Sometimes it's important to keep reading a book you completely disagree with. It will just make you a more interesting person with an even more diverse outlook on life.

Bibliography

A bibliography provides source material for a book and is usually found at the back of a book. In some scholarly works and textbooks, you will find endless pages of bibliographical references. These bibliographies can be invaluable to your own studies. If you are looking for source material for your own academic work, or just for further reading on the same topic, a great place to find it is in someone else's bibliography. Nonfiction is not the only reading material to have a bibliography. You will find that novels that have been read, analyzed, critiqued, and studied by literary scholars (commonly referred to as the *classics*) often have a bibliography at the end.

In Regina's copy of *The Scarlet Letter* there is a bibliography. It's not Hawthorne's bibliography, however; it's that of the person who wrote another introduction to her particular edition. This can come in very handy if you are looking to read more about Hawthorne and his work.

Further Reading

Many modern-day books contain appendixes indicating other resources to read for further information. Suppose you have a question about something the author has written and you wonder where you can learn more about that topic. At this point, you can flip to the back again and check out some of the suggested reading material.

The suggested reading list will be arranged in a bibliographical format. That means it is in alphabetical order by author's last name.

Another example of an appendix may be a list of questions that may be pertinent within book group settings. Even reprinted books, such as *The Scarlet Letter*, contain such appendixes.

Reading the extra material provided in any book will guide you to a deeper understanding of how the book was written, why it was written, and what was going on in the author's life and times. In the case of Hawthorne, you will even find out what led him to write this story.

Inspecting Nonfiction

Now let's take a look at some nonfiction, which includes books about science, philosophy, history, biography, autobiography, art, music, and a full range of special interests.

Regina enjoys reading about science and looks for books that will appeal to the regular person—those of us who are not scientists. We're just enthusiasts who read out of curiosity. This kind of reader does not have any kind of specialized training in the subject but wants to know more about it. You can find books like this for the layperson in almost all specialized fields of knowledge.

Format at a Glance

Regina has a stack of books she is getting ready to read. The next science-related book she plans to delve into is *The Elegant Universe* by Brian Greene.

Brian Greene is one of the world's leading physicists, and the reason Regina picked up his book is that he promises the reader (on the inside dust-jacket flap) the opportunity to "look at reality in a completely different way." Now, what better offer could any reader ask for? This intrigued Regina, so she immediately turned to the table of contents where she noticed that the book was divided into 5 parts, 15 chapters, author notes, a glossary of terms, suggestions for further reading, and an index. The combination of the construction of the book, the back flap, and a glance at the author's style of writing were proof enough that this was an eminently readable book and one not meant for scientific professionals. And the glossary was the icing on the cake because she'll be able to understand certain scientific terminology as she reads along.

This nonfiction book is a good example of a fully developed, well-organized format for a lay reader to pursue the subject of physics.

The index, found in the back of the book, comes in handy because if you want to read about something specific, you just go to the back and look for it. It lists topics, names, and terms in alphabetic order with page numbers so you can easily find what you are looking for. For example, if you want to find out about quarks, you can look it up in the index under the letter Q, go to the indicated pages, and see what the author has to say about that subject matter.

Checking References

Some nonfiction books may also contain *footnotes*, which are stylistically presented differently than bibliographical material.

If footnotes are supplied, they are numbered in the body of the text and then matched with the corresponding number and additional information about a topic, in smaller print at the bottom of the page.

Look It Up

A **footnote** is used to emphasize and/or expand a point the author is making in a textbook or book on a particular subject. You will also find footnotes or endnotes in some older novels, which usually explain a reference that may not be commonly expressed in modern times. When the notes come at the end of the book, they are called **endnotes**.

What you will find in the notes is the source of the thought, quote, or information. The notes list the author's first then last name, the title of the book, and the page numbers the author took the information from.

There is no set guideline for how any nonfiction book should be constructed. For example, Regina's copy of *A Source Book of Chinese Philosophy*, translated by Wing-Tsit Chan (Princeton University, 1963), is 856 pages long. A "source book" is usually very comprehensive piece of literature, and Regina's book certainly fits that description. It's illustrative of a comprehensive overview that provides information about historical developments in China, comparisons with western humanism, and specifically introduces the reader to Chinese philosophers over a long period of time.

In addition to the extensive information contained in the text, the book provides a foreword, preface, acknowledgments, chronology of Chinese dynasties, and chronology of philosophers. These pages are numbered with Roman numerals— a stylistic indication that this material is separate from the rest of the book. This book is so comprehensive that it even includes a glossary with Chinese words and their English translations.

One of the things nonfiction books have in common is the inclusion of extra information to help you have a complete and comprehensive reading experience. You don't have to look beyond the binding of the book unless you really want to. Other nonfiction material such as autobiographies, biographies, and memoirs—books about people's lives—are often constructed similarly to a piece of fiction.

Grabbing and Holding On

What an author wants more than anything is for the reader to keep on reading. What's the point of writing a book that readers will put down after the first 10 pages? There's no guarantee that this *won't* happen; after all, you might like one author's style while another reader prefers a different kind of style. The author knows that some people will like the book and others will not. That's one of the beauties of subjectivity. Each author will appeal to different kinds of people.

For example, there are writers who might open their book with 10 pages of description before getting to the actual story. This will appeal to readers who want to have a feel for the atmosphere before they get into the action. Other readers want to get right to the heart of the story and are only interested in description that applies directly to the story line.

The important thing for any author is to hold on to one kind of reader and try to lure in others. Authors use strategies involving narrative voice, humor, point of view, and even foreshadowing to keep you reading. You read more about these techniques in Chapter 9.

Once you find an author whose work you enjoy reading, you will probably look for more of his or her books. You may even find yourself rereading some of your favorites. The more books you read by specific authors, the more able you will be to identify the style of writing you prefer.

The Least You Need to Know

- You can determine whether a book is right for you by examining its various parts, such as the cover, table of contents, foreword, and introduction.

- Nonfiction (as well as some fiction) often includes extra material to help you further understand the text.

- Fiction and nonfiction books are formatted differently.

- Authors employ different techniques to grab and hold the reader's attention.

Chapter 5

Developing Your Critical Eye

In This Chapter

- ◆ What makes a work of fiction absorbing
- ◆ Learning to read nonfiction
- ◆ Start asking (more) questions
- ◆ Uncovering author techniques
- ◆ Backing up your reading with even more reading and research

Reading is a growth experience. As you change, so do your reading tastes. Now that you've made the conscious decision to learn more, it is inevitable that you will start to look deeper into the literature you choose to read. But what exactly are you looking for?

There's the rub! It's simple, really; you're looking for connections in the text: between events, between thoughts, between ideas, between the author and his era, between the author and his readers … and the list goes on. In this chapter, we take a deeper look at the techniques authors use to get their point(s) across, both in fiction and nonfiction.

What to Expect from Fiction

Let's begin with some definitions and some criteria. A work of fiction is a piece of imaginary prose that can be in the form of a novel, novella, or short story. A novel is a long work of fiction, whereas a novella is longer than a short story but shorter than a novel. The writer of a piece of fiction may draw on his or her own experiences or imagination to create the story. What makes it fiction is that strictly speaking, it is made up—created out of the thoughts and feelings of the writer.

> **Between the Lines**
>
> Even if a piece of fiction is based on or inspired by actual events or people, it's still considered fiction, not fact.

You should approach reading fiction as you might approach any adventure (such as a vacation, for example). Reading a work of fiction is like taking a trip to an unfamiliar location. You are entering a world of the unknown.

I Just Can't Put It Down!

As a reader, there's no better feeling than picking up a book that's so absorbing you can't put it down. Some book lovers will read very slowly to put off the inevitable end of a book. It's an amazing feeling when a book grabs you so completely that you find yourself walking down the street, book in hand, knocking into lampposts and fellow pedestrians. (Well, it might not be so amazing for those people you bump into!)

What is it that makes a particular piece of fiction so absorbing? Generally speaking, it's the element of surprise, the author's ability to tell the story in such a way that you just have to know more. You have a secret desire to skip ahead and find out what happens next (but resist the temptation to do that—you'll ruin the surprises along the way!).

The Able Author

A story should be interesting or funny enough to hold your interest and make you want to know more about what happens next. The author should care enough about his characters (or at least be involved enough) to make you care about them, too. The plot should flow and make connections between events, thoughts, and feelings as it moves along. It should contain the basic structure of rising action, climax, and falling action that leads to some kind of resolution.

Fiction is sometimes written strictly for entertainment purposes without expecting to teach you much of anything. Other times the author has a larger message that he depicts through allegory, a symbolic statement of an idea, philosophy, emotion or feeling, or all of those elements combined. We talk more about allegory in Chapter 7.

What you should come away with by the time you close the book is a new perspective, a new insight into a universal theme. Isn't that what you expect from a vacation—to come back with new images and new ideas?

How to Read Fiction

You've already learned the basic structure of fiction. But what makes fiction different from any other form of writing, aside from the fact that it is imaginary?

In addition to identifying the structure of a piece of fiction, it's essential to ask yourself two questions as you read:

- Who is telling the story?
- How is it being told?

In answering these questions, you're identifying the narrative voice and the point of view. The narrative voice is the voice of the person telling the story (not to be confused with the author). Point of view determines how much the narrator knows and how the story is told. These concepts are discussed in detail in Chapter 8. For now, however, just be aware that the narrator has a great influence on how the story ultimately unfolds.

Accepting the Author's Choices

As the reader, try to begin every fiction-reading experience with an open mind. Even if you don't necessarily learn something new, and even if you don't particularly like the book, authors are quite adept at depicting old ideas in completely new ways. The story line, the characters, the atmosphere, and the descriptions of a new book just might show you a different way of looking at things.

Bookmarks

Consider an old adage that, as far as anyone knows, is true: There are no new ideas, only new ways of stating them. This is certainly true for fiction. How many stories do you know of that depict the battle between good and evil, for example? The list is endless.

The author's creative process helps you see things in new ways. The reader's creative process involves going along with the author for the ride.

I Don't Get It

If the author is successful in translating his or her ideas to you through the story, the author has done what he or she intended to do. If you walk away scratching your head, there could be one of two things going on: either the author failed to communicate with you, or you failed to grasp the intended meaning. Just as there are bad readers, there are bad writers. So don't jump to the conclusion that the inability to connect to the author or to the story is your fault. Sometimes it just happens.

Understanding Nonfiction

Now it's time to switch gears. Nonfiction is a completely different from fiction in form and style of writing. Rather than finding its origins strictly in imagination, nonfiction is based on facts. Whether it it's a how-to book, biography, autobiography, or a book about a specialty area such as physics or computers, the author's purpose is to convey information to you — real information in as "true" a form as possible.

When you pick up a nonfiction book, you are usually looking for specialized information, and the one thing you may demand of the writer is that he or she be clear. If the book is assigned to you for a class, you might have to trudge through difficult information to get to the root of what you need to learn; if it's a book of your choosing, however, the style of the writing and how the information is presented will be important in making your selection. Your choice of book has everything to do with your personal preferences.

Specialty Books

If you are choosing a book in an area of special study, clarity should be your first criteria. Regina knows a person who recently lost her job and needed to update her computer knowledge and skills to find new employment. She took some computer classes, but, unfortunately, she couldn't keep up with the class because the teacher was racing through the material like he was trying to make the *Guinness Book of World Records* for speed teaching. So she went to a local bookstore to pick up additional texts that she could follow at her own pace.

Regina's friend knew that some of the material might be over her head and she would need a text that would start with the basics. What she found, to her surprise, was not so much that the books were over her head, but that many of them were disorganized and poorly written. She had to really look around before she found something she could follow and that would help her update her computer skills on her own.

Although some of these how-to books may have appealed to one person, chances are there are a lot people like Regina's friend who would not have been able to follow these texts. The point is that the material must be clear, which means it must be organized in an easy-to-follow style, and it must be written so that a beginner can understand the content.

Who Is This Author, Anyway?

The second criteria for choosing nonfiction is to expect help from an author that goes beyond the style of writing. Check out the information on the back cover or inside the dust jacket, or look for a section called "About the Author." (In this book, the "About the Authors" section is on the inside back cover.) Knowing about the author's background and knowledge base will help you make your choice. If you are confident in the author's expertise in the subject, you may be more likely to want to read the book.

There may be other references in the book that will convince you that what you are reading is based on a solid knowledge base and therefore as accurate as you would expect a work of nonfiction to be. You may find a preface, introduction, glossary, bibliography, as well as footnotes and/or endnotes. The more information the book contains, the more credibility you are likely to feel it holds. (See Chapter 4 for more on how a book is structured.)

The reason for all of these extras is that the author wants to help you to understand the material more completely. It's important that the author add additional references and information to back up the text and to show you that he or she is a reliable source that you can count on for accurate information. The author also wants you to have the sources so that you can further your study of the topic. Just keep in mind that just because a book references many different sources and seems to have all the elements required of a work of nonfiction, the most important thing is that you understand the text.

Biographies

You have to be especially careful about whom the author of a biography is. (Remember, a biography is the story about someone's life told by someone other than the person who lived that life.) Who is telling the story exactly? A family member? A friend? A housekeeper? Or someone who simply has an interest in studying that person's life? Is the person still alive? Is the author writing the life story from historical documentation or from eyewitness observation? You need to do your research before you accept a biography as fact.

CAUTION

Take Note! _____

Sometimes biographies are faulty because they are lacking critical archival material to back them up. If a person is famous enough, his or her estate often insists that records be kept sealed for many years before anyone can access them. This has been true for records related to the death John F. Kennedy, for example. It may be years before all the records regarding his time in political office will be available to writers and researchers.

Unauthorized biographies are written without the subject's consent or cooperation. Although these books claim to tell the true life story of someone, you really need to check out the author and his credentials before you can trust the story being told. Usually, there's some hidden agenda involved in these books, whether it's money, revenge, or the author's quest for fame. So although you might enjoy these juicy reads, keep in mind these books should really be classified as entertainment.

Let's look at the one of the most notorious biographies, *Mommie Dearest*, about the life of the legendary screen actress Joan Crawford, star of many films from the 1920s through the 1970s. *Mommie Dearest* was a book before it hit the big screen in the early 1980s. As you may know, Joan Crawford was depicted in both the film and the biography as anything but a loving mother of her adopted children. In fact, she was portrayed as an obsessive-compulsive egomaniac who often used her children to show what a great benefactress she was. In the end, when she died, she left daughter Christina absolutely nothing in her will.

Consider who the author of this biography is: Christina Crawford herself. Now ask yourself, was Christina trying to get in the last word as revenge against her mother's lack of generosity, or was she finally free to tell the world the truth about what went on behind the closed doors of Joan Crawford's "perfect" world? Was she trying to make her own name known? (She went on to publish a novel shortly after *Mommie Dearest* came out.) *Mommie Dearest* was published in 1978, a year after her mother's death. Did Joan Crawford know that her daughter was writing this book and subsequently cut her out of the will? No one can know the truth for sure.

In the case of *Mommie Dearest*, knowing the identity of the author is critical to being able to believe the content of the book. This is true for many biographies.

Autobiographies

Again, with autobiographies, it's important to consider who the author is. Obviously, because an autobiography is a book written about one's own life, you would expect it to be as close to the truth as possible. (This applies to memoirs as well, which tell of significant events in a person's life. Like an autobiography, a memoir is written by the person who experienced the life events.) Keep in mind that those who write a book about themselves believe they have something of interest to say. Anyone can write an autobiography, but readership will depend on the level of interest in that person, and the more interesting the story, the more likely it is that the book will sell well (and make the author oodles of money). Most autobiographies are written by someone in the public spotlight.

Sometimes writers of autobiographies feel they have something to explain about themselves. Perhaps a person believes he or she has been misunderstood by the public and writes a book to set the record straight. Maybe the author is a person who has been gossiped about and feels he or she needs to respond to some of the things that have been said. In some cases, autobiographies are written because the person just wants to be remembered from his or her own point of view rather than that of someone else or a collective audience.

Asking Questions and Finding Arguments

What fiction and nonfiction have in common is that you begin both reading experiences with a desire to know more. With a work of fiction, you have chosen to read it because, for some reason, the story appeals to your senses, or to your personality, or to your life circumstance at any given time. Maybe you picked it up because it had an interesting title or a pretty cover or because you enjoyed other books by that author. It doesn't matter *why*, really; what matters is that the book is in your hands and you're reading it. The same is true for nonfiction material. Something caught your attention, and now it's in your grasp or on your bookshelf.

What Do You Want to Know?

The most important thing is to start asking questions as soon as you develop the desire to know more about the topic. Suppose you have an interest in the war in Iraq and want to know more. Do you want to hear the answer from someone in the Bush administration or do you want to hear it from a political activist's point of view? What is it that you want to know? Are you looking for a reliable and informed viewpoint? A scholarly viewpoint? Or a radical viewpoint? You don't even have the book in your hands yet, and you've already begun to ask yourself questions about what you want to read in regard to the topic.

Maybe you're interested in furniture and want to learn how to build your own mahogany dining room set. Whose book will you read? One written by a professional furniture crafter or one written by a self-taught carpenter?

Again, we get back to you and the kind of questions you bring to a subject and to an author. These will ultimately lead to whatever opinions and arguments (which support your opinions) you are going to develop. Not all works of nonfiction will lead you to forming such strong ideas, however. Sometimes a nonfiction book is just a book that will satisfy a curiosity you have. Maybe you want to know more about growing African violets. In that case, you'll pick up the book with the most appealing style. There's no need to form an opinion or an argument supporting the theory behind growing African violets. You will just want to satisfy a curiosity and learn something new.

On the other hand, you may have always wanted to read the Roosevelt-Churchill letters because you wanted to find out how these two heads of state dealt with World War II. These are actual letters, so what you see is what you get. There is no interpretation of the letters unless you dig deeper. You will likely find that many political historians have interpreted these letters in several different ways. But without any background material, you are left on your own to read and comprehend what these two men said to each other and how their words led to action that would affect the world from that point on.

It is inevitable that you will form questions as you read the letters. (Why didn't Roosevelt or Churchill see what Stalin was up to? Why didn't Roosevelt go to war sooner?) Your questions may not be answered by the letters themselves. You will either have to find the answers on your own through research or you will have to research what others have to say about the letters in order to formulate further opinion on the material. While you are reading, however, it is up to you to form your opinions, build your arguments, and develop your own interpretations. Sounds like some serious work, but this is exactly why you're reading in the first place.

When you are able to make up your own mind about the material, you will find new doors opening to you everywhere you turn in your reading experiences. This is why we call it a voyage of discovery. What you are discovering is what you believe and what you decide for yourself by means of reading the ideas and opinions of someone else.

> **CAUTION**
>
> **Take Note!** _____
>
> All facts are subject to interpretation. When an author begins to interpret those facts, that's when you need to apply your critical eye and begin to formulate your questions and arguments.

Fact or Fiction?

With fiction, you know that what you're being told isn't being presented as true. When you read nonfiction, it's important to have a system of checks and balances so that you can stop and evaluate the author's point of view from time to time to determine whether he is being objective. Here are questions to consider as you read nonfiction:

♦ What are the facts being presented?

♦ How are they being presented? Are they clear and straightforward or muddled and perplexing?

♦ Is the author expressing an opinion? If so, what is it?

♦ How is he or she interpreting the facts?

♦ Do I see a particular bias or perspectives in the text?

♦ How does that perspective compare against what I already know or believe?

♦ Is this the first time I've read this point of view?

♦ Do I need to find further reading material to make up my mind about this author or the subject matter?

Take Note! _____

It's not enough to just disagree with an author. You need validation to back up your argument. Be careful if the topic is highly specialized. You wouldn't want to challenge Stephen Hawking's theory of black holes, for example, unless you had the credibility to back up your argument with other sources and your own expertise.

◆ Have I read enough about this topic to formulate my own arguments or do I need to do more research?

If you just accept the author as an authority on the topic and don't ask yourself questions such as these, you're not doing your job as an active reader or as a thinker. You should question everything that is stated as a fact. Question the point of view, research the background, and find your own answers. You may or may not come to the same conclusions as the authors. What is most important is that you have come to a conclusion that is your own—otherwise you might just be regurgitating someone else's biases or points of view.

Putting It All in Perspective

Who knew there was so much involved in reading? Not many of us, or we wouldn't need reference guides such as this one to help us along. There is so much more involved in reading than what you could possibly have learned in high school.

Now that you have all this information, it's time to make it work for you. Try following this simple list of questions (yes, more questions …) to guide you in your reading. Some apply to fiction, some to nonfiction, and some to both:

◆ Based on what I know about it, why did I pick this book?

◆ Who is the narrator?

◆ What is the point of view?

◆ What is the author's point of view?

◆ What is the author trying to tell me?

◆ What is the theme?

◆ How does the author's opinion differ from what I already know and believe?

◆ What do I think about the story or book?

◆ How has this reading experience affected me?

So, What Do You Think?

This is the most important question of all, because that's the whole point, isn't it? When all is said and done, what matters most is what you take away from the book. The author's opinions and feelings are still out there waiting for another reader to interpret. Although two people may walk away with many of the same thoughts, their own experiences and personalities will make one reading experience different from the next.

If your curiosity leads you to further explorations, the books you are choosing and learning from are helping you to grow, be it in the area of politics, physics, or growing African violets. More than anything else, your reading experiences should make you a better you.

Drawing Conclusions

Be cautious when it comes to drawing conclusions. At best, you should draw only tentative conclusions, at least at first. No book can give you everything you want or need. There can be gaps in information or too much said about one topic and perhaps not enough about another. That's to be expected. The best you can do is pick up some information from a single text, which hopefully will lead you to formulate more questions that another author addresses in a different book.

Life is a never-ending process of learning. If you could pick up all the information you would ever need on a particular subject from one book, you would be all set. But that's not likely to happen. Even when an author is an expert in a given field, he will usually lean toward a preferred theory, which you may completely disagree with. It's up to you to find out about the other theories out there and then come to your own educated conclusion.

Your conclusions will be largely based on your expectations from a piece of writing, whether it's fiction or nonfiction. And what you may be looking for can be found in pieces and parts of several different books. Be patient. Keep looking. Keep reading. There isn't any book that you pick up that you aren't going to get something out of, if, at least, it's written in an interesting and engaging way.

The Least You Need to Know

- Asking questions of yourself and of the author and his or her subject matter is the first step toward developing as a reader.

- Fiction and nonfiction differ in the questions that you ask yourself before, during, and after your reading experience.

- It is important to pay attention to an author's techniques and expertise. It is another way he or she is trying to communicate with the reader.

- Never take anything an author says at face value. Learn to recognize biases and opinions in yourself as well as in the author.

- Don't expect one book to be all things to all readers. It is almost always necessary to go looking for more information either about the author or about the subject matter.

Chapter 6

Relating to the Material

In This Chapter

- ◆ Learning what to look for in the writing
- ◆ What the author expects from you
- ◆ Subjectivity, objectivity, and emotional involvement
- ◆ What history teaches us as readers

In this chapter, we delve a little deeper into what you need to be looking for in literature in terms of expectations, emotions, and mood. You will begin by getting a better understanding of an author's intentions and figuring out your own expectations so that you will develop confidence in your conclusions.

Then, using references to Nathaniel Hawthorne's *The Scarlet Letter*, you will learn about the complexities of a good piece of fiction and historical context. You will learn about how historical writings reflect societal development and what that means for you, the reader today.

What Does the Writing Mean to You?

As you become a more experienced reader, you will discover that people read differently. Obviously, by now you know we don't mean how you hold the book or position your elbows on the arms of your chair. Because we are all different people, we interpret the reading differently. What you interpret as one meaning, someone else may interpret as something else entirely. This is another reason it's nice to have an outlet, such as a book group, to talk about what you've read. What the writing means to you has everything to do with who you are. And choosing any book, to begin with, has a great deal to do with what the writing will mean to you. You've chosen the book for a specific reason. It called out to you in some way and you were drawn to it.

The Task at Hand

Let's return to Nathaniel Hawthorne's *The Scarlet Letter*, a story about a woman accused of adultery in seventeenth-century Massachusetts. She is humiliated in front of her community by being forced to wear a scarlet letter *A* on her dress as punishment for her "crime."

Bookmarks

You can read *The Scarlet Letter* without being well versed on either the nineteenth or seventeenth centuries, but to have a full understanding of the work, it's best to do some background research about the time and place in which it was written.

What is interesting here is that because Nathaniel Hawthorne lived in the nineteenth century, you have two questions to ask yourself in this reading: What was life like in the nineteenth century when the story was written, and what was life like in the seventeenth century, the time that Hawthorne is writing about? Your task is to try to understand how a nineteenth-century writer might imagine life two centuries prior to his own. So you are actually reading a historical perspective of another historic time.

What Do You Expect?

As with any book, your reading experience will begin with interest and curiosity. Your first step when approaching a novel such as *The Scarlet Letter* should be to examine your own expectations of the topic itself. Based on what you already know about the story and based on what you have read of nineteenth-century western culture, what do you think Hawthorne will have to say about his character's situation? What kind of statement, if any, is Hawthorne trying to make about the moral issues of that society versus his own and how does that differ from the issues in your own society?

As a twenty-first-century mind (that's you), it might be difficult to picture that there's any huge difference between the two societies; but try to imagine two centuries prior to the times in which you live.

While you read *The Scarlet Letter*, for example, here is a list of questions you might keep in mind about our society's moral expectations of its citizens (and in turn, about your own moral expectations):

- In what way does religion play into the morals of American society?

- How are women treated compared to men when accused of committing adultery?

- How much say does our society and government have in our private and personal lives?

- Where do the Puritans in *The Scarlet Letter* get their moral code from, and does that kind of code exist in any part of American (or even world) cultures today?

- Can you compare Hester Prynne and Rev. Chillingworth to any modern-day heroes or victims, either literary or factual?

Now try replacing the questions regarding your society with nineteenth-century society—the time during which Hawthorne was writing. See how different your answers are and try comparing all three centuries and cultures (the seventeenth, nineteenth, and twenty-first). Obviously, this is where the research comes in!

After you read *The Scarlet Letter*, you will acquire meanings from the book based on your focus and expectations of the author. The outcome of this particular reading experience for you will be whether the author fulfilled your expectations. Is this what you were looking for? If not, how was it different? Maybe the author exceeded your expectations. When that happens, it's always an adventure—and an exciting one at that!

Reader Response and Author Intention

Hawthorne has something to say, and it's up to you to figure out what it is by examining the life of the author himself. We won't keep you in suspense, and we'll even help you a little with your research here.

Hawthorne carried the tainted heritage of a hanging-judge uncle who sentenced many innocent women to die for all sorts of reasons—and ultimately condemned them for witchcraft, based on paranoia, irrational suspicion, and the fertile imaginations of people eager and swift to judge others. This should make you wonder (without even getting an answer to the question): Was this piece of writing by Hawthorne intended to be an act of reparation for his shameful relative's behavior back in the seventeenth century? Was there a thriving Puritan heritage calling out to the author? Or, more simply, maybe he just wondered what it was like to be alive back then. What did people think and feel? And what did the Puritans do to those who did not live by a standard moral code? What *was* the standard moral code, for that matter?

Like most fiction writers, Hawthorne drew from his own life and his own questions about life to create an imagined world that strives to answer many of these questions. These may be questions Hawthorne asked himself, and by writing the novel, questions he is asking you to consider as well. However, whatever answers you come up with are your own. There may be no one answer to these life issues in the end, but there certainly are *your* answers.

Between the Lines

Nathaniel Hawthorne (1804–1864) was born on the fourth of July in Salem, Massachusetts, the infamous region of early American "witch" burnings and hangings. He wrote *The Scarlet Letter*, his best-known work, in about a month. Clearly he knew what he had in mind to say. He had lived with this book inside of him just ready to go.

Hawthorne evoked his questions about life, and maybe even about his own ancestry, by humanizing history. He gave names to faces, feelings to characters, and description to places. This is what makes fiction. This is what teaches us. And this is how we grow.

The Scarlet Letter is charged with emotional and intellectual issues, making it a very good example of how literature can push you to look very closely at your own responses. Reading *The Scarlet Letter* will inevitably force you to contemplate your own code of ethics, your sense of morality, and the religious and spiritual influences in your life. How do *you* see the novel? How does it reflect what you believe or do not believe? How does it compare to the modern-day view of "morality" or "honor," for that matter? What is your opinion on adultery? Do you think Hester has done anything wrong? Is she a hero or a victim—or both? What kind of person do you think Hester is? What do you think of the outcome?

On the other hand, and maybe more importantly, what was Hawthorne trying to say to the reader?

Emotion Versus Subjectivity

We all have likes and dislikes as well as things we're just not so sure about. We have emotional responses to difficult as well as happy situations, to the people around us, and about ourselves. We are human beings with biases and prejudices, and we all have things that trigger our reactions. But to get stuck in those emotional places leaves us at dead ends. It would be hard to read anything subjectively or objectively if you're stuck in certain emotional places.

If you can understand that, it will be easier for you to grasp the difference between emotional and subjective responses.

CAUTION

Take Note!

It is as important to be an emotionally developing person as it is to be an intellectually developing one. Learning to be a good reader allows you to work on both aspects of yourself.

The Emotional Reader

An emotional response is often a knee-jerk reaction. It comes from the gut—it can happen in an instant and always speaks to how we feel in the immediate. In many ways, it speaks to our biases and things with which we are familiar. Sometimes the feelings don't hit us in the here and now, but when they do, they can often be powerful and eye opening.

For example, if you are reading a story about a mean dog that is shot by a member of an unsympathetic community, you could have one of two reactions: Maybe you're relieved because that dog was a total menace to society—in this case your bias may be in favor of society. On the other hand, the dog had been treated cruelly, so you sympathize with him and feel sad when he dies—then perhaps your bias is with the dog and against a conceivably uncaring society. Both are emotional responses.

A Subjective Perspective

Subjective responses are grounded more in the kind of person you have become to this point as opposed to what you feel at any given moment. From a subjective perspective, you bring your inner reality to your reading, which will either be expanded or more limited depending on what it is you choose to read.

You bring values and points of view of your own; they are all hopefully going to be challenged by the reading. That is usually what the author intends to do: challenge the norm and shake up the status quo.

In the case of the dog in the previous example, maybe you were the owner of a dog who had been cruelly treated by a group of local hooligans and as a result you have had to muzzle the dog and have people look at you and the dog with trepidation. To you it's a loving, friendly animal, much like your own dog, while to the rest of the world it's a monster. You cannot see the dog as just good or bad, you know that it's more complex than that. It is your own life experience that affects this read.

Intellectually Speaking

Intellectual response is geared toward bringing your analytical skills to bear on your reading. Reading intellectually will allow you to see the writing more objectively. Look objectively at how the author shapes his or her characters, develops the plot, or uses descriptions. What is the point of view? Who is telling the story? Does the narrator have an opinion about the events or about the characters? And what about the author? Why did he or she write the book in the first place? What does he or she want you to get out of it?

Okay, let's go back to that dog for a moment. Try thinking about it this way: "Personally, it troubles me that this society did not understand the dog, but objectively, I understand that they needed to get rid of the dog or face the loss of more human lives within the community."

Bookmarks

Try to keep your emotions in check when you are trying to look at literature from an intellectual perspective. Emotions can be very powerful and could block open-mindedness or clear-sightedness regarding the other issues in the story. To be a good reader you need to develop this skill as well.

Looking at the story from the dog's perspective, the owner's perspective, the community's perspective, and the individuals within the community and their various perspectives allows you to look at a situation—in real life or in a book—from an intellectual standpoint so that you can draw objective rather than subjective conclusions.

While you will find answers from your own reading of the material, you will also gain perspective from outside sources such as book reviews and literary criticism, which will also examine and interpret literature. Although this will help you formulate some of your own questions, it is important that you not stray too far from yourself and your initial responses when you read the thoughts of others.

What About Those Gray Areas?

A subjective response to *The Scarlet Letter* may allow you to see that Hawthorne reveals not so much the opposites of good and evil as the shadowy in-between areas—the subtle, nuanced complexities that make it difficult to see things in extremes the way the Puritan community in *The Scarlet Letter* does. Maybe, for reasons in your own life, you have come to realize that life is all about the gray areas—the middle zone. Not everyone can be categorized as angelic or evil the way law and society may try to make things seem sometimes. So in the end your focus might actually be philosophical, ethical, or even theological.

If you are looking for an objective read of *The Scarlet Letter*, you need to keep your own opinions at bay as best you can and look strictly at the story, the characters, the themes, the symbols, and the author. This may be harder to do if the topic charges you and makes you feel strongly about your own ideology and philosophy of life. But that's all the more reason to try to see the story objectively.

Walking a Fine Line

In *The Scarlet Letter*, Hawthorne provides insight into the battling forces of fear, ignorance, jealousy, revenge, suffering, redemption, and the transcendence of love by means of the characters in the book and the community in which they live. It's not like those attributes only apply to seventeenth- or nineteenth-century societies. Those are timeless topics that apply to human nature and society in general.

While you read *The Scarlet Letter*, do you feel sympathy for Hester? That's interesting if you were raised to believe that adultery is wrong, no matter what the circumstances. Let's say you hold firm to that belief. Does that mean everyone has to believe what you believe? Or does it mean people should be ostracized for not believing what you believe? Maybe you believe in the laws of society, no matter who the society is made up of, but somehow you feel that Hester wasn't wrong in breaking the laws of her own society. What does this say about you?

> **Between the Lines**
>
> Although it helps to know the author's intentions, it is not absolutely essential that you fulfill them. The most important thing is what you conclude for yourself. If you have grown into a confident reader, you will stick by your conclusions with the author's intentions always close by as a reference point.

Now, you can see it—your world has turned upside down and sideways, and that's the whole point! That's what makes a good reader!

Putting Together the Pieces of the Puzzle

Your life and opinions aside, what does Hawthorne do to make his reader see the gray areas—the middle ground between good and evil, right and wrong, justice and injustice? How does he show us that the power of love with a huge dose of strength of character can help transcend all adversity? By the use of symbolism and metaphor, the author gives us all the meanings, and like a puzzle it's up to you to put them together.

Here are some examples of complex layers of symbolism and metaphor in *The Scarlet Letter* all relating to the letter *A*. One layer leads to a deeper layer not only within the story, but within the text, which helps us see what Hawthorne is trying to say:

- The letter *A* stands for adulteress, as the town sees Hester. Forcing Hester to embroider her own *A*, as though she is making her own prison uniform as punishment, actually allows her the freedom to make a statement.

- The letter *A* also stands for Arthur, the hidden first name of the father of the child—hidden because Hester keeps his identity a secret from the community to protect him.

- The letter *A* also comes to stand for *angel*, as Hester becomes a caretaker within her community, after she is let out of prison, bringing solace and help to those who need it.

- Angel also refers to the father of the child, Arthur (Dimmesdale), when Hawthorne tells us about him in the middle of the book: "… and thus kept himself simple and childlike; coming forth, when occasion was, with a freshness and fragrance, and dewy purity of thought, which, as many people said, affected them like the speech of an angel."

Look It Up

Irony is a form of expression (and a commonly used literary technique) in which the meanings of words are actually the literal opposite of what they are intended to mean.

Hawthorne is focused on that scarlet letter from many perspectives, as you can see, and along with symbolism and metaphor, Hawthorne throws in a healthy dose of *irony*. That ever-present letter *A* is supposed to be a daily source of humiliation for

Hester Prynne—a scourge on her soul—as she is forced to wear it. But instead she wears her *A* as though it is a medal of honor—her own private symbol of pride and integrity as one who bears the punishment of the community but will not give them what they want.

The community in *The Scarlet Letter* wants Hester to publicly reveal the name of the father of her child. She refuses because he is a respected member of the community— the minister. To identify him to the public would destroy his life, her life, and the life of her child, and equally important to her, it would be bending to a rigid and restrictive society.

It is no shrinking, humiliating *A* that she wears as her community would like to believe. Splendidly embroidered by her own hands, the *A* has layered emotional and spiritual meanings for Hester having to do with her character and integrity, her world of private meanings, and an inner beauty and richness. Despite public humiliation, she proudly wears the first initial of the father's name. The symbolism of the way she has embroidered it refers to her undying resolve. In the elaborate embroidery, she shouts in the face of her community that she has done nothing wrong.

We look at symbolism and metaphor in greater detail in Chapter 9.

Hearing the Author Loud and Clear

Hawthorne speaks to us in parables about our very human nature—about the beauty, character, and strength of spirit within each individual as represented in the character of Hester Prynne. He looks at the vulnerability and weakness of individuals in the character of Arthur Dimmesdale, and tells us about corrupted human nature in the character of Roger Chillingworth (Hester's estranged husband from the Netherlands). The thread that binds the whole story, and perhaps the reader to the writing, is the wondrous power of love woven throughout the novel.

The meanings you get from the writing depend on your own expectations, and on your particular focus when you read. Of course, the more you are looking for, like a detective, like a literary archaeologist, the more you are apt to find, and the more meanings a book is likely to hold for you.

Bookmarks

It's up to you to search, look, think, and assemble all the pieces of what you read. The more you bring of yourself to your reading, the more questions you will be able to formulate, and the more meaning you will discover from what you read.

Writing and Societal Identity

Keeping all of this in mind regarding *The Scarlet Letter* and Nathaniel Hawthorne's own historical perspective on the society from which he and his family originated, it's important to understand where you have come from as well. As Americans, we all originally come from somewhere else. But American society as we know it today originates with the early colonists, and these are the times of which Hawthorne writes. To understand modern American society, you need to look at American history and culture and how it plays into your world and into your reading experiences.

Back to the Beginning

If you look at the United States, the process of shaping a national identity has been astonishing. The country started as a vast landscape of mountains, rivers, lakes, and trees, home to the Native Americans, who were storytellers but not writers. They had no printing presses to share their knowledge—it was all by word of mouth and works of art.

With the arrival of the Europeans in the seventeenth century, the society we have grown into today began. They changed the nation of the Native Americans into what was familiar to them—in terms of religion, law, and societal morality.

To understand the kind of society we are today, we should think back to the seventeenth century, specifically to Massachusetts Bay, where middle-class British subjects settled to build John Winthrop's "city upon a hill." In his famous emotional sermon to the colonists as they sailed to the new world, Winthrop, one of America's first Puritan settlers, told the weary travelers how they would be part of building a model Christian community. Based on education and good living far from the persecution of the Church of England against the Christian reformers, the Puritans would finally have the life of which they dreamed.

This sermon, which reflected Winthrop's principles and ideals, became the national metaphor that has inspired literary and political thought well into our times.

Despite the desire for freedom from persecution, this was not a time of great liberal thinking. There were rules—lots of rules. In fact, the only writing that was

> **Between the Lines**
>
> Not everyone paid attention to the rules. Puritan Anne Bradstreet, wife of Massachusetts governor Simon Bradstreet, is considered America's first American poet. She is best known for her collection called *The Tenth Muse Lately Sprung Up in America, By a Gentlewoman of Those Parts.*

allowed were letters, diaries, and pious sermons. But on the other hand, these were times of survival and hard work. Even storytelling was forbidden unless they were stories from the Bible.

History and Modern Thought

Who we are today stems from where we came from—who we were yesterday, so to speak. The only references we have for understanding this are the writings of the times. And as you can see, what happened in the seventeenth century was still affecting Nathaniel Hawthorne in the nineteenth century, and affects us today in the twenty-first century.

Historians say that to know your history is to learn from it, to be ignorant of it is at one's own peril. The same can be said of masterpieces of fiction. They don't only tell us who our cultural ancestors were, they tell us about who we are right now. So the thinking of one century to the next is witnessed mainly in the writings of the times. By the twentieth century we had film and videotape to help us document our times so we now have a new way of looking at the past and the present, but there is no better keeper of history than the writings of its people.

The Least You Need to Know

- The author has something to communicate to the reader, and it's up to the reader to figure it out.

- There are different ways to look at a piece of writing, including objectively, subjectively, and emotionally.

- How you interpret literature has a great deal to do with who you are and what your life experiences have been.

- Authors use different techniques, including symbolism, metaphor, and irony, in an effort to reach the reader.

- The history of American society greatly influences who we are today as a nation and what we can expect and learn from our writers.

Part 2

All About Fiction

Fiction is a means of seeing life through the art of storytelling. By reading fiction, you are seeing life through the eyes of someone else in a way that you can (or in some cases cannot) identify with. That's not to say that you'll relate to every single story you read, but within every story you will most likely encounter something that calls out to you—a theme, concept, or emotion—that will help you see yourself more clearly.

Emotions expressed in the fictional story should be reflective of a universal theme. We find these reflections in novels, short stories, plays, and poems. When we read this kind of literature, we are really looking for pieces of ourselves. Do we really care about a bunch of fishermen chasing after a whale? Perhaps not, but we do care about battling our inner demons. Do we care about a woman branded with a scarlet letter *A* on her dress? Maybe ... or maybe not ... but we do care about injustice within society. This is why we read fiction: to dig out the bits and pieces of what we do care about and relate them to our own existence.

Chapter 7

Reading Imaginative Literature

In This Chapter

- ◆ Telling a story with meaning: parables, allegories, and fables
- ◆ How the characters fit in
- ◆ Exploring the themes
- ◆ The importance of setting and imagery

When a writer sits down to work on a piece of fiction, he or she doesn't necessarily know what devices will be applied throughout the story. The devices tend to grow as the piece of writing develops.

In this chapter, you learn what it takes to write a piece of fiction so that you have a better understanding of how it needs to be read. It's not just about what the author wants you to take away from the book, but how the message is presented.

Creative Minds at Work

What do you think happens when an author sits down in front of a computer screen or with pen and paper in hand (the old-fashioned way) and decides to write a story? Well, it depends on the author, that's for sure, but they all have one objective in mind, which is to uncover a deeper truth about life that you can relate to.

Some writers will just think for hours before they ever put a single word on the page. They develop characters in their minds; they hear them speak; they give them hair and eye color and physical gestures. Sometimes a writer will start with an outline— a rough idea of the story line (the plot) and who the players will be (character sketches). But not everyone is that organized. Sometimes a writer sits at a computer (or in front of that blank white sheet of paper) and starts to write anything and everything that comes to his or her mind. Or, if you're a writer like Amy's father (an author of historical novels), you might have put yourself to bed as a child every night with a story you made up about Native Americans and Jesuit priests. The story grows and grows until it has to be written, and what appears will often surprise everyone, especially the writer.

> **Between the Lines**
>
> It's rare that a book is published after the author submits the first draft. Some authors have to write dozens of drafts before their novel, novella, short story, or poem is deemed ready for publication.

If a writer were to stop and think every few sentences about what writing techniques to use, the piece would probably never get written. Most writers concentrate first on getting the story on paper. While the writer thinks about the story on her way to a day job, or before falling asleep at night, thoughts about creative storytelling devices will certainly come to mind and will eventually be employed to move the story along, but at the outset all that matters is that the words make it to the page.

Allegory and Parables

To convey your feelings, ideas, beliefs, thoughts, and dreams to another human being is never easy. Some people are better communicators than others, but it is difficult to tell someone how you feel in such a way that they will feel it, too. That's the job of the fiction writer and the power of *allegory*.

Some of the most notable allegorical storytelling can be found in the Bible. This book contains countless stories that have not only been the foundation of Christian belief, but have taught people meanings and feelings for centuries. For example, take a look at this passage:

> Then he ordered the crowds to sit down on the grass. Taking the five loaves and the two fish, he looked up to heaven, and blessed and broke the loaves, and gave them to the disciples, and the disciples gave them to the crowds. And all ate and were filled; and they took up what was left over of the broken pieces, twelve baskets full. And those who ate were about five thousand men, besides women and children. (Matthew 14:13–21 NRSV)

Look It Up

An **allegory** is a story that appears to be one story on the surface but hides a secondary meaning underneath. This secondary meaning is called a metaphor. A **parable** is an allegory that teaches a moral lesson and is usually somewhat plausible.

What does it mean that Jesus Christ was able to feed thousands of people with just a little bit of food? To take the story literally (the surface story), it would be one of the many miracles performed by Jesus Christ in the Bible. When you take a closer look at the story and dig at the metaphor contained beneath the surface, you will most likely find several meanings, one of which is that every person has the power to nurture others with prayers and hope. In other words, the faith of one can influence many. For Jesus Christ to make himself understood to the people, he had to speak in *parables;* in other words, teach his truths by means of stories with embedded metaphors.

There are many religions that use allegory and parables to help people understand deeper meanings. Examples include stories of Hindu gods and goddesses; stories about Buddha; and the ancient religions of gods and goddesses worshiped in Greece, Rome, Egypt, and more.

If religion were simply preached at you without giving you a story behind it, it might not be as easy to understand—or as interesting, for that matter. Theologians understand the power and conviction of the allegory as much as fiction writers do. The more metaphorical the story the more likely it is that the reader will absorb the deeper meaning. Many storytellers try to communicate an idea or belief to you by disguising the theme in the form of a story. By doing so the writer is asking you—the reader—to figure it out for yourself, because all answers that bear any meaning for you must ultimately come from you.

A Whale of a Story

Moby-Dick, by American author Herman Melville (1819–1891), is one of the best examples of allegorical American fiction because of its depth and subject matter. On the surface *Moby-Dick* is a story of the whaling industry and one sailor's search to destroy an infamous sea legend, a whale named Moby Dick. However, look a little deeper and you will find much more than a simple fish story. In *Moby-Dick*, Melville takes on the age-old philosophical theme of good versus evil.

> ### Between the Lines
>
> You may notice that while the title of Melville's book has a hyphen between Moby and Dick, the name is not hyphenated in the body of the text. This is because there were countless editorial errors when the book was originally published in 1851. There were also hundreds of discrepancies between the American and British publications. Melville had supposedly edited the British edition on his own without sending the manuscript to an editor for review.

Is Melville right in his hypothesis? Do we all have to confront the darkest sides of ourselves at some point in our lives? That's what you need to decide for yourself when you read the book. What truths, if any, does the author touch inside of you?

After you have uncovered the mystery that Melville has set before you, you will reach an understanding with the book and with the author. Uncover the metaphors and see what you can relate to. What are your feelings about good and evil? Are they innate qualities or are they acquired through living? How does the struggle of good versus evil affect your life? What does Melville say about the strength of the individual through Ishmael's tale of the captain and that white sperm whale?

What's in a Name?

Often characters represent something allegorical within the story. Sometimes they are represented as subtle symbols, whereas at other times they just scream out at you either by name or by action. In other words, sometimes you have to search for the symbolism, and other times the author makes it more obvious to the reader. Let's return to *Moby-Dick* for an example of characters used as symbols—and there is nothing subtle about them!

Melville approaches the issue of good and evil in a symbolic way by relying on several biblical references, the most obvious of which are the names *Ahab* and *Ishmael*. These are carefully chosen names that point us in the direction of further inquiry. Why would Melville use these names instead of, say, Will and Sam?

From its origins in the Bible, the name Ishmael has become synonymous with the orphaned outcast of society. In the Bible, Ishmael was the son of Abraham and a slave girl. Abraham's wife, Sarah, thought she could not have children despite the fact that she was promised a child by God. When Sarah finally did have her promised child, Isaac, Ishmael and his mother were cast onto the streets.

Ishmael in *Moby-Dick* is new to the world of whaling and he is the eyes and ears of the reader. He is the outsider on the ship and therefore can see the events aboard the whaling ship with a fresh eye. As he sees it, we see it. As the reader, you are as new to this world as Ishmael himself.

In the Bible, Ahab is the king of Israel known for being evil, vengeful, and bloodthirsty on the one hand, although other references refer to him as one of the greatest kings that ever ruled Israel! So which is it? Was he great or was he evil? Or … was he both?

> **Between the Lines**
>
> "Call me Ishmael" is one of the most famous opening lines of all literary texts. It's right up there with other famous opening lines such as "I am born," from Charles Dickens's *David Copperfield*, and "It was the best of times, it was the worst of times," another Dickens opener, from *A Tale of Two Cities*.

Captain Ahab in *Moby-Dick* is not unlike King Ahab in his lust for revenge. Captain Ahab searches the globe for the white sperm whale that had previously maimed him. Moby Dick is known by all sailors for his ferocity—he has destroyed everyone who has attempted to destroy him. Yet Ahab will not be deterred and is willing to risk his ship and the lives of his crewmen in an effort to quell his anger and hatred.

Fables

Some of the most memorable nonbiblical allegories can be found in the form of the fable. A fable differs from a parable in that a fable usually includes some unbelievable action or some strange characterizations such as talking animals. Fables hide a metaphor for one of life's many lessons. One of the most well known of Aesop's fables is *The Fox and the Grapes*, a story about a fox (of course) who stumbles across a grapevine. He's thirsty and would really like a nice fresh juicy grape or two. But the ripest of the bunch is on a higher limb and he can't reach it no matter how hard he tries. Finally he gives up and haughtily says to himself, "I bet they were sour anyway." Have you ever heard someone say "it sounds like a case of sour grapes"? That's where that expression comes from, as do many of our English expressions.

Every fable has a meaning that can usually be summed up in one easy sentence. In the case of this story, the underlying meaning is "It is easy to despise what you cannot get."

Between the Lines

Aesop (or Aisopos in Greek) is believed to have lived about 600 years before Christ. His fables are still taught in schools as morality lessons. It's possible Aesop may never have written down any of his stories, but they were passed along through great philosophers and writers including Socrates. Some scholars say Aesop didn't exist at all. Try telling that to the fourteenth-century monk Maximus Planudes who spent years putting Aesop's stories into one collection.

So That's What It Means!

If you read into a story and find the hidden meanings, they are your own discovery and will hold a more valuable and deeper meaning for you. Even if you don't personalize the message, you will see and understand it, and that means everything when you are trying to become a critical reader.

As you know from living your life every day, the most valuable lessons learned are the ones you learn on your own. Sometimes you need a little nudge, but until you figure it out for yourself you will never fully understand the messages that are handed to you.

Fiction is often allegorical. It is the good fiction writer's task to give the work a deeper, more global meaning than what is happening in the surface story. That, and the ability to allow the reader to find the hidden meaning, is what make writing fiction an art. On the other hand, some fiction writers write purely for entertainment. What you take from the book and how you relate to it may not go any deeper than the surface—and it's not supposed to. There may be smaller life lessons in the story, but the writer is not necessarily intending to do anything but allow you to relax and absorb.

Tools of the Trade

Like a carpenter needs tools and a painter needs paints and a paintbrush, a writer uses tools as well. These are different tools, they are not ones you pick up and hold; but without them, a story would not be complete. Here is a list of just a few of the literary devices and techniques writers frequently use in allegorical stories. They fall into the category of figurative language, or language in which the literal meaning of the words is different from the intended meaning. (We take a closer look at figurative language in Chapter 9.)

- **Metaphor.** A direct relationship in which one idea or thing substitutes for another without being directly stated.

- **Simile.** An indirect relationship comparing one thing or idea to another usually using the words *like* or *as*.

- **Personification.** Human thoughts, perceptions, and actions are attributed to inanimate objects or to ideas.

- **Symbolism.** The use of objects or images to represent abstract ideas. A symbol must be a visible or tangible thing, whereas what it represents must be universal.

- **Hyperbole.** An exaggerated description.

Characters Make the Story

One of the most important things a writer will do for his or her story is invent memorable characters. Characters can't exist just for the sake of the action. Characters exist in a story for a far bigger purpose. The characters are an integral part of the story—the part that the reader will attempt to identify with or even judge or deny. The characters tell the story, live the story, have the relationships within the story, and judge the action and other characters; they are what makes a work of fiction come alive.

Every book you read will use characters to help you find a bigger meaning. Characters in a book will always be representative of you, of people you know, of relationships you've had or will have, or of people in the world that you may have encountered or will encounter. They are the observers and the actors. Without them we would be left with little more than descriptions of places or seasons. Without characters in whatever form they take, there can be no story. (See Chapter 8 for more on choosing characters.)

Some characters will not shout "symbol" as loud as Ahab and Ishmael in *Moby-Dick*, but have more subtle messages for the reader. In Virginia Woolf's *Mrs. Dalloway*, for example, we are confronted with far more subtle characterizations. But the way Woolf has developed the main character in this book speaks volumes about character and metaphor. In *Mrs. Dalloway*, Woolf offers us a character whose personality and purpose is evident from the first line of the story to the last. In the first line of the story—"Mrs. Dalloway said she would buy the flowers herself"—Woolf gives us an immediate impression of a gentle woman of possible means. The very idea that someone else could buy her flowers for her implies that she could have sent someone else.

Of course, that person could be anyone, but one of the many scenarios is that someone works for her. We, of course, must read on to be sure. We know right away that there is a reason for buying flowers that day. Does she buy flowers every day or is there a special occasion involved? And why does she need to choose her own flowers? Does she normally buy flowers? If so, what is different about this particular day? Mrs. Dalloway has some kind of purpose, which will also make us wonder whether taking charge is part of her personality, generally speaking. Literally, all we know from this first line is that Mrs. Dalloway will buy flowers, but this one sentence implies so much more, from who Mrs. Dalloway is to what is going on in her life.

> ### Between the Lines
>
> Virginia Woolf was born in 1882 and died in 1941 (the same years in which James Joyce, another famous fiction writer, was born and died). A feminist, essayist, and fiction writer, she is one of the most popular women writers of the English language to this day. In 1941, fearing madness, she committed suicide by drowning herself in a river.

While Mrs. Dalloway is blissfully ignorant of her own sense of loss in the life she has chosen, we—the readers—see it and feel it for her. In the novel, her situation is comparable to another seemingly unconnected story line and character in the book. Septimus Warren Smith is a World War I veteran suffering from the trauma of his war experiences and makes a conscious decision to kill himself rather than face life in an asylum. Mrs. Dalloway in her ignorant bliss and Septimus in his tortured mind have both made similar decisions. Mrs. Dalloway has committed emotional suicide, whereas Septimus has committed physical suicide. With her last line of the book, Woolf brings the character of Mrs. Dalloway full circle: "For there she was." This was her life. This is the one she chose, and this would be the one she lived, whereas Septimus, too, chose the life he would not live.

Basically the story of Mrs. Dalloway is one big character sketch. Mrs. Dalloway goes through life sampling what it has to offer. Each delight is a joy in its own right. She never has a yearning to specialize or to be "superb" at anything, she just longs to live and be herself. Being able to enjoy life is Mrs. Dalloway's gift and what makes her character come to life. That's how Virginia Woolf wanted her readers to experience her, but at the same time there's a bittersweet sadness that meanders its way through her life based on the decisions she has made.

The use of characters in a work of fiction is not a device in itself, but how they fit together using symbolism and theme is a device. For example, the last line of *Mrs. Dalloway* ("For there she was") reflects the meaning of the first line ("Mrs. Dalloway said she would buy the flowers herself"). This is a device that Woolf uses to solidify your understanding of who this character is—one line parallels the other and helps you make a conclusion about the personality of Mrs. Dalloway.

Dissecting the Theme

When an author begins to write a story, it's essential that he have a concept of the theme he's trying to communicate to the readers. It's fine to have an exciting story and lots of great characters, but what's the point of assembling them all in one plot if there is no real meaning to the story? What "truth" about life does the author want to convey to the reader? Everyone has a set of truths that they hold as a means of identifying themselves—there are personal truths, and there are general truths. These "truths" that the author attempts to convey to the reader are what constitute the overall theme of the story.

The best way to try to identify a theme is to try to state the theme in a single sentence. For example, In Mark Twain's *Huckleberry Finn*, the surface story is about a young boy, Huckleberry Finn, a child of nature—unschooled, without the manners of society, with a good heart and wild spirit—who travels down the Mississippi River with Jim, an escaped slave. They are two different people, of different ages and races, but they are equal in every other sense—they are both human beings and they both seek freedom (Huck from his cruel, greedy, drunken father, and even the Widow Douglas and her "siviliz-ing" ways; and Jim from slavery). The raft becomes their home, the river becomes their world, and as they float along, they learn about life from each other.

There are many other themes and truths to be uncovered regarding Mark Twain's thoughts

> **Between the Lines**
>
> A story doesn't have to have just one theme, but the best ones have a major theme with several other smaller themes contained within the story line. The theme of Shakespeare's *Hamlet*, for example, has been argued for centuries. Is it the act of vengeance that leads to Hamlet's downfall or his indecisiveness? Well, a little bit of both. *Hamlet* has more than one theme.

and feelings about hypocrisy, religion, the role of imagination, about racism and prejudice, and finding one's own truth as Huck is always trying to do—a kind of model for the rest of us who try to make sense of the same things. But the main theme is this: All human beings are free and equal no matter what rules society puts in place.

Personal Themes

Maybe an author is fascinated by his own family history because of the interesting stories he heard in childhood, or because of the interesting family members who were very much like characters he could imagine in a book. When combined, these real-life experiences can make for some wonderful stories.

Contemporary author and *New York Times* correspondent Rick Bragg tells us about the loved ones in his life in at least two of his books, *All Over but the Shoutin'* and *Ava's Man*. He tells the story of his mother in one book and of his father in the other. His truth is about coming to terms with what his family and what his connections to his family mean to him. The theme of his work is developed around how his protagonists lived their lives. He wants us to know them as he knew them or learned about them. But why would we care about his family? What can we learn from what his family meant to him?

This is where the art comes in. Rick Bragg uses real people from his own life history to tell us something about life in the rural South during the twentieth century. But he also tells us about suffering, sorrow, and the struggle to survive by using humor and wit. He shows us how his family made their way in this world in terms of stories told to him—stories both real and imagined.

> **Between the Lines**
>
> Not all readers will relate to the same themes in a novel. We all personalize different aspects of a book, picking and choosing the parts that makes sense within our own lives. That's why having a discussion about the book with others later will open your eyes even more to the themes. What someone else saw in the book, you may not have—so you can learn more through the reading experiences of others.

What Bragg has written is a fictional autobiography. In other words, he is writing about what he knows to be true through memory and storytelling, but he fills in the blanks to make the story complete and readable for those who do not know him, or his family, or anything about the South for that matter. He does this by creating conversations, characters, scenes, and settings. He is not attempting to re-create facts as they occurred but to tell us a story he imagines.

Taking it beyond the realm of fact into imagination is what makes his work fiction. Like any work of good fiction, Bragg hides both truths and mysteries for us to discover beneath his story lines. He touches his readers by writing about a particular theme in such a way that allows us to relate to the aspects that have touched all of our lives in one way or another: being poor, sad, overworked, provoked, angry, jealous, vengeful, feeling foolish, or trying to make others feel foolish. He looks at flaws in his own world that have universal meaning for everyone.

Universal Themes

Although some themes appear only in individual books, other themes are taken on by many authors. There is a saying that there are no new stories, only new ways to tell them, and you can apply that when you think of some of the pervasive themes in literature.

There are countless universal themes that everyone in the world can relate to, and these are what fiction writers try to communicate when they construct their stories.

One universal theme in literature is the victimization of women. Female and male writers have explored this theme for centuries. Leo Tolstoy's *Anna Karenina*, Thomas Hardy's *Tess of the D'Urbervilles*, more recently Margaret Atwood's *A Handmaid's Tale*, and (as you read earlier) Nathaniel Hawthorne's *The Scarlet Letter* all take on the theme of female victimization. What happens to women if they so much as attempt to break societal rules and live their lives with the same freedoms that the men in their society have? Well, there is rarely a happy ending to these stories. Many of the women die at the end of these stories, either by suicide or by execution—and if they don't die, someone else suffers the agony of their desire to be free individuals.

The women in most of these novels are not shrinking violets. They are strong-willed, intelligent women who find it hard to deny their desire for independence and the need to pursue their happiness despite a society that does not allow women access to the same freedoms as men. The message is, in many cases, that the desire to be free is even stronger than the threat of suffering if they attempt to break the rules of society.

The reason the theme of female victimization is still so prevalent in fiction is because it touches so many societies worldwide. Perhaps these authors were trying to make a statement not only within their respective societies, but also to the world at large.

What was the statement? Well, when you read these books, you can figure it out for yourself. If we tell you here, how will you ever incorporate the message into your own knowledge base of global understanding?

Okay, okay ... how about this: The desire for freedom and equality is so powerful that people are willing to risk everything, even their lives, to achieve it. Or to be more specific to the plight of women, you could say that the imposition of societal law on only one part of the population in an effort to establish control and assert male dominance is unjust and cruel, especially when it defies the innate desires and the rights of women.

Cultural and Regional Themes

Whereas some themes are personal or universal, others are cultural. For example, some themes are specific to a certain country or region of the world. There are even themes within one society that some relate to more than others. African Americans, for example, will most likely relate to a story about racism and slavery in a different way than a Caucasian person or an Asian person might.

A good example of a regionalized theme is American fiction. The United States can still be considered a new country when you compare it to the age of the rest of the world. With a new world comes new ideas, beliefs, and dreams, and therefore new literary themes. In the next section, we take a look at how regional themes played a part in James Fenimore Cooper's writings.

Imagery and Setting

Where a story takes place is as important to the theme as character and any literary device. The setting will determine who the characters are and how they interact. A setting can be symbolic in itself, as can the details of the location. For example, go back to Huck and Jim on that raft: a Caucasian boy and an African American man isolated together on a raft—a symbol of freedom, the vehicle that takes them away from their oppressive lives. The river gives them samplings of what life in that region of America is all about—the good, the bad, and the ugly. If they were floating down the Hudson River rather than the Mississippi River, they would have to have been different characters, and their experiences would be completely different.

The imagery that any author describes is a symbolic device used to help move the story along and make the theme more evident to the reader. Why did Melville feel the need to set his story of good versus evil on the sea? What imagery does he use to push his theme forward, to lift it from the confines of life beneath the surface to a place more obvious to the reader? Although it is true that the author wants to obscure the theme so that you can figure it out for yourself, he or she doesn't want the theme to be lost. He wants it within your reach, and will employ devices to make the theme pop out at you here and there throughout the story. In *Moby-Dick* the whale is larger than human beings while the ocean is larger than life itself. It is unpredictable, beautiful, dramatic, and cruel all at the same time—not unlike the struggles of human existence.

James Fenimore Cooper (1789–1851) is a uniquely American storyteller of the nineteenth century. Thematic concerns about the young country of America are taken up by this author in many of his tales of the American wilderness. *The Leatherstocking Tales* is a work that contains five novels (and you may have heard of some of them thanks to Hollywood): *The Pioneers* (1823); *The Prairie* (1827); *The Last of the Mohicans* (1826); *The Pathfinder* (1841); and *The Deerslayer* (1842).

Setting is vital to Cooper's writing. If Cooper had lived in England, perhaps he would never have been a fiction writer at all. Perhaps the new world was his creative inspiration, because Cooper enjoyed showing off the "new country" to his readers (which is now what we would call the "old country"). His writing about the Native Americans and early pioneers contrasted the old world (Europe) and the new world (America). Cooper's descriptions and themes are important for people to read even now because they take you back to what the original colonists may have seen, known, and felt. He gives you descriptions and vivid imagery of what America looked like in its earliest stages of transformation—the age before skyscrapers and superhighways. Not only is his writing important to us historically, it also contains themes of survival and concepts regarding tolerance of unfamiliar cultures that hold true to this day.

The Least You Need to Know

- Authors employ literary devices in fiction writing to help the reader identify the meaning of the story.

- Allegorical literature is used to help readers find answers for themselves.

- Character analysis is essential to discovering theme.

- In addition to universal themes, there are cultural and regional themes in fiction.

- Imagery and setting are as important to the theme as the characters themselves.

Chapter 8

Novel Ways to Pull the Reader In

In This Chapter

- ◆ Who's telling the story?
- ◆ What dialogue really tells the reader
- ◆ Using style, tone, and tense to shift meaning and mood
- ◆ Using new characters to recycle old themes
- ◆ The basic structure of plot

What does an author do to make his or her work memorable? Part of it is the story itself, but even more important is the way the story is told. Why does the author choose a character in the novel to tell the story versus telling it himself, for example? What about dialogue, plot, and tone? Do these things simply fall into place, or are each of them carefully constructed by the writer?

To read a novel, it's important to understand how it is put together. In this chapter, you learn why the author makes certain choices about the way he or she will tell the story, and how being able to identify those choices will make the story clearer for you.

Find the Point of View

When you tell someone a story, it's always told from your point of view. You were there; you witnessed or were directly involved in the action—the only way to tell the story is the way you remember it happening. You can try telling a story from someone else's point of view, but you can only say what *you* think and feel and not what the other person is thinking and feeling.

One of the first things a fiction writer must do, after figuring out the plot and characters, is to figure out who will tell the story. The narrator is the heart of the story, without whom the text would not hold together and the tale would not hold authority.

The author has a few choices with regard to who will tell the story. Will it be a character within the story? Will it be an objective observer to the action? Or will it be an active participant in the action? Sometimes the story is told by someone who is not involved in the story at all, but who seems to know about everyone and every-thing happening in the book. (This is called the omniscient narrator.) When you read a novel, the narrator will either be so obvious that he screams off the page at you or will be so subtle that you barely notice who is telling the story. None of this is an accident. Writers make very conscious decisions about how they want their stories to be told, and a great deal of consideration is always given to narrative voice and point of view.

There are a number of different narrative voices an author can use, and the final choice will be for both stylistic and artistic purposes, which we discuss further after you have a handle on some specific terminology. Narrative voices are referred to as first, second, and third person.

Here's a summary of some commonly used narrative techniques in fiction:

- **First person narrator.** The narrator is a character in the story and tells the story from his or her point of view. He or she is an observer of events with a subjective point of view. Writing in the first person limits the narrator's ability to be objective and therefore limits his or her reliability in the telling of the story.

- **First person observer** (or first person reporter). Again, the story is told from the narrator's point of view, most likely by a character in the story, but as more of an observer than a participant in the action.

- **Second person.** Second person is most commonly found in letter format and when a narrator switches gears to address the reader. Second person allows the narrator to address the reader by using "you." Authors do not usually feel the need to write in the second person. It is actually a difficult voice to use and is not always executed effectively.

- **Third person.** The third person narrator is not necessarily a character in the piece of writing. Writing in the third person allows the author to have an objective party telling the story.

- **Third person reporter.** Writing with this voice allows the narrator to be close to one character, telling the story through that person's eyes. The third person reporter has a limited point of view, but allows the reader to identify with one character throughout the story.

- **Third person omniscient.** This might be the favorite voice of any fiction writer. It allows the narrator to be anywhere at any time. The author can use the omniscient narrator to tell you what anyone is thinking. It gives the author godlike powers to tell the story from any character's point of view.

Although it's the fiction writer's job to establish the narrator and to be consistent with the narrative voice in the telling of the story, it's your job as the reader to try to understand what the writer intends to say to you through the use of a particular narrator. Often the best way to figure this out is to identify the point of view and to consider the reliability of the narrator.

Exceptions to the Rules

There are very rare exceptions when a first person narrator can be omniscient, but one good example is in a recently published novel called *The Lovely Bones*, by Alice Sebold. It is about a young girl who is murdered and watches her family lead their lives from her bird's-eye view in heaven. Because she is in heaven, she has the ability to be omniscient—so she is able to see, hear, and know things that she normally wouldn't be able to if she were alive on Earth.

Young Suzie Salmon, in that case, can be considered Sebold's first person omniscient narrator:

> Hours before I died, my mother hung on the refrigerator a picture that Buckley had drawn. In the drawing a thick blue line separated air and ground. In the

days that followed I watched my family walk back and forth past the drawing and I became convinced that that thick blue line was a real place—an Inbetween, where heaven's horizon met Earth's. (pg. 34)

Another good example of this type of first person omniscience was used in the recent Jeffrey Eugenides novel called *Middlesex*. The narrator tells the story of the lives of his parents and grandparents as he awaits his own birth, so his narrator is able to see, hear, and know all:

Meanwhile, in the greenroom to the world, I waited. Not even a gleam in my father's eye yet (he was staring gloomily at the thermometer case in his lap). Now my mother gets up from the so-called love seat. She heads for the stairway, holding a hand to her forehead, and the likelihood of my ever coming to be seems more and more remote. (pg. 11)

This was a clever technique for the author to use because it allowed him to tell the story from the main character's point of view in first person while giving the narrator reliability by putting him in a position of omniscience. In other words, the back story can be told with credibility by the main character in the story.

Point of View and Dialogue

Another way an author can sneak in more information about characters when the book is written in third person is through the use of dialogue. This proves especially helpful when writing in third person limited, where the narrator is particularly close to one character. If the narrator has a limited scope in ability to tell the story from different character perspectives, dialogue is a good way to alert the reader about what is going on in a character's mind, allowing you to get a more complete story.

Look It Up

The **protagonist** is the main character in the story who goes through a transition by the end of the novel based on the action that takes place within the plot. The **antagonist** is a main character in the story whose actions spur the protagonist to his or her transition.

The following exchange comes from Ursula Hegi's *Stones from the River* (which uses a third person limited narrator) and takes place between the *protagonist*, Trudi Montag, and her *antagonist*, Max:

"Look at me," he said. "I haven't seen her in years."

"You're divorced then?"

"Not legally. But I will be, if we ever agree enough to sign papers."

Her body felt stiff as if her heart had stopped beating.

"Come here." He opened his arms to her. "Please, Trudi?"

She shook her head. One of his hairs lay on her arm, dark and curled. She couldn't bear to touch it and blew it away.

"Ask whatever you need to know."

"You wouldn't have told me …"

"I promise you the truth."

"You would never have told me …"

"I don't think of her, Trudi. I don't think of myself as married."

"But you are."

"People don't always tell each other everything right away."

Her face felt hot. "What do you mean?"

"Wouldn't you agree that it's better to wait to reveal some things until you know the other person's ready to hear them?"

"I-I'm not sure."

"Well, you wanted to know if I had faults."

"And you do."

"You said I was too perfect."

"I would have settled for something less dramatic than a wife." (pg. 394–395)

Through the dialogue, with very few narrator interjections, we see the struggle between the two characters. The narrator doesn't tell us this directly; the characters do, as though they have taken on the role of the narrator. By not interceding, the narrator allows us to draw our own conclusions about who these characters are.

For example, from this dialogue we know that Trudi is hurt as her lover, Max, explains his situation to her. Although he is loving and honest, it doesn't stop Trudi from feeling betrayed and angry. That's a lot of information to receive based on the words of two characters. What the author is doing here is showing us, rather than telling us, what is going on between these two people.

Is the Narrator a Character?

If the narrator is a character in the novel, the author will have a good sense of the tone and mood of the character, and that makes it a little easier to determine how the author wants the character to convey the story to you.

But what happens when the narrator is not a character in the story? Where is this mysterious voice coming from? The logical answer to that is that it is the author telling the story, but this is not always the case. Sometimes the author and the narrator are one in the same, but most often authors choose a different voice from their own because they have a plan in mind for the way they want the story to be told. When the story is told in the third person, and not by a character within the story, the narrator is invisible but will still have a mood and a tone and a particular way of telling the story.

> **Bookmarks** _____
>
> It can be difficult at first to understand the difference between the narrator and the author unless the narrator is a character within the story. When the story is told in third person, keep in mind that the narrator and author are rarely one and the same. To the author, the narrator is as much a character as any other character taking part in the action.

Narrator Reliability

The reader doesn't have to agree with the narrator, but the reader needs to believe that the narrator is telling the real story from whatever perspective the story is being told. If the author is not consistent with the mood and tone of the narrator, the narrator will not be convincing and the reader may not stay with the book.

> **Take Note!** _____
>
> To really understand the reading, you must know who is telling you the story. As you read, consider the narrator—your source. Who is this narrator and what is his or her relationship to the story and how is he or she relating the story to you so that it is believable and readable?

Sometimes, however, the author _wants_ to use an unreliable narrator. For example, if the character is a child, you will hear the story from the child's point of view. Although children are certainly as able as anyone else in telling stories, you may not be getting as close to the truth as possible because you will have a more innocent and inexperienced voice telling you what is going on.

Choosing an unreliable narrator, such as a child, is a deliberate author technique. The writer wants the reader to have to dig a little further to find the truth, and yet the writer still wants us to hear the story from the perspective of this particular observer. But because we have to read so much more into the narrator's story, we are dealing with what is called an "unreliable narrator" and have to be sure we don't take the story at face value or we will completely miss the author's intention.

One of Amy's favorite unreliable narrators is Daisy Fay Harper from Fannie Flagg's book *Daisy Fay and the Miracle Man.* Daisy Fay is 11 years old and has some interesting perspectives on life as she sees it—or on the stories she's been told:

> When I was being born, I kicked Momma so hard that now she can't have any more children. I don't remember kicking her at all. It wasn't my fault I was so fat and if Daddy hadn't choked the doctor and made him nervous, I would have been born better. (pg. 14)

Although the readers will never know where Daisy got this story from unless she tells us, it is likely she heard it from one of her parents and has put her own spin on it. So not only are we hearing the story from a child narrator, we are hearing her own retold version of it, which makes it even more unreliable.

So why did the author do this? Well, Daisy is a very creative and amusing child. What we learn from this short paragraph is that Daisy is confident and strong-minded in her ability not to blame herself for her mother's hard delivery; we also learn that her mother can't have any more children. It is unlikely that that is because Daisy kicked her, even though that's what Daisy is presenting to us as fact. We may never know the truth, but we are getting information from her, and she does tell us the story with humor, which makes the reading experience a lot of fun.

Another type of unreliable narrator would be someone who is not mentally stable, as in Vladimir Nabokov's novel *Lolita.* The story is about a grownup man's obsession with an adolescent girl told from his point of view. Humbert Humbert is clearly delusional and portrays the girl, Delores (or Lolita), as a temptress.

If we were to take the story at face value solely based on what Humbert tells us, we would believe that Lolita is largely to blame for her plight. But as logical and objective readers, we know that we are reading the story from the point of view of a pedophile and Lolita is probably not the seductress Humbert would like us to believe she is. This is where it is the reader's responsibility to read between the lines.

Keep in mind that at the very beginning of Lolita, Humbert, as the narrator, tells the reader that he is not a normal man. He gives you definitions of his obsession and even compares himself to "normal" men. It is important not to lose sight of this as he moves into the actual story or you run the risk of taking his story as the truth instead of just his point of view.

Know Your Narrator

To read more deeply means making some kind of acquaintance with who the narrator is. You may have to get a few pages into the story before you understand what kind of narrator you are dealing with. From page one, you will know what point of view the story is being told from: first, second, or third. It may take a little more reading to know whether this is third person limited or third person omniscient, but after you've figured it out, you should keep it in mind as you read. Just remember: It may take you even more time to figure out whether the narrator is reliable—sometimes it isn't apparent until the end of the book.

Autobiographical Narration

In some cases, especially in the case of the autobiographical novel, it's helpful to compare the author with his or her narrator. The more you know about the author, the easier it will be to understand the narrative voice.

The story of Edna Pontellier as told by Kate Chopin in *The Awakening* was based on Kate Chopin's true-life story. When we say "based on," we don't mean that the story is word for word the life of the author, but Chopin takes her own thoughts and feelings and uses them to bring her character to life. Chopin lived her life in pursuit of independence with the desire to validate her identity apart from being a mother and apart from the men who admired her. Chopin took these characteristics and made them a part of Edna's psyche in order to tell her story.

Chopin takes some daring and innovative risks in her writing. For example, she switches the narrative voice between third person limited and omniscient. She uses third person limited when she wants us to understand what is going on inside of Edna's mind. It's as though we are privy to the inner workings of the protagonist, almost as though the story were written in first person. When Chopin wants you to see Edna's external world she dips back into the omniscient narrative. This allows the reader to take a peek at what the action outside of Edna's mind is all about. This is important because if we stayed inside Edna's mind too long, we wouldn't be able to get a complete picture of her circumstances. Viewing the action through the omniscient voice allows the plot to move along while enabling the reader to stay with the story.

Between the Lines

Kate Chopin was born Kate O'Flaherty in St. Louis in 1850, the third of five children. Her sisters died as babies, and her brothers died in their 20s; Kate was the only sibling to live past the age of 25. In 1870, she married Oscar Chopin, a man of French Catholic descent and a wealthy cotton grower in Louisiana. Because of her innovative thinking and outspoken writing, Chopin's essays and short stories were consistently subject to criticism and controversy.

What we know of Edna Pontellier is that she is an independent woman, much like the author herself. Although Chopin invented Edna, she is really telling you her own story—thus making the novel autobiographical in nature but not necessarily true to life with respect to the details of Chopin's life.

When Chopin switches to an omniscient narrator, she relies upon an observer to tell you the story of Edna Pontellier. You know now that the story is autobiographical, so in choosing to tell us part of the story in third person omniscient, Chopin allows herself some distance from her own reality to tell us her self-inspired story in a fictionalized form. If the story is her own, or close to her own, why wouldn't she tell it in first person? Well, that was a personal choice for Chopin; if you think about it, however, it makes sense to tell it through the eyes of an observer.

To tell the story in first person would make it seem as though she were writing a memoir and she may not have been able to communicate the story to the reader quite so powerfully. By telling the story in third person, she gives it a more universal appeal. If she told the story in first person, the reader might see the story as only applying to the author and might not relate to it or understand it in the same way.

By taking her story outside of herself, she can observe it in a similar way as the reader—with some element of distance and objectivity.

Consider the Tense and Tone

An author can use many techniques to affect your reading experience. Sometimes these choices will surprise you, as when a writer fiddles around with narrator, tense, and tone. For example, in *The Awakening*, when Chopin relies on the omniscient narrator, and she uses the past tense and changes it only when she is emphasizing details. Here is an example, in which she speaks about her husband:

> Mr. Pontellier had prepared for bed, but he slipped on an extra garment. He opened a bottle of wine, of which he kept a small and select supply in a buffet of his own. He drank a glass of the wine and went out on the gallery and offered a glass to his wife. She did not wish any. He drew up the rocker, hoisted his slippered feet on the rail, and proceeded to smoke a cigar. He smoked two cigars; then went inside and drank another glass of wine. Mrs. Pontellier again declined to accept a glass when it was offered to her. Mr. Pontellier once more seated himself with elevated feet, and after a reasonable interval of time smoked some more cigars.

The omniscient narrator has set a scene almost in the same way a camera might pan the details of this man's moments in a film. And then, the narrator shifts the tone to a much more personal one in telling us about Edna:

> Edna began to feel like one who awakens gradually out of a dream, a delicious, grotesque, impossible dream, to feel again the realities pressing into her soul. The physical need for sleep began to overtake her; the exuberance which had sustained and exalted her spirit left her helpless and yielding to the conditions which crowded her in.

First of all, notice that Edna is no longer referred to as Mrs. Pontellier in this second paragraph. By switching tenses and tone, the narrator seems to have drawn herself into Edna's mind, bringing us closer to her and further away from the world outside of herself. By using her first name and changing the tense, it's as though the narrator is standing side by side with Edna, allowing the reader to feel the closeness and giving you a sense that this story really is about Edna's inner world. The narrator has entered into Edna's mind and body and describes her feelings intimately and personally. Do you notice how the change to the present tense gives us an immediate experience in connection to Edna's feelings and her state of mind?

This change of tense from the detached, distant, cameralike view to the intimate, deeply personal is done throughout the book and has a powerful dramatic effect on the story and therefore upon the reader. It might not be something you would have caught if you were unfamiliar with author techniques. Now that you know what to look for, it might be easier to spot and will allow you a more complete and fulfilling read of the book.

Choosing the Characters

Like the plot (which we discuss later in this chapter) and the selection of the narrator, the characters the author chooses to use in the story have a place and meaning in relation to the story. Each character is carefully selected and has a specific role in the story to make the plot reliable and complete. Sometimes the character's place is easy to identify, whereas at other times you have to ask why the author feels such a character is necessary. It's not enough, for example, to throw in a character who is funny just to make the reader laugh. The character has some greater purpose. Ask yourself why the author feels you need this *comic relief*. Never take any character for granted. They're all there for a reason.

Look It Up

The term **comic relief** is used when an author uses humorous action or a humorous character to break up dramatic tension. This is commonly used in theater and is also used quite naturally in our everyday lives. We all know someone who has the ability to make a tough situation lighter by using humor.

Old Themes, New Characters

In Chopin's *The Awakening*, the story follows an unconventional married woman who finds herself stifled in her conventional marriage and takes a lover. But it really isn't as simple as that tired old theme suggests. This book is about growing and changing through the experiences life offers. It's about wanting a sense of fulfillment in life. This has been a common literary theme concerning stories about men and women alike, and similar examples can be found in novels about class and race, as well.

So why do writers bother with tired old plots? Well, because they aren't yet worn out; otherwise authors would stop using them. These plots and characters are based on what human beings are still struggling with and will probably always struggle with. We can relate to them.

The art of repeating themes lies primarily in the characters used to depict the story and the plot that drives them in their actions. In other words, it doesn't matter whether the same theme is stated over and over again in book after book. It bears repeating as long as people continue to evolve and change and try to find solutions to age-old problems. What makes old themes recyclable are the characters we read about, who point to the larger society and culture that bred them, and to ourselves personally.

Character and the Common Bond

Although it is true that characters in their various plots and settings can carry a common bond, what makes them unique is the way they tell the story. For example, Becky Sharp from William Thackeray's *Vanity Fair* and Scarlet O'Hara from Margaret Mitchell's *Gone with the Wind* are similar characters living in completely different places and times.

Becky Sharp uses her femininity and conniving abilities to keep herself afloat amid the upper class. What use is it to be beautiful and poor? She wants attention and money, which for her means the good life and, ultimately, survival. She'll stop at nothing to get what she wants. Scarlet O'Hara is the same type of character with different motivations. Scarlet doesn't dream so much of wealth and the upper classes—she was born and bred in that world. Scarlet most wants love, a home, and attention. To her, these things define survival.

So what do these two character types tell us about their respective stories? What are the authors trying to say to us by using these characters? Well, that selfish manipulation doesn't always have the same outcome. Although Becky Sharp and Scarlet O'Hara are often compared as character types due to their abilities to get what they want through using femininity and manipulation tactics, their personalities and their needs are not the same, and the outcomes of their stories are completely different. Scarlet winds up virtually unchanged and trying to figure out to weasel her way back to Rhett Butler. Becky, on the other hand, winds up with the desire to be a respected woman.

Characters following a common (and well-used) theme may not arrive at the same place at the end of their respective stories. As long as there are clever authors out there who are able to put new and unusual twists on a character "type," the reader will want to keep on reading.

Scarlet's story ends with the realization that the love she had sought was hers all along, but instead of winding up happy, she winds up losing the man she realizes she loves too late.

Building a House: Plot Structure

Every good piece of fiction will be comprised of a specific plot structure. This is a basic truth for novels, short stories, film, plays, television programs, and sometimes even in poetry (depending on the style of the poem). Although it might sound like a dull concept for every piece of fiction to have the same basic foundation, it is the very structure of the work that makes it understandable.

A common teaching method to help readers and writers understand the structure of fiction is to picture a piece of fiction as a house. That's right—four walls, a roof, rooms, closets—everything that makes a house a complete structure, although plans for that interior may vary greatly from book to book just as they do in real homes.

How does the concept of architecture apply to fiction writing? The house represents the entire structure—the whole story. Inside the house there are rooms, and each room is a plot point, meaning a particular action that takes place within the story. The action of the story is the movement that takes place within the house, and, of course, the people moving within the house are the characters. Without these elements a house could never be a home—it would just be a skeleton with no life.

Between the Walls

In addition to having an overall structure, the story must follow a certain movement, which you can remember by thinking about the alphabet. Well, part of the alphabet anyway:

> A – Action
>
> B – Background
>
> C – Conflict, crisis, climax (in that order)
>
> D – Dénouement (resolution)
>
> E – End (conclusion)

Action

Every story needs action to move the plot forward and lead the characters toward growth and transition. If there is no action, the story cannot go anywhere and we probably wouldn't be interested in reading it anyway.

Background

To fully understand the story and the motivations of the characters, we need to know some background. Who are these characters, where do they come from, why do they do the things they do and feel the way they feel? It's no different than understanding your own life or the lives of other people. We really get to know the people in our lives when we know where they come from, what makes them tick, and what drives them.

From Conflict to Climax

The purpose of a piece of fiction is to show how the protagonist changes. This is best done when there is a conflict. How the conflict builds comes from the action in the story. A conflict leads to a crisis where the protagonist is usually faced with choices. How that character deals with the crisis helps us understand the protagonist's psychological, moral, social, or even physical transformation. The climax of the story is the pinnacle of the crisis and the point at which the character transition occurs.

Dénouement or Resolution

As readers (and as people) we need resolution to a given conflict. In fiction, we need to know what the character makes of this transition. Is the character aware that there has been a change inside himself or herself? If so, what are these internal changes? Is the character at peace? Does he or she have any better understanding of himself or herself within the situation? Or does he or she have more work to do and have simply passed through the initial stages of change?

Conclusion

Although an author can easily end a book with the *resolution*, sometimes he or she will take it a step further with a *conclusion*. It really depends on what the author is trying to say. If the most important development in the story is the resolution of the conflict, the author may choose not to tell you what happens to the character next. By ending the story at the point of resolution, the author is telling you just that: You don't need to know where the character goes from there; the important thing is how he or she got there.

Look It Up

A **conclusion** will usually contain what becomes of the character, while a **resolution** involves the character's development as a result of the conflict.

Think of this in terms of the fairy tale that ends in "happily ever after." What does that mean, exactly?

The story is really about how the hero or heroine got to the "happily ever after" and not what the "happily ever after" actually refers to—which we assume to be comfort and family.

All of these elements, if constructed well, should lead the reader to a sense of both satisfaction and loss—satisfaction with the resolution and loss that it is over. That's what makes fiction reading worthwhile.

Putting the Pieces Together

If you take the narrative voice, tone, mood, setting, plot, theme, point of view, and characterizations and put them together, they complete an intricate puzzle of meaning. If the craftsmanship is there, you will be in for a wonderful reading experience. It's an art form and a skill for a writer to put all the bits and pieces together and have them make sense to a total stranger. You have no idea what the author was thinking when he or she set out to write the book, but by the time you close the book, if the author has done his or her job well and you are knowledgeable enough to see it, you will have completed a journey you may never forget. But now, not only will you be able to feel excited about it, you'll also be able to say why.

The Least You Need to Know

- Narrative voice is a deliberate storytelling device.
- The tense the author chooses to use (past or present) pulls us into the story or backs us away from it.
- Dialogue is used to reveal character detail.
- Following a basic plot pattern is essential for fiction.

Digging Beneath the Obvious: Figurative Language

In This Chapter

◆ The difference between symbolism and metaphor

◆ How to spot hyperbole

◆ Religion, myth, and superstition as literary devices

◆ How authors incorporate wit and humor into their work

Like every other part of a carefully constructed novel, an author is always searching to tell the story in unique ways. To help you find the meaning, the author will incorporate clues in the form of symbols and metaphors. Sometimes these clues are bold and obvious, whereas other times they meander through the story like secret passageways left open for readers to discover on their journey.

In this chapter, you learn what you could be getting from a novel beyond the obvious. It's not just the characters, the plot, the themes, and the numerous narrative techniques that make the work come together, but the symbols, metaphors, and myths incorporated in the text that make the story complete and fulfilling.

Getting Definitive

We touched on *figurative language* in Chapter 7, but it's time to take a closer look. Somehow over the years the meanings of the words *symbolism* and *metaphor* have crossed paths, and one term is often mistakenly used for the other. So before you read any further, the first thing you need to do is establish the definition of the two words so that you can spot them within the text of a piece of fiction. (Allegories—symbols that reveal a larger metaphor—were covered in Chapter 7.)

Look It Up

Figurative language is used to convey something other than the literal meaning. Metaphors, similes, and hyperbole are all examples of this literary style.

Here are the definitions of the two words according to the *Dictionary of Cultural Literacy (Second Edition)*:

♦ **Symbol.** An object or name that stands for something else, especially a material thing that stands for something that is not material. For example, the symbol of America is an eagle.

♦ **Metaphor.** The comparison of one thing to another without using the words *like* or *as*. For example, "The road was a ribbon of moonlight."

Literature and Symbols: Unveiling Mysteries

Why is it important to understand symbols? Symbolism, as we have discussed in previous chapters, is frequently used in fiction as a creative literary device to give the story more depth and complexity, which of course means that there will be more for you to understand.

Sometimes symbols are blatant—they will stand out and scream their meanings—but the more interesting symbols are the ones you have to dig for. Some authors are heavy on the use of symbolism, whereas others tend to be more subtle. For example, it's fair to say that one of the most blatant symbols in *The Scarlet Letter* is the letter *A*. As you remember, in Chapter 6 we looked at the many different ways that simple letter took on very specific symbolic meanings in that novel.

Because some symbols have become so much a part of our everyday lives, many authors try to keep their ideas and writing fresh by creating unique symbols and using them to tell stories in new ways.

For example, Amy recently read the novel *The Secret Life of Bees* by Sue Monk Kidd, which builds itself up primarily by heavy use of symbolism and metaphor to make the story complete and fulfilling. The story is about a young girl's search for the truth about her mother's life. Lily Owens's mother dies tragically when Lily is a child, and she is left to be raised by her brutish father and a strong-willed African American nanny. In Lily's search for understanding of who her mother really was, she encounters several other symbolic mothers along the way.

A picture of a black Madonna leads Lily to the home of her mother's own nanny, named August, who lives with her two sisters, May and June—a household of women nurturing women. August, the oldest of the three, is a spiritual and wise woman who uses the image of the black Madonna on the label of her jars of homemade honey. In the hive, there is the Queen Bee, of course, the mother of the hive without whom all the bees would be lost. August, her sisters, and their female friends worship the Madonna (the ultimate Christian symbol of motherhood) by using their own physical relic of a black Madonna in their living room services.

The symbolic breakdown would be as follows:

- Lily uses a symbol representing the Virgin Mary to find her own mother.
- A mother (the Madonna image) leads Lily to another mother (August).
- August cares for yet another mother (the Queen Bee) and all of her offspring.

The Queen Bee and the black Madonna are two of the most significant symbols in this book, and they are used deliberately by the author to help you understand what the book is about. It is not only Lily's story, but a story that calls out to everyone who seeks love, nurturing, and unconditional acceptance. In the big picture, the global meaning is that we all need to be nurtured. The concept of "mother" is the very essence of ultimate nurturing, but we can also find that nurturing in the most unlikely places, whether it is in the house of three unwed beekeeping sisters or within the hive itself.

From the Serious to the Ridiculous

Authors have so much fun with names in their works of fiction on many different levels. Think about all the great names in literature—there are so many! Remember Ahab and Ishmael in Herman Melville's *Moby-Dick?* In Chapter 7, we discussed how their names have particular symbolic meaning to the story. We also discussed why Melville chose those names.

Think of the character Huckleberry Finn for a minute. The name conjures images of nature but perhaps in a more playful way. A huckleberry is a wild berry that grows in mountain regions, and a fin is the part of a fish's body that allows it to move. So immediately, through his name as a symbolic reference, we have a sense of Huckleberry Finn as being something good, natural, and free.

> **Between the Lines**
>
> John R. Greenfield put together a reference guide called the *Dictionary of British Literary Characters* (Facts on File, 1993) that lists thousands of famous fictitious characters from the eighteenth and nineteenth centuries. In it, he says that Charles Dickens created an astounding 989 individual characters in his career!

Charles Dickens consistently used names to represent character type—in fact, it is one of his many claims to fame. Some of the names of Dickens characters are so familiar to us now (does the name Ebenezer Scrooge ring a bell?) that they have taken on a life of their own in the English language, and we often use them as symbolic references. We might call a stingy person "a Scrooge," for example.

Metaphorically Speaking

Using *The Secret Life of Bees* as an example again, although the bees and the Black Madonna are symbols, what they represent in conjunction with the story is a metaphor. In other words, when you put all the symbols together and connect them to the story, they become pieces of the overall concept.

> **Bookmarks**
>
> Sometimes you will find something in a book that maybe the author didn't even see himself or herself, but chances are very good the references in the book are deliberate.

The *concept* of the beehive and its beekeepers is metaphorical in relation to the theme of the story. Although there is order and nurturing within the hive, in the same breath there is also fragility. This is a metaphor for what we experience as human beings. In the story, the narrator explains what happens to the hive if the Queen Bee disappears—the workers would be lost. Likewise in life, if we are not nurtured we will suffer a sense of tremendous loss and grief.

So how on earth did the author put together all these ideas in the first place? The answer is simple: by living, observing, and thinking creatively. These are the qualities that make the author an artist.

Hyperbole? Stop Exaggerating!

Using hyperbole is another way both poets and prose writers sometimes express an emotion. Hyperbole is an exaggerated expression used to show the depth and strength of an emotion. We use hyperbole in our everyday language, certainly more than we would ever use metaphors or similes. For example, how many times have you heard someone say, "I'd give my right arm for a hamburger" or "I'm so hungry I could eat a horse"? This use of language to demonstrate the strength of emotion is called hyperbole.

Some believe that hyperbole is just melodrama and sounds a little ridiculous and clichéd at times. Although this may seem true if the device is overused (as it tends to be in some gothic and romantic literature), when used in moderation hyperbole can actually be very amusing and quite profound.

Hyperbole Then

Many older pieces of poetry and prose tend to be rich in hyperbole. The romantic writers loved to use hyperbole because it allowed them to break away from the conventions of past generations of writing. They could express passionate emotion in their writing that might not have been so well received in previous literary eras.

Gothic horror in the romantic literary era is most recognizable in the use of hyperbole for effect:

> The murderer discovered! Good God! How can that be? Who could attempt to pursue him? It is impossible; one might as well try to overtake the winds, or confine a mountain-stream with a straw.
>
> —Mary Shelley, *Frankenstein*

Jane Austen, the Brontë sisters, Samuel Taylor Coleridge, Alfred Lord Tennyson, and William and Dorothy Wordsworth are some of the most well-known writers of hyperbolic text in the history of the English language.

Hyperbole Now

Human beings cannot resist the temptation for melodrama. Although hyperbolic text is not nearly the fashion now as it might have been 200 years ago, it's still commonly used by modern-day authors.

> **CAUTION**
>
> ### Take Note! _____
>
> Magical realism as a category of Spanish-language literature has faced a great deal of criticism by Spanish-language authors themselves. The concern is that the genre is limiting and marginalizes authors by removing their work from the realms of serious literature. Some say magical realism is just a passing literary trend, but most agree the genre is here to stay.

Colombian author Gabriel García Márquez's writing is rife with hyperbole, as are many works by Spanish-speaking authors. In fact, hyperbole is so commonly used in the writing of Latin authors, that it falls into its own literary genre known as "magical realism."

When Márquez writes in *One Hundred Years of Solitude* "… it rained for four years, eleven months, and two days …" what does he mean? Did it really rain all that time? No. It's an exaggerated and humorous tone that tells us that it had rained very heavily. It is highly unlikely that any place would ever get that kind of consistent rainfall, but Márquez is trying to describe the devastation to an area as a result of a storm.

Let's look at some samples of hyperbole from both old and new works of literary prose, with some explanation of what the author is trying to do.

Here we get a sense of the newness of the place through exaggeration and humor:

> The world was so recent that many things lacked names, and in order to indicate them it was necessary to point.
>
> —Gabriel García Márquez, *One Hundred Years of Solitude*

Whereas here we just get a wonderful sense of Mark Twain's consistent and beloved caustic wit through narrative voice:

> There did not seem to be brains enough in the entire nursery, so to speak, to bait a fishhook with.
>
> —Mark Twain, *A Connecticut Yankee in King Arthur's Court*

(Ahh, Twain and his humor … what would we do without them?)

Hyperbole is often used to describe someone's physical features:

> The skin on her face was as thin and drawn as tight as the skin of an onion and her eyes were gray and sharp like the points of two icepicks.

> —Flannery O'Connor, *Parker Is Back*

As you continue your reading journey, try to pay attention to hyperbole, especially in modern works of literature. We seem to be in a current literary trend of finding great meanings in understatement, so when you find exaggeration in a newly released novel, ask yourself why it's there; it may lead you to a greater understanding of the story.

References to Religion and Myth

With every page you turn in various works of fiction, you will find references to myth and religion. And if you don't find these references, you will often find their antithesis—meaning a denial of these religious or mythical references.

In Thomas Hardy's *Far from the Madding Crowd*, Hardy sets the scene of a passionate, idyllic, and even tragic pastoral countryside where nature is representative of life with all its good and bad. In the midst of this rural, almost pagan setting, Hardy introduces Bathsheba Everdene, who shakes up everyone's world with her strength, independence, and beauty. It's interesting to note that here, too, you will find symbolic names. The characters who are part of the pastoral setting have names such as Oak and Boldwood, which are strongly connected to nature by bringing to mind the image of trees; whereas Bathsheba is a biblical name taken from the Old Testament. Both her name and her very presence as an outsider automatically create a contrast between religion and culture.

If you decide to read *Far from the Madding Crowd*, keep your eyes open for another surprise. An outsider by the name of Sergeant Troy comes into the picture. What do you know about the word Troy? It's associated with myth. Your next step would be to research the story of Troy, which would lead you to the story of the Trojan horse, a decoy that led to murder and mayhem. When you understand the reference, you'll understand the character and you may even get a sense of *foreshadowing*.

Look It Up

Foreshadowing is a technique authors use to give you a hint as to what may happen later in the novel. Sometimes the foreshadowing is obvious, like when a narrator says "I didn't know this would be the last happy day of my life." The narrator is telling you point blank that there is bad news ahead in the story. Sometimes the foreshadowing is buried in the text, as in the case of Sergeant Troy.

So in one novel, Hardy uses both religion and myth to move the story along. It's a device that is frequently used in fiction, so pay attention to the signposts as you read—names, settings, symbols, and metaphors will soon jump off the page at you if your mind is curious enough to find them.

Superstition as Metaphor

Superstition is a term used to describe a belief that is not based on reason but more on magical thinking. Sometimes a superstition is faith-based or has simply arisen from the beliefs of a particular culture or society, meaning it has folkloric origins. Some people say that superstition comes from ignorance or fear, whereas others say it stems from an unenlightened religious mindset. In actuality superstition can be any or all of these things.

So how do authors incorporate elements of superstition in their writing, and how is it different from religious metaphors? For a good example, let's revisit *Huckleberry Finn*. After all, Huck was one of the most superstitious characters in literary history.

Hairballs and Snakeskins

Superstition is a powerful force that drives Mark Twain's writing in *Huckleberry Finn*. Both Jim and Huck have their own sets of superstitions that stem from their own cultures and life rituals. Although Huck initially writes off Jim's superstitions as ridiculous, he eventually comes to see the relevance and wisdom in what Jim says. And although you, as the reader, may not relate to these superstitions, what Twain is doing is showing the breakdown of differences between the two characters. The more they understand about each other, the more they respect each other.

Here are just a few examples of superstitions referenced in *Huckleberry Finn:*

♦ A hairball can tell the future.

♦ A loaf of bread can point out the whereabouts of a dead body.

♦ Touching a snakeskin with your bare hands will give you the worst kind of luck.

There are countless others. It's a wonder these two don't scare themselves to death with all of their superstitions!

Nature, Superstition, and Metaphor

Nature is used as symbol and metaphor most frequently for Huck's state of mind. For example, when Huck feels lonesome and wishes he were dead, his mood is captured with superstition references:

> The stars were shining, and the leaves rustled in the woods about somebody that was dead, and a whippowill and a dog crying about somebody that was going to die; and the wind was trying to whisper something to me, and I couldn't make out what it was, and so it made the cold shivers run over me.

The stars and the leaves and the whippoorwill and the wind and all they represent superstitiously to Huck seem to extend his mood of deep sadness and dread.

Read on:

> I got so downhearted and scared I did wish I had some company. Pretty soon a spider went crawling up my shoulder, and I flipped it off and it lit in the candle; and before I could budge it was all shriveled up. I didn't need anybody to tell me that that was an awful bad sign and could fetch me some bad luck, so I was scared and most shook the clothes off of me. I got up and turned around in my tracks three times and crossed my breast every time; and I tied up a little lock of my hair with a thread to keep witches away.

All of these references from *Huckleberry Finn* demonstrate the use of extended metaphors using nature and superstition to symbolize Huck's various emotional states. By using superstition as Huck's and Jim's belief systems, Twain further reminded readers that these two people are almost untouched by "civilization," education, and religion. This makes them appear to be as pure as the nature around them, which makes their transitions in the novel all the more poignant to the reader.

The Art of Wit and Humor

Mark Twain is famous for his sense of humor as evidenced in his fiction and essays. Twain loved to take the seemingly normal and conventional world and turn it on its head to show the reader just how ridiculous we can be. In doing this, he helps us laugh at ourselves.

Mark Twain posts a notice at the very beginning of *Huckleberry Finn* warning his readers that if they take any of the story seriously, they will be punished. In writing this "notice" to the reader, he is really asking his readers to find the humor before they get all riled up over any presumed messages.

Of course, Twain wants you to see the seriousness of the subject matter, really, but what he asks the reader to do is to see the humor first. In fact, this is another way that Twain breaks conventional literary traditions. He is not asking you to look beneath the surface by using metaphor and symbolism; rather, he wants you to find your way to the top by seeing the humor in his writing first, because then and only then will the hidden meanings be clear. He would rather the truth as he sees it be revealed to the reader by playing on the reader's own human qualities and sensibilities, one being, of course, a sense of humor.

Here is Twain's "notice" to the reader:

> Persons attempting to find a motive in this narrative will be prosecuted; persons attempting to find a moral in it will be banished; persons attempting to find a plot in it will be shot.

> By Order of the Author

The Joy of Discovery

There is no end to what authors can do to reach their readers, and there is nothing more pleasurable for a reader than to spot the hidden treasure that lies within the text. If you are the kind of reader you want to be, you will be able to find the name, the symbol, the metaphor that opens doors wide for further understanding. When that happens, you will experience a joy in reading fiction that you may never have expected. It's like being the archaeologist who finds the skull of a previously unknown dinosaur. You will relish your discoveries and use them to forge ahead to further understanding about yourself and the world around you.

The Least You Need to Know

- ◆ Symbolism and metaphor are two different comparative devices.

- ◆ Hyperbole is exaggeration used to express strong emotions.

- ◆ Superstition, myth, and religion are commonly used as metaphors in fiction.

- ◆ Humor is a clever device used to help readers see deeper meanings in literature.

How to Read a Poem

In This Chapter

♦ Demystifying poetry

♦ How subjectivity affects the reader

♦ A look at poetic terminology

♦ Understanding the different types of poetry

♦ The structure, form, and style of the poem

♦ Poetic twists and turns

Some people find it difficult to relate to poetry, whereas others delight in it. Think of poetry and visual arts in the same light. Whereas an artist uses a paintbrush to have color, texture, and shape come alive for the viewer, a poet uses a pen to create the same effect.

In this chapter, you learn not only how to read poetry, but why you should read it. If you've never been much of a poetry reader, ask yourself "Why not?" What is it that you are not getting from this kind of writing and how do you find it? You'll learn that here—now—finally. And if you're already a poetry reader, you will learn even more about how poems are put together and how to better absorb them.

Poetry Is Art

Poetry probably falls through the cracks of English and literature courses so often because it's overlooked as an artistic expression of emotion in the same way that the visual arts are. Poetry is most often not taught in any hands-on kind of way, the way it really should be.

Some people may find poetry tricky to read—in fact, many voracious readers tend to pass right by poetry. Why? Is poetry really so mysterious? Is it because people need to be told a story directly without having to put too much of their own thought into it? Is it because it's too abstract?

Poetry can be compared to painting. When you look at a work of art, you first see it for what it is—a depiction of a person, an animal, a place, or a thing. You'll notice the colors and the textures, and maybe how the light shines through a window or highlights a patch of flowers. These are the things you see on the surface. Then you look a little closer at some of the fine details. How did the painter make white paint look silver against blue drapery? How did the artist catch that sad look in the eyes of the child? How on earth did he actually make an apple look so real you could almost reach out and grab it off the table?

Now what about abstract art? What do you see in these paintings? Strange shapes and images—are they recognizable? Do they make you feel a certain way? When you look at abstract art, maybe you don't necessary see as much as you are actually feeling.

To some people, poetry is like abstract art. Some people feel that poetry is too subjective to the artist for the reader to be able to fully understand it. How can you make sense of words that don't necessarily tell a story? To appreciate art, you must first appreciate your own sensibilities, then you must appreciate

Look It Up

If you look up the word *poem* in various dictionaries, you will find many different definitions, but most of the time you will find something like "a highly developed and imaginative expression of emotion." And a *poet* is often defined as a writer who "has a gift of artistic sensitivity." Basically, **poetry** is a compressed form of writing that conveys emotion or ideas to a reader.

Bookmarks

If you really want to understand poetry, it's a good idea to start a poetry-reading group. Most book groups concentrate on prose fiction reading only. Why not break away and join a poetry club? If you can't find one, start your own. It will definitely help with your understanding of poetry to see what others get from their own readings.

form and texture. With poetry, you start with an appreciation of and trust for your own feelings, and then you examine your appreciation of words and the magic they make when they're used together.

Up Close and Personal

You do have to know some terminology in order to study poetry, but it shouldn't be the be-all and end-all of your understanding of the subject. You should just have enough information to make understanding the art and form of poetry a little easier. It's really not so important that you be able to analyze the structure of a poem unless you're in school and it's on an upcoming exam. The most important thing is that you can feel the poem. If you can't feel the poem, you need to look closer to find what you might be missing.

Understanding the terminology will make this task easier for you, but ultimately the understanding has much more to do with whether you can relate to the poem and find a place for it within your own sensibilities.

Coming to Terms with Poetry

Here are some terms commonly used in the study of poetry and a few examples to help you along:

♦ **Alliteration.** Repetition of consonant sounds at the beginning of words: "flags flapping ferociously in the wind" (note the three f's).

♦ **Assonance.** Repetition of similar vowel sounds in a sentence or within a line of poetry or prose: "I took a look at a book that I found in the nook."

♦ **Couplet.** A pair of rhyming lines that often separate one stanza from another (but there is no rule that they have to).

♦ **Meter.** A pattern of rhythm syllabic accents in the lines, verses, and stanzas of poems.

♦ **Foot.** A unit of poetic meter consisting of both stressed and unstressed syllables—usually one unstressed syllable is followed by one stressed syllable. Read this example aloud from Robert Frost's *Stopping by Woods on a Snowy Evening* and as you do, notice the syllabic emphasis:

Whose woods these are I think I know.
His house is in the village though;
He will not see me stopping here
To watch his woods fill up with snow.

- **Iamb.** A metrical foot—one unstressed syllable is followed by a stressed syllable. The adjective is "iambic."

- **Iambic pentameter.** Because one iambic foot consists of one unstressed syllable follow by a stressed one, iambic pentameter is a poetic measurement consisting of five iambic feet per line (the unstressed syllables are in bold):

  Was this **the** face **that** launch'd **a** thous**and** ships
  And burnt **the** top**less** tow**ers of** Ili**um**?

  —Christopher Marlowe, *Dr. Faustus* (sixteenth century)

This piece of Marlowe's poem is also a good example of blank verse, which is iambic pentameter without rhyme.

- **Closed form.** A form of poetry where structure is characterized consistently in terms of rhyme, line length, and metric pattern. Robert Frost frequently wrote in closed form.

- **Free verse (open form).** We live in an era of free verse, where poetry does not necessarily contain any patterns of meter or rhyme. It is free in that it is not bound by any traditional poetic rules. (We take a closer look at free verse later in the chapter.)

- **Verse.** One line of poetry.

- **Stanza.** A poetic paragraph. Note that not all poems are necessarily broken into stanzas.

You don't have to memorize these terms, just be aware that poetry doesn't consist of words thrown together; it's an art form, with guidelines and rules.

Get With the Rhythm

Most poems have a rhythm that depends on the emphasis on syllables within the lines, verses, and stanzas. Take a look at a few poems and note how important the syllables are to the movement of the poem. The most obvious poems to help you see this are children's rhymes and song lyrics. If so much as one syllable is missing or one too many syllables added, it will throw off the rhythmic pattern of the poem. (Think back to the Dr. Seuss books of your childhood.) Although some types of poems such as limericks and haiku have very strict rules about syllabic use, most poems are pretty free flowing.

To understand the rhyming patterns in poetry, a rhyming meter devised of a, b, c is commonly used. The first rhyme at the end of the first verse is given the letter *a*. If the last word in the second line does not rhyme with the word in the first verse, you give it a *b*, and so on. When you find a rhyme within the stanza, you give it the letter it matches. Then you start again with the next stanza.

Note that the ability to format meter by using this method only applies to poems that rhyme. You will have to study other types of poems and poetic terminology to analyze nonrhyming poetic form and structure.

Types of Poems

Now that you have a handle on some basic poetic terminology and concepts, let's take a look at how these elements are used in various types of poetry.

Poetry, like all art forms, is international: It crosses all borders, language barriers, age groups, and eras. (The British have their sonnets, for example, whereas the Japanese have their haikus, and children have Mother Goose.)

The following sections describe some types of poetry and include excerpts from notable poets who wrote within these genres. There are many more types of poems, but these are among the most common.

Bookmarks

For extra guidance, look for an anthology of poetry, which is a collection of selected writing that also contains a great deal of helpful background information. You'll find a wealth of information on poets, poetry, poetic eras, and poetic terminology in these books. You can find anthologies in any bookstore or online.

Ballad

A ballad is a story told as a narrative, rhythmic saga of something that happened in the past. Sometimes the themes are heroic, sometimes satirical, and other times romantic. The ballad almost always has an unhappy ending. Ballad and ballade are two different types of poetry. The ballade is a fourteenth- and fifteenth-century French poem written in verse form consisting of three stanzas written in a particular rhythmic format.

Take Note! _____

It's important to find good translations if you are reading poetry written in a language other than your own. Much of the beauty of the words and meaning of the poem can be lost in the translation if it is not done accurately.

It was in and about the Martinmas time,
When the green leaves were a-falling,
That Sir John Graem, in the West country,
Fell in love with Barbara Allen

He sent his men down through the town
To the place where she was dwelling;
"Oh hast and come to my master dear,
Gin ye be Barbara Allen."

—Anonymous, *Barbara Allen* (medieval Scottish ballad, first two stanzas)

Cinquain

Influenced by Japanese poetry, the cinquain was developed by American poet Adelaide Crapsey. It is a short, nonrhyming poem that consists of 22 syllables with a certain number of syllables per line.

Listen …
With faint dry sound,
Like steps of passing ghosts,
The leaves, frost-crisp'd, break from the trees
And fall.

—Adelaide Crapsey, *November Night* (early twentieth-century cinquain)

Elegy

An elegy is a poem that is written to mourn the death of someone. It is a reflection either upon death or some other great sadness.

The curfew tolls the knell of parting day,
The lowing herd wind slowly o'er the lea,

The ploughman homeward plods his weary way,
And leaves the world to darkness and to me.

—Thomas Gray, *Elegy Written in a Country Churchyard* (eighteenth-century elegy, first stanza)

Epic

This type of poetry has a very broad definition. An epic is a continuous narrative of the life or lives of a heroic person or persons. These heroes can be fictional, historical, or mythical.

So toward that shrine which then in all the realm
Was richest, Arthur leading, slowly went
The marshalled Order of their Table Round,
And Lancelot sad beyond his wont, to see
The maiden buried, not as one unknown,
Nor meanly, but with gorgeous obsequies,
And mass, and rolling music, like a queen.

—Alfred, Lord Tennyson, excerpt from *Idylls of the King* (nineteenth-century epic poem)

The first known epic poem is the Sumerian poem *Epic of Gilgamesh.* The longest is the great Indian mythical poem *Mahabharata*, which contains more than 100,000 verses—making it four times the size of the Bible.

Haiku

One of the most important Japanese poetic forms is the haiku. This is a short poem that consists of no more than three lines, with the first line consisting of five syllables, the second line consisting of seven syllables, and the third line consisting again of five syllables.

While the traditional Japanese haiku consists of a strict structure of sounds, when written in English the haiku has taken on all sorts of forms. The artistic value of the haiku exists in simplicity of language that creates images or evokes ideas. Both the contemporary and traditional haiku should consist of only three lines with a total of no more than seventeen syllables—or in the case of Japanese, sounds.

The Haiku Society of America defines the haiku as "A short poem that uses imagistic language to convey the essence of an experience of nature or the season intuitively linked to the human condition." While this may be the official American definition, great liberties have been taken in the art of haiku writing over the years.

Here is an example of a traditional Japanese haiku (translated into English) which was written by one of the most notable Japanese poets of the seventeenth century, Matsuo Basho. Note that the structure, in its English translation, does not follow the 5-7-5 syllable rule—but in its original Japanese it would! Translators predict that 17 sounds in Japanese correlate to about 12 syllables in English.

> An old pond!
> A frog jumps in
> The sound of water.

A traditional Japanese haiku should also contain at least one word that will indicate a season. This word is referred to as the "kigo" in Japanese. In English the "kigo" is often omitted and replaced with the concept of juxtaposing two images or ideas—referred to in Japanese as "renso." Other literary techniques commonly omitted from haiku writing is the use of titles, similes, and metaphors.

Here is contemporary haiku written in English by Amy:

> Setting sun
> Sandcastles wash away
> A seagull lingers

Limerick

Limericks are poems that consist of a strict meter. In fact, without the structure of the lines and the rhyming patter, the limerick would simply be just another poem.

> There was a Young Person of Smyrna
> Whose grandmother threatened to burn her;
> But she seized on the cat, and said, "Granny, burn that!
> You incongruous old woman of Smyrna!"

> —Edward Lear (otherwise known as the poet laureate of the limerick), untitled limerick (nineteenth century)

Between the Lines

Although Limerick is a county in Ireland, the limerick poem did not originate there. Nobody knows for sure why the limerick poetry form has adopted the name of an Irish county. There were several nineteenth-century Irish limerick poets who may have ended their poems with the final line of "come all the way up to Limerick?" This is disputed by other historians who believe the word *limerick* may have been a derivative of Edward Lear's last name.

Lyric

When we think of the word *lyric*, we often think of a song, which is where the word originates: A *lyre* is a Greek musical instrument often used to accompany someone singing a song. The common and academic use of lyric, as a poetic form, means a poem that expresses a subjective point of view.

> Thou still unravish'd bride of quietness,
> Thou foster-child of silence and slow time,
> Sylvan historian, who canst thus express
> A flowery tale more sweetly than our rhyme:
> What leaf-fring'd legend haunts about thy shape
> Of deities or mortals, or of both,
> In Tempe or the dales of Arcady?
> What men or gods are these? What maidens loth?
> What mad pursuit? What struggle to escape?
> What pipes and timbrels? What wild ecstasy?
>
> —John Keats, opening lines of *Ode to a Grecian Urn* (late nineteenth century)

Although an "ode" is most often a love poem, it is also a type of lyric poetry. The actual definition of an ode is the praise of a person or an object in a poetic form that is not subject to any definitive rhyming scheme or iambic line lengths, as is true with this particular ode and lyric poem by Keats.

Nonsense Verse

Often used for comic effect or as children's verse, a nonsense poem can be silly and witty—but it can also have a serious meaning beneath the surface.

The Owl and the Pussy-Cat went to sea
In a beautiful pea-green boat;
They took some honey, and plenty of money,
Wrapped up in a five-pound note.
The Owl looked up to the stars above,
And sang to a small guitar,
'O lovely Pussy! O Pussy my love,
What a beautiful Pussy you are
You are,
You are!
What a beautiful Pussy you are!

—Edward Lear, *The Owl and the Pussycat* (nineteenth-century nonsense poem, first stanza)

Ode

An ode is a long form poem usually of a serious nature on an exalted subject matter. In Pablo Neruda's *Ode to My Socks*, he seems to lightheartedly worship a particular pair of socks. While to most people a pair of socks is not worth any exaltation at all, this poem is an ode, not only because of its structure, but, well, because of his heightened appreciation of his new socks!

Maru Mori brought me a pair of socks knitted with her own shepherd's hands, two socks soft as rabbits. I slipped my feet into them as if into jewel cases woven with threads of dusk and sheep's wool.

Audacious socks, my feet became two woolen fish, two long gangly sharks of lapis blue shot with a golden thread, two mammoth blackbirds, two cannons, thus were my feet honored by these celestial socks. They were so beautiful that for the first time my feet seemed unacceptable to me, two tired old fire fighters not worthy of the woven fire, of those luminous socks.

—Pablo Neruda, *Ode to My Socks* (1950s)

Look a little deeper and you will notice that, despite its title, the poem is a sort of love poem. Neruda is not really worshipping the socks, but rather, the comfort and beauty and everything else a pair of warm socks in winter means to a couple of cold feet. And although it's not stated, maybe Neruda was even worshipping the woman who made the socks.

Quatrain

A quatrain is a poem or stanza of a poem that contains four lines of verse.

> Tyger! Tyger! burning bright
> In the forests of the night,
> What immortal hand or eye
> Could frame thy fearful symmetry?
>
> —From William Blake's "The Tyger" (eighteenth century, first stanza)

Rondeau

A form of poetry that makes use of song-type lyricism. It is based on a strict rhythmic meter and contains refrains repeated in a specific style. A good example of a rondeau is Lieutenant Colonel John McCrae's "In Flanders Fields." As you read it, notice the sing-song quality in its rhyming pattern:

> In Flanders fields the poppies blow
> Between the crosses, row on row
> That mark our place; and in the sky
> The larks, still bravely singing, fly
> Scarce heard amid the guns below.
>
> We are the Dead. Short days ago
> We lived, felt dawn, saw sunset glow,
> Loved and were loved, and now we lie
> In Flanders fields.
>
> Take up our quarrel with the foe:
> To you from failing hands we throw
> The torch; be yours to hold it high.
> If ye break faith with us who die
> We shall not sleep, though poppies grow
> In Flanders fields.
>
> —Lieutenant Colonel John McCrae, M.D., "In Flanders Fields" (1915)

Sonnet

The word *sonnet* comes from the French word meaning song. It is a poem consisting of fourteen lines within a strict rhyming pattern. One of the most famous sonnet writers was William Shakespeare.

> Let me not to the marriage of true minds
> Admit impediments. Love is not love
> Which alters when it alteration finds,
> Or bends with the remover to remove:
> O no! it is an ever-fixed mark
> That looks on tempests and is never shaken;
> It is the star to every wandering bark,
> Whose worth's unknown, although his height be taken.
> Love's not Time's fool, though rosy lips and cheeks
> Within his bending sickle's compass come:
> Love alters not with his brief hours and weeks,
> But bears it out even to the edge of doom.
> If this be error and upon me proved,
> I never writ, nor no man ever loved.

—William Shakespeare, *Sonnet 116* (sixteenth century)

Structure and Form

When we think about structure and form in poetry, we look for patterns of meter, lines, and rhymes. You're an expert on all that now, right? Well, it's one thing to understand the terminology and another to put it in context as you read.

Structure and form involve how the poem is actually put together. What kind of poem is it? What kind of rhythmic patterns does it contain? How is punctuation used? Are there stanzas? Does the break in stanza have any kind of reason to it?

These are the questions you must ask yourself after you've read the poem—but not so much while you're reading it. We are firm believers that you should read the poem for pleasure first, then for understanding, and then a third time for an even deeper understanding—to get an up-close-and-personal look at it.

The Poet's Purpose

William Wordsworth, the English poet whose work spanned from the eighteenth century into the nineteenth century, gave us a definition of poetry that has lived through the ages in the scholarly world. Wordsworth defined poetry as "the spontaneous overflow of powerful feelings" and went on to say that the poem originates from "emotion recollected in tranquility."

Wordsworth was particularly concerned that a poem be judged directly by the standard of "the emotional and moral integrity of its language," which basically means that in his time, a poet not only had a responsibility to himself as an artist but to society on the whole. In his *Ode: intimations of immortality from recollections of early childhood*, it almost seems like he is lost in himself—lost in his own sense of missing something that is gone. That is true—he is—but as he speaks through his own emotion, he implores every adult to reflect on these sentiments of lost youth:

This particular portion of the poem highlights this point:

> Then sing, ye Birds, sing, sing a joyous song!
> And let the young Lambs bound
> As to the tabor's sound!
> We in thought will join your throng,
> Ye that pipe and ye that play,
> Ye that through your hearts today
> Feel the gladness of the May!
> What though the radiance which was once so bright
> Be now forever taken from my sight …

But he brings the sentiments back to the reader by expounding on a bigger message:

> Though nothing can bring back the hour
> Of splendor in the grass, of glory in the flower;
> We will grieve not, rather find
> Strength in what remains behind;
> In the primal sympathy
> Which having been must ever be;
> In the soothing thoughts that spring
> Out of human suffering;
> In the faith that looks through death,
> In years that bring the philosophic mind.

It is important to read what authors and poets have to say about their own works in order to fully understand what they are trying to say to you through their writing. As with a work of fiction, you need to study the background of the writer, study the times in which he or she lived, and try to get a sense of what the poet wanted to communicate to the audiences. Does the message still hold true for modern-day readers? These are all the factors to consider when reading any piece of literature, but especially poetry, because a poem will never spell its meaning out directly—instead, it calls to you to discover it for yourself.

Bookmarks

Because you will never know what Wordsworth was thinking and feeling when he sat down to write a poem, you really only have his words to go by. Therefore, his definition of poetry gives you clues as to how to read his poems. If you are intent upon understanding a poem, keep in mind you are about to be deeply immersed in the poet's art of truthfully communicating to you his or her deeply felt feelings and ideas. Reading a poem in a heightened state of your own awareness of feelings and thoughts is what you bring of yourself to the poem so that you can meet the poet (and his or her poem) halfway.

Understanding Free Verse

If you read all the poetic definitions earlier in the chapter, you will have noted the reference to "free verse." Simply stated, free verse is poetry that does not ascribe to any set structure. It is a type of poetry that is written without rules pertaining to rhythm, iambic line length, or any set rhyming pattern. Even though free verse (or open form, as it's also called) is popular with contemporary poets, it's not a new idea. In fact, poet Walt Whitman inaugurated "the free verse movement." Whitman was influenced by Ralph Waldo Emerson's essay called *The Poet* (1844), in which Emerson says:

> The poet is the sayer, the namer, and represents beauty. He is a sovereign and stands in the centre... Beauty is the creator of the universe. Therefore the poet is not any permissive potentate but is emperor in his own right ... he writes what will and must be spoken ... he is the true and only doctor; he knows and tells; he is the only teller of news ... he is beholder of ideas and an utterer of the necessary and casual.

Whitman was so moved and inspired by these words that he added to what Emerson had to say and applied it directly to his own society:

> Yet America is a poem in our eyes, its ample geography dazzles the imagination and it will not wait long for metres.

In a time when the United States was in the midst of transition to a freer society, Whitman saw an opportunity to free his verse from convention when he wrote *Song of Myself*, a lyric poem about America and the individuals who live there. The poem is considered one of the greatest poems written in the English language, not only for the beauty of the words, but because of its pure subjectivity and introspection:

> I celebrate myself;
> And what I assume you shall assume;
> For every atom belonging to me as good belongs to you.
>
> I loafe and invite my Soul;
> I lean and loafe at my ease, observing a spear of summer grass.
>
> Houses and rooms are full of perfumes—the shelves are crowded with perfumes;
> I breathe the fragrance myself, and know it and like it;
> The distillation would intoxicate me also, but I shall not let it.
>
> The atmosphere is not a perfume—it has no taste of the distillation—it is
>   odorless;
> It is for my mouth forever—I am in love with it;
> I will go to the bank by the wood, and become undisguised and naked;
> I am mad for it to be in contact with me.

What makes the poem so remarkable is that it is so full of mystery (and we mean that in a good way!). The mystery lies in the fact that we have no idea what Whitman's really talking about. Is he remembering something? Is he relishing a moment that is special to him? We may never know the true emotional sources he called upon when creating this poem, but that doesn't mean we can't connect with him in the same kind of introspective way.

The Poet Speaks to You

As you know now, lyric poems are known to be particularly subjective, which means that the author is not necessarily writing it with the intention of relaying any specific messages to an audience. By being subjective, it is as though he is painting a picture of a place you may have never seen, smelled, or even imagined, but he writes it so that you share his emotional state of mind.

Whitman tells you this at the beginning of *Song of Myself.* He lets you know that you are invited to experience this emotional state right along with him whether or not the experience is yours. He is sharing it with you.

In the very first line of this poem, Whitman is saying: I am the center of my creation as I write this poem, but at the same time I am aware of you, my reader: ... *And what I assume you shall assume/For every atom belonging to me as good belongs to you.* In other words, he is telling you directly that you can easily understand his poem because we all have similarities within our sensibilities. We are separate beings, but we are also alike if we choose to be.

You become immersed in his subjectivity. And when he has your attention, he continues: *I loafe and invite my soul, I lean and loafe at my ease observing a spear of summer grass.* Here he invites you to settle yourself down with him—"loafe" a little yourself and pay attention.

He uses his subjectivity to bring you toward him. Don't forget, he has already told you that everything he is saying about himself is also true of you.

What else seems to matter to Whitman in this section of the poem? Well, the senses. Read this line out loud and listen to it carefully. What does this bring to mind for you?

> Houses and rooms are full of perfumes—the shelves are crowded with perfumes;
> I breathe the fragrance myself, and know it and like it;
> The distillation would intoxicate me also, but I shall not let it.

He enjoys these senses but does not intend to let them overtake his mind.

And here is your first mystery from this section of the poem:

> The atmosphere is not a perfume—it has no taste of the distillation—it is odorless;
> It is for my mouth forever—I am in love with it;

> I will go to the bank by the wood, and become undisguised and naked;
> I am mad for it to be in contact with me

Here is where the poem turns more toward the reader—there is really no mystery here, only a small element of surprise as he lets the reader a little further into what he wants to say. What he is telling you here is that we hide ourselves—we don't allow ourselves to dissolve into our own senses. He is telling us to relax and allow our senses to awaken to the world of sounds, smells, tastes, and memories that surround us.

If you continue with this poem, we can almost guarantee that you will get to many new places inside of yourself. It will be impossible for you not to gain new understandings and awareness through this poem.

The Element of Surprise

Don't take for granted the fact that Whitman is inviting *you* into his very subjective piece of writing. This is a pleasant surprise and should make you feel like the poet needs you there to experience these feelings with him. You will not get this invitation very often when you read lyric poetry (or any poetry for that matter). But remember, if you are really absorbing a poem, it is impossible to separate yourself from the poet or the poem, even if you are not as blatantly and intimately included as Walt Whitman allows in this particular poem.

Meaningful Twists

Oddly enough (or maybe not so odd given the close-knit circles in which poets travel), poets often write for other poets, despite the reference to *you*. Poets drop little clues and throw in surprises here and there. What makes a poem wonderful despite the language and the meaning you take from it is that element of surprise.

For example, although this next poem by Rainer Maria Rilke clearly speaks directly to other poets—surprise!—he's also talking to you. He's giving the reader a little insight into what makes a poem and the poet. Rilke had this to say in translated verse form (he wrote his poetic works in German):

> You must construct an image for each feeling
> You wish to give to many strangers;
> For one must firmly frame what one imparts;
> In children's words or summer lime trees

There be some likeness that will shape it.
You mustn't 'say' what secretly you 'have',
Your life mustn't trickle out upon your lips,—
You must bear your blossoms like a bough,
Then all breezes will proclaim you …

—Rainer Maria Rilke, from *Diaries of a Young Poet* (1898)

> ### Between the Lines
>
> Rainer Maria Rilke (1875–1926) was born into a noble family in Prague. He traveled the world, and on his journeys he met Russian author Leo Tolstoy and worked as a secretary for Auguste Rodin. He was a prolific poet in the German expressionist style, in which artists began to reject past conventions and write with freedom of emotion.

Rilke says that as the poet, you must consider whom you are speaking to and put together clearly what you want to say. Keep it clear and direct the way children do. Use images that frame exactly what you mean, but don't say it all or you will spoil it for the reader: *Your life mustn't trickle out upon your lips/You must bear your blossoms like a bough/Then all breezes will proclaim you …*.

What's more wonderful than a pleasant surprise, and what's more dramatic than an unpleasant one? Poetry has the ability to startle as well as to please by taking twists and turns into the unexpected. We sometimes will have preconceived notions shattered when we follow along with the poem—as it builds we fall into its rhythm, its heartbeat, its movement, we begin to think we know where it will take us, when *wham!* The whole thing changes with a single line of verse, or even a single word. This is what can make the difference to any reader of poetry—when the expected gets flipped on its head, forcing us to see something that we never knew was coming our way.

The Perfect Fit

Although we want to believe that every poem will speak volumes to us, open new doors, and open our hearts and minds to new thoughts and feelings, as with fiction and the visual arts, not all poems speak to us. That's okay, though. We all have different tastes, and once again, we have to emphasize that you not get frustrated as you forge ahead with poetry reading. What will probably happen is that you'll find a poet who does speak to you, whether it's a poet from the eighteenth century or someone more contemporary. The important thing is to find the right fit for you.

Is bliss, then, such abyss
I must not put my foot amiss
For fear I spoil my shoe?

I'd rather suit my foot
Than save my boot,
For yet to buy another pair
Is possible
At any fair.

But bliss is sold just once;
The patent lost
None buy it any more.

—Emily Dickinson, *Poem 340*

As Dickinson is telling you here, not every poem will suit you or fit just right. You need to keep looking until you find those that do. There are poems that tickle with laughter, and ones that draw us close to the universe. There are those that ponder and contemplate, and those that float like the breeze. There is no "one size fits all" in any art form—and that is equally true for poetry.

The poems you do wind up choosing will vary with your mood and where you are in your life. Well, that's just all to the good because then you will fit yourself right in with what suits and feels best to you.

The Least You Need to Know

- Poetry is a subjective art.

- You can't know what the author was thinking, but the clues the author leaves should lead you to understanding.

- There are many different types of poetry. Some types have strict structural rules, whereas others have no rules at all.

- Poets have developed their styles and ideas through the centuries.

- The element of surprise is a key way for a poet to reach the reader.

Chapter 11

How to Read a Short Story

In This Chapter

- ◆ What is a short story?

- ◆ Short on words, but not on meaning

- ◆ Structure of the short story

- ◆ The short story's origins

- ◆ Where you can find short stories

Sometimes the short story gets shortchanged. Many people who read fiction never consider reading short stories. Instead, these readers forge right into those novels, hoping to be taken away on grand, long adventures. But can't a day trip be just as fun and enjoyable as a long vacation?

The writer of the short story specifically needs to know how to use point of view, style, plot, and structure with a compressed writing technique. Basically this means the author can't dilly-dally with words. The art of the short story is in the author's ability to use as few words as possible in just the right ways to make the story complete its arc and evoke the desired emotional and intellectual responses from the reader.

In this chapter, you learn not only how touching, poignant, and amusing short stories can be, but also where they came from, why you should read them, and what you can take away from them that will not only make you a better reader but a more insightful person.

Keeping It Short but Sweet

When an author writes a novel, he or she has a great deal of "wiggle room" to explain the actions or a character, a personality trait, or the dynamics within relationships. *Short story* writers are not allowed the same liberties because they are attempting to tell a focused story with a limited number of words.

Whereas a novel can span hundreds of pages over several volumes, if need be, a novella is longer than a short story and shorter than a novel. Anything over 20,000 and less than 50,000 words is considered to be a novella. A short story has fewer than 20,000 words but must have more than 500.

Look It Up

Shorter than a novel or novella, a **short story** usually develops around a single central theme, and is limited in scope and number of characters.

As you know, a novel can give you lots of introductory material before getting to the heart of the story. The author of a short story doesn't have that kind of luxury. She has to use as few words as possible to keep the piece of prose within the short story genre of prose fiction writing.

So the author must employ her words efficiently to produce this tight piece of writing. A limited number of characters are introduced, and they have to be sharp from the get-go—in other words, they have to be well developed and the reader needs to know them right away.

If you are the sort of person who enjoys getting down to the nitty-gritty of a story as soon as possible, the short story is for you. If you enjoy expert artistry with regard to the writing process, you'll especially enjoy this form of writing because the author's ability to accomplish an effective piece of short writing depends on her being highly skilled at her craft.

No Time to Waste

The short story usually begins very close to or even on the verge of the climax. Everything is kept to a minimum, such as details of the setting and other descriptions, and the complications are kept to a happy minimum. The central incident is selected to reveal as much as possible of the protagonist's life and character, and the details are devised to carry maximum significance. The short story is sharper and clearer than longer prose fiction because it is written so economically. This kind of writing is meant to be spare, neat, and clean.

Up-Front Focus

When you begin reading a short story, one of the things you should pay attention to is the very first paragraph. A well-written piece of short fiction not only gives you a great deal of information in the opening paragraph due to the compressed style of writing, it also grabs your attention so that you're eager to read on.

In his 1919 story titled *Hands*, in the very first paragraph Sherwood Anderson tells us the following:

> UPON the half decayed veranda of a small frame house that stood near the edge of a ravine near the town of Winesburg, Ohio, a fat little old man walked nervously up and down. Across a long field that had been seeded for clover but that had produced only a dense crop of yellow mustard weeds, he could see the public highway along which went a wagon filled with berry pickers returning from the fields. The berry pickers, youths and maidens, laughed and shouted boisterously. A boy clad in a blue shirt leaped from the wagon and attempted to drag after him one of the maidens, who screamed and protested shrilly. The feet of the boy in the road kicked up a cloud of dust that floated across the face of the departing sun. Over the long field came a thin girlish voice. "Oh, you Wing Biddlebaum, comb your hair, it's falling into your eyes," commanded the voice to the man, who was bald and whose nervous little hands fiddled about the bare white forehead as though arranging a mass of tangled locks.

Right from the start, Anderson makes us want to read more about Wing Biddlebaum. As you read this paragraph, think about what makes you want to know more. There is one key word that should grab you—the word "nervous." There is nothing particularly nerve-wracking about this scene, so you may immediately be hooked by that one simple word because it instills a sense of anticipation. The driving force to continue reading the story is the desire to know why Wing is nervous. Knowing that the title of the story is *Hands*, you may also immediately notice that this opening paragraph ends with not only a repeat of the word "nervous" but incorporates the title of the story buy describing a small action involving Wing's hands.

Bookmarks

In some ways, the author of a short story is trying to reach the reader in the same way a poet does—by using just the right words to get a point across. The difference is, a poem can easily be as long as a novel.

The second question you may ask yourself, then, is "Who is Wing Biddlebaum and why are his hands significant?" Anderson's choice of words (in conjunction with the story title) has been deliberately constructed to hook the reader into the story. This is the art of the short story—hooking the reader and holding him or her to the end by using carefully chosen words within carefully constructed paragraphs. We take a closer look at Anderson, a master of the short story, later in this chapter.

A Different Kind of Structure

The structure of a short story is similar to that of the novel and novella. There is a theme, a plot line, characters, and a climax. Technically speaking, however, the short story does not follow the same structural format as longer prose fiction.

The basic elements of the short story are as follows:

- **Setting.** Time and place
- **Conflict.** Usually between the protagonist and antagonist
- **Main character.** Protagonist
- **Theme.** The point that evokes both an emotional and intellectual response

One of the main differences between the structure of the novel and that of the short story has to do with what is known as the "arc" of the story, meaning the way the story comes full circle. It opens with a setting, a character, and a mood, and the conflict is evident from early on. The story builds to its climax and resolves and concludes rather quickly. The arc of the story is the skeleton of the overall structure.

Between the Lines

Short stories are usually set in present times because they are published predominately in popular magazines and literary journals. Readers of magazines usually look for matters that concern them in the here and now.

Setting the Scene

Short stories are usually set in the present day, but the places can vary from the rural to the urban and even to outer space. A short story also focuses on one main character, the protagonist, who faces some sort of transition within the story. The conflict in the story (leading to the transition) is usually between the protagonist and another character, the antagonist. On the other hand, the protagonist may struggle with an internal conflict—maybe a spiritual or psychological dilemma.

Subject and Theme

The subject and the theme are not one and the same in the short story. The subject matter of a short story is the groundwork—the roots from which the theme grows. Modern-day subject matters relate to feminist, race or gender, or class issues as well as drug abuse, poverty, and relationships.

The theme is the heart of the story, which is highlighted by the subject matter. Modern-day themes include loneliness, isolation, and alienation; personal trauma; love and hate; emotional and physical relationships; family troubles, including generational conflicts; growing from innocence to self-realization; illusion versus reality; self-denial versus self-indulgence; self-delusion; self-discovery; conflicts of morality and spirituality; and immigration and cross-cultural issues. These are themes that seem to hit home in modern times and themes that publishers most commonly look for.

You know that in any piece of fiction you are ultimately looking for the theme(s). In a short story, the best way to understand the theme is to pay attention to the climax. The entire story is built around one central theme rather than the multiple and layered themes within a novel. While you might have to dig for subthemes in a novel, in a short story, the theme will be hard to miss, especially if you can pinpoint that climax. Keep in mind, that, unlike the novel, the climax may not be in the middle of the story, so keep your eyes peeled and mind open.

Experimenting with Structure

A short story is a tale or what is known as a "story of incident," in which the focus of interest is on the course and outcome of events. In just a few pages, you'll be moved very swiftly through the beginning, middle, and end. That is the standard, but many authors have experimented with this writing style using different techniques where the structure may seem more subtle but the theme hits home nonetheless.

For example, Anton Chekhov's 1899 story titled *The Lady with the Pet Dog* explores both the simplicity and complexity of a relationship between a man and woman after they meet on a beach in Yalta. They become lovers, and while there is an ease and simplicity in their bond, the outside pressures of their lives cause complication, struggle, and pain. This is not an extraordinary theme, but the way that Chekhov presents it to us evokes tremendous feeling. There is not a great deal of action in this story, but there is heightened emotion between the characters, which is transferred to the reader through the carefully constructed story.

That doesn't mean the story is about nothing. The story is about two people who meet by chance in a most ordinary way and are attracted to each other. The result of their attraction is the real action of the story in that it is what evokes response in the reader.

The narrator ends the story by giving us a sense of wistful hopefulness but no real conclusion. The story is not about these two people winding up together or not winding up together. It's about the beauty in desire and the hopelessness in the characters. It's about longing. We have all felt that at some point in our lives. The point of the story is for the reader to share the experience of the characters' emotions. The conclusion lies within our emotional state and not in what happens to these two people.

It is important to note the title of this story as well. Chekhov gives it the most mundane of titles as an ironic gesture. While the title is as mundane as the chance meeting of these two characters, the action within the story is anything but mundane.

The Short Story Becomes Popular

Short stories have existed from the beginning of humanity, with fables and storytelling—some of which have survived to modern times. The first written short story is believed to be an entry in the *Anglo-Saxon Chronicle* of 755 C.E., compiled by King Alfred the Great. It included one particular entry involving sex, revenge, and loyalty that was written in rather an artistic and thoughtful way. Despite this introduction of short prose told as fiction, poetry was still the literary choice of the times.

Edgar Allan Poe (1809–1849)

Edgar Allan Poe has been called the founder of the short story as a specific genre. He believed that a story (or tale) should be able to be read in one half to two hours. Born in the United States but raised mostly in England, Poe is credited with elevating the short story from mere anecdote to an art form. He is the originator of the short fiction form of the psychological thriller and detective story. If you are familiar with Poe, your first reaction may be to get a chill up your spine. Although Poe is famous for his spooky and sometimes grisly plot lines, he is just as famous for his sad but passionate poetry.

Poe's short fiction often dealt with the concept of paranoia rooted in story lines involving obsession, fantasy, and horror. He didn't use your typical tools of witches, vampires, and demons; rather, he used the psychology of the human mind—in other words, the horror and sadness we create for ourselves by virtue of being human.

Here is an excerpt of one of Poe's scariest short stories, *The Tell-Tale Heart:*

> TRUE!—nervous—very, very dreadfully nervous I had been and am; but why will you say that I am mad? The disease had sharpened my senses—not destroyed—not dulled them. Above all was the sense of hearing acute. I heard all things in the heaven and in the earth. I heard many things in hell. How, then, am I mad? Hearken! and observe how healthily—how calmly I can tell you the whole story.
>
> It is impossible to say how first the idea entered my brain; but once conceived, it haunted me day and night. Object there was none. Passion there was none. I loved the old man. He had never wronged me. He had never given me insult. For his gold I had no desire. I think it was his eye! yes, it was this! He had the eye of a vulture—a pale blue eye, with a film over it. Whenever it fell upon me, my blood ran cold; and so by degrees—very gradually—I made up my mind to take the life of the old man, and thus rid myself of the eye forever.

Poe was also able to laugh at the human condition in stories like *The Devil in the Belfry:*

> EVERYBODY knows, in a general way, that the finest place in the world is—or, alas, was—the Dutch borough of Vondervotteimittiss. Yet as it lies some distance from any of the main roads, being in a somewhat out-of-the-way situation, there are perhaps very few of my readers who have ever paid it a visit. For the benefit of those who have not, therefore, it will be only proper that I should enter into some account of it. And this is indeed the more necessary, as with the hope of enlisting public sympathy in behalf of the inhabitants, I design here to give a history of the calamitous events which have so lately occurred within its limits. No one who knows me will doubt that the duty thus self-imposed will be executed to the best of my ability, with all that rigid impartiality, all that cautious

examination into facts, and diligent collation of authorities, which should ever distinguish him who aspires to the title of historian.

In this story and others, Poe not only laughs at the common people but makes use of the devil as an object of humor rather than anything particularly evil. (You'll have to read the rest of the story to see where exactly the devil fits in.)

Poe's poem *The Raven* brought him to national fame in 1845 but he did not live much longer to enjoy it. Edgar Allan Poe suffered spells of depression that led him to attempt suicide in 1848. He did not succeed that time, but he died just a year later after a three-day drinking binge.

Folktales or Folk's Tales?

In his book of short stories titled *Winesburg, Ohio*, writer Sherwood Anderson (1876–1941) brings the folktale back to life. Anderson is essentially an oral storyteller. His art is a very special type of writing that blends the two traditions of oral and written storytelling.

Within the oral tradition, Anderson had his own picture of what a story should be. He was not interested in telling conventional folktales—those in which events are more important than emotions—but rather *his* stories written in *his* voice—a traditional American Midwestern–style drawl.

Twain, Condensed

Mark Twain is one of the greatest authors of American short stories. (Yes, he wrote those, too!) As you already know, Twain was also a novelist and essayist.

One of Twain's favorite techniques was to grab the reader at the end rather than at the beginning of a story. After starting with the plausible, Twain's stories progress through the barely possible to the flatly incredible, and then, true to Twain's style … just wait for the punch line. We see this in *The Notorious Jumping Frog of Calaveras County*:

Jim Smiley was a bettin type of man—

Well, thish-yer Smiley had rat-tarriers, and chicken cocks, and tom-cats and all them kind of things, till you couldn't rest, and you couldn't fetch nothing for him to bet on but he'd match you. He ketched a frog one day, and took him home, and said he cal'lated to educate him.

Jim named that frog Dan'l Webster and he was going to "learn that frog to jump."

The story unfolds around Smiley and the frog and a jumping contest. All Mark Twain wants to do is tell us a little bit about gullibility. Jim Smiley bets a stranger that his frog is very special and can outjump any frog in the country. But the stranger doesn't buy Smiley's line:

I don't see no p'ints about the frog that's any better'n any other frog.

Smiley, not backing down, says:

Maybe you don't … Maybe you understand frogs and maybe you don't … I'll resk forty dollars that he can out-jump any frog in Calaveras County.

The stranger finds his own frog and the bet is on. They set it all up, and good old Dan'l …

… couldn't budge; he was planted as solid as a church, and couldn't no more stir than if he was anchored out. Smiley was a good deal surprised and he was digusted too, but he didn't have no idea what the matter was, of course.

The stranger takes the money and takes off after making his point that Dan'l was no better than any other frog. Okay, now here's the good ol' Twain punch line:

… he ketched Dan'l by the nape of the neck, and hefted him and says "why blame my cats if he don't weigh five pound!" and turned the frog upside down. Dan'l belched out a double handful of shot. And then he saw how it was, and he was the maddest man.

The gist of the story is that Jim, who thinks he's a super conman, got conned himself when he wasn't looking. His rival loaded poor Dan'l Webster with tiny lead pellets so he couldn't jump. Not quite the outcome Jim had expected!

Twain's short-story writing is rooted in the storytelling tradition of the West, Southwest, and the rugged American frontier. His tales are folktales, and they are great stories because they show that not only was he an observer, but also a listener.

Between the Lines

Mark Twain (1835–1910) was born Samuel Langhorne Clemens in Florida, Missouri. The name Mark Twain was a pseudonym and a Twain pun (surprise, surprise). "Mark twain" is a riverboat depth measurement meaning "two fathoms" (12 feet) or, in other words, "safe water" (where the boat will not hit ground).

His knack for dialogue was extraordinary as he demonstrated consistently in almost all of his writing. The actual way people spoke was like music to his ears, and he was able to translate the sounds to the page like no one else in American literary history. We get some of our best slices of real life from Mark Twain's short stories. We get the sounds, rhythms, myths, stories, points of view, and character types.

As some musicians remember melodies, Twain recalled spoken speech. And he wrote it like he heard it, as seen in *The Notorious Jumping Frog of Calaveras County*. And as foreign as it may sound within your own English dialect, he was able to make the sounds not only readable, but essential to his overall writing technique.

Although you already got a taste of Twain's ability to capture dialect with both realism and humor, here is another good, long sample from *The Notorious Jumping Frog of Calaveras County;* try reading it aloud and hear it for yourself:

> Thish-yer Smiley had a mare—the boys called her the fifteen-minute nag, but that was only in fun, you know, because of course she was faster than that— and he used to win money on that horse, for all she was so slow and always had the asthma, or the distemper, or the consumption, or something of that kind. They used to give her two or three hundred yards' start, and then pass her under way; but always at the fag end of the race she'd get excited and desperate like, and come cavorting and straddling up, and scattering her legs around limber, sometimes in the air, and sometimes out on one side among the fences, and kicking up m-o-r-e dust and raising m-o-r-e racket with her coughing and sneezing and blowing her nose—and always fetch up at the stand just about a neck ahead, as near as you could cipher it down.

Why is this so important with regard to the short story? Through the use of dialect, Twain is telling you a story as though he is actually speaking it aloud and not writing it on paper. He was able to bring back the flavor of the oral tradition of storytelling before pen, ink, or the printing press. He gives the reader a sense of what a story should sound like in addition to how it should move you. He brings it alive with pen and paper in his own special way.

Where to Find Short Stories

Short stories are everywhere; you just have to look a little harder than you might have to for books; but don't worry—not *that* much harder.

You can find short stories in several different magazines such as *The New Yorker* and *Harper's*. You can find these two magazines in your local bookstore or library. You can also go online and look for literary journals in which you'll be able to read what some fresh, new authors have to say.

If you decide to go to the bookstore or library to find short stories, look for anthologies or collections. Anthologies usually contain works by many different authors, whereas collections usually contain stories written by one particular author. An anthology allows you to read several different authors, enabling you to decide which ones you like the best. Then maybe you can head for a collection of one particular author who stands out in your reading.

Depending on the anthology you find, you will mostly be reading the works of famous short-story writers through various periods of history. Some anthologies may just contain works from the twentieth century, whereas others will span through the centuries.

> **Between the Lines**
>
> You may be surprised to learn that several well-known novelists (for example, Ernest Hemingway, Margaret Atwood, and Leo Tolstoy) have also written short stories. And did you know that Sir Arthur Conan Doyle not only wrote novels about his fictitious detective Sherlock Holmes, but also more than 50 short stories?

The Heart of the Story

Reading a short story is like unpacking a time capsule. Condensed into a small space are intriguing objects—things that make you think and wonder. In totality, they present a bigger meaning, an experience, a moment. Through careful thought and planning, the author has put these things together to hold you in place and set you on a path that leads to someplace you've never been before. A short story should strike you in the same way a poem does—quickly and suddenly.

The Least You Need to Know

- A short story has fewer than 20,000 words.

- Short stories are centered on a single theme.

- Edgar Allan Poe is credited as the founder of the short story.

- Short stories are rooted in the oral folktale tradition.

- Short stories can be found in magazines, literary journals, and anthologies.

How to Read a Play

In This Chapter

- ◆ The difference between seeing a play and reading one
- ◆ Playwright intention and reader interpretation
- ◆ What to expect from a play
- ◆ The importance of character
- ◆ Dialogue as narrative

"What do you mean, *read* a play? I thought I was supposed to see a play!" We can hear you thinking that as you open to this chapter. Well, you're right; a play is supposed to be seen. Because they *have* been written and you *can* read them, however, you should. There are mysteries to uncover for yourself as you investigate this style of creative writing.

In this chapter, you learn all about reading theatrical drama for yourself—and not because your tenth-grade English teacher told you to. This is a reading experience that will teach you a great deal about dialogue and how to see the world through monologues, conversations, and even stage direction.

Shouldn't a Play Be Seen and Not Read?

Probably the most interesting thing about reading a play is the very fact that it was written to be performed and not simply to be read. That might sound odd, but think about it this way: What you interpret on paper will not necessarily be the same as what is interpreted on stage. In the theater there are actors, directors, staging, and an audience. (Sometimes there will also be special lighting or special effects onstage.) A play is a story, but when you include interpretation from various sources, the story can take on completely different meanings.

Look It Up

A **playwright** (or dramatist) is an author of plays performed in a theater. (A **screenwriter**, in contrast, writes for film and video productions.)

The *playwright* writes the script for the use of professional performers on whom he is dependent to get a point across to an audience. The playwright may not necessarily provide a great deal of information or detail within the text of the play; and even if he does, the actors and the directors are under no obligation to follow anything the playwright may have intended.

Action!

When you sit down to read a play, you will notice stage directions in italics from time to time. (The amount of direction varies from writer to writer.) Here is a list of terms you should know when reading a play:

- **Script.** The playwright's "book"—the written play itself—that includes the text, dialogue, and stage directions.

- **Monologue.** A speech by one character either directed to the audience or to another character in the play.

- **Dialogue.** Scripted conversation between two or more actors.

- **Epilogue.** A speech given by an actor to himself or herself at the end of a play.

- **Soliloquy.** A speech the actor makes to himself or herself while onstage.

- **Exeunt.** Stage direction meaning that more than one person will leave the stage.

- **Exit.** A stage direction indicating which person leaves the stage.

♦ **Preferred reading**. The original intentions of the playwright as stressed by the author or by the text itself.

There are many other stage directions, as well, that you might study if you were to perform a play. (You would want to know which way "stage left" directs you, for example.) These are the basics, though, and will give you a good idea of what's going on in the script.

The Writer

A playwright writes in a much different way than the author of prose fiction or poetry. The playwright's vision is to bring a theme to an audience through the use of dialogue. The playwright depends on the actors to get his meanings across to an audience through a series of acts and scenes. (If plays are unfamiliar to you, think of acts as a means of sectioning off the play. Acts are dividers used in the same way as the parts in this book, for example, and the scenes can be thought of as chapters.)

Think of the position a playwright is in for a moment. He spends months, maybe even years, writing a play and then turns it over to a director, who will then entrust the script to a group of actors. The playwright's work is interpreted by middlemen, in effect, and if they don't do it in such a way that the audience can relate to, the play could be a flop. Imagine a playwright waiting to see how his work will be received by audiences and critics when much of the presentation is out of his hands.

> **Between the Lines**
>
> The earliest known playwrights (with plays that have survived the ages) are from fifth-century B.C.E. Greece. They include Aeschylus, Sophocles, Euripides, and Aristophanes.

The Reader

Did you have to read Shakespeare in high school? Most of us did. In Amy's high school classes, everyone had to pick a part and read it aloud. What were we really getting out of it (except, possibly, the dread of being asked to read and the sheer humiliation as we stumbled over every line)?

> **Bookmarks**
>
> There are theater "book" shops that sell only scripts. You can find stores like this in cities where theater is a major form of entertainment or where drama education is prevalent. You can also buy scripts online. Try stageplays.com—they have an extensive library of theatrical scripts.

Despite promoting youthful angst over the possibility of being exposed as a nonactor (or maybe, as a thespian at heart) before a roomful of people, teachers really do have the right idea in having students read plays aloud. Reading the words aloud takes the play off the page and turns it back into the spoken word, the way it was originally intended to be.

You can read a play aloud to yourself or read it as part of a group. Either way, a playwright is counting on the performance to tell the story and divulge the meaning to the audience. But understanding a play through a reading is also essential for the growth of the creative imagination.

What the Actors Know

Regina used to belong to a play-reading group in New York City. Real actors attended the group to try out new scripts. Those who were not actors were invited to participate in the readings, not just for fun, but so the actors could hear the readers' perspectives.

Bookmarks

You don't have to be a professional actor to start a play-reading group. You just need a bunch of people who enjoy performing, love drama or comedy, or simply like hearing the sound of their own voices.

Interestingly, it wasn't just important for the actors to hear the words spoken aloud by other actors. To hear the words read aloud by the nonactor readers gave the actors the opportunity to hear how the script might be interpreted differently, which gave them new and different insights into the work. So the actors learned from the readers just as the readers learned from the actors.

Different actors prepare for plays in different ways. First they usually concentrate on the words in the script itself. They may also need to do some historical or cross-cultural research. An actor from one part of the country (or world) may have to research another area, and perhaps even mimic the accent of persons in that other area, while preparing for a play to help make an onstage persona more believable. Some actors are even fortunate enough to meet personally with the playwright as they develop their characterizations.

In the end, what you see on stage will be a collaborative, well-prepared effort on the part of the actors and the director—whether it matches up to the playwright's original intentions or not.

Imagine That!

When you are reading a play, it helps to imagine the sound of the spoken words and to imagine the kinds of characters who would be speaking them. The difference here is that the characters are the narrators; the stage is the setting and the atmosphere; the plot is the action; and the theme … well, the theme is always the heart of the story—the part that speaks directly to you.

If your own reading (interpretation) of a play differs from what you see onstage, don't worry. That's why you're reading it. Don't doubt your intelligence or your ability to read critically in general. There's nothing wrong with having a different interpretation. After all, actors and directors have different interpretations of the same script all the time (sometimes at the same time within the same performance, which can be real trouble!).

You can also get different interpretations of a play from one performance to another. Whereas one actor may play a character one way, another actor in a separate performance may play that same character in a completely different way. They are using the same script, but the play takes on new definition because of the actors' delivery of the lines. This is true regarding the direction of a play, too.

A good example of this is Shakespeare's play *Hamlet*. Amy studied Shakespeare in Oxfordshire, England, where she saw the character of Hamlet portrayed differently in two different theaters. In Shakespeare's home of Stratford-Upon-Avon, Hamlet was portrayed as a madman; in another interpretation performed simultaneously in London, Hamlet was portrayed as someone pretending to be mad. While the actors spoke the same words and the action was true to Shakespeare's original script, their different interpretations of the play led to completely different meanings for the audience.

Expectations Run Amok

The element of expectation in theater is so great that in twentieth-century playwright Samuel Beckett's play *Waiting for Godot*, the characters and the audience spend the entire play anxiously awaiting the arrival of the mysterious Godot, who never shows up. You don't know who he is or why you are waiting for him, and neither do the characters. Beckett took the concept of expectation and turned it upside down right on the collective heads of the audience. The action in a play lies completely within the expectation, but you don't always get what you expect—in fact, sometimes you never get anything at all. In that sense Beckett is saying that a play is just like life:

> Vladimir: But that is not the question. What are we doing here, that is the question. And we are blessed in this, that we happen to know the answer. Yes, in this immense confusion one thing alone is clear. We are waiting for Godot to come—

It's not the playwright's intention necessarily to give us what we want (as witnessed in *Waiting for Godot* especially), but it is his or her intention to make us wait for it.

Royal Expectations

Similarly, Shakespeare sets us up for expectations right away in his play *Henry VI.* Scene One is set in London's majestic Westminster Abbey, where we find ourselves in the company of dukes and bishops at the funeral of Henry V. We know that people have a lot to say at funerals—both good and bad—and this regal crowd is no different. It only takes a small amount of dialogue during the play's opening scene to arouse our curiosity of what's to come.

The duke of Gloucester speaks at the funeral:

> England ne'er had a king until his time.
> Virtue he had, deserving to command:
> His brandish'd sword did blind men with his beams:
> His arms spread wider than a dragon's wings;
> His sparking eyes, replete with wrathful fire,
> More dazzled and drove back his enemies
> Than mid-day sun fierce bent against their faces.
> What should I say? his deeds exceed all speech:
> He ne'er lift up his hand but conquered.

Between the Lines

In the theater, the audience can be just as much a part of the atmosphere as anything happening on the stage. Laughter, silence, gasps, and even yawns can all play a part in creating the atmosphere of the performance and the interpretation of the story itself.

The duke of Gloucester is praising the king's heroism and complains that no English king had ever survived to the end of his natural life span. Immediately, our attention is piqued. A hero king is dead. He is beloved and mourned by his peers. What will happen next? If no king has lived out his natural life span, is that foreshadowing that the next king might not either? Between the rich and extravagant opening of this play at the funeral of a king, Shakespeare is setting up the audience to want to know what happens next without even telling us what had happened before.

Expecting the Inevitable

In Arthur Miller's *Death of a Salesman*, Miller does not surprise us with the unexpected but tells us flat out what to expect. All we do as the reader is wait for the inevitable.

The process of how we get there is driven by the inner workings of the main character's mind. The ending of the play is announced right from the start when Willy Loman says he will die the death of a salesman, and every moment of the play thereafter leads us to this inevitable outcome.

Here Miller has played a sort of a playwright's trick on us. We know what will happen from the start—the action is a result of the preexisting turmoil on the part of the main character and not necessarily the result of the action within the play. We are even lucky enough to have the words of Arthur Miller to help us understand his intentions in this respect:

> The play was begun with only one firm piece of knowledge and this was that Loman was to destroy himself ... if I could make him remember enough he would kill himself, and the structure of the play was determined by what was needed to draw up his memories like a mass of tangled roots without end or beginning.
>
> —Arthur Miller, Introduction to *Collected Plays* (1957)

Intensity of Character

Let's stick with *Death of a Salesman* for now. The play focuses on an intense character sketch of Willy Loman. This is a tragic story about the downward spiral of a proud man who is devastated by a tremendous sense of failure.

What was Arthur Miller's process that led him to the creation of this character? Listen to the words of the playwright himself:

> The first image that occurred to me which was to result in *Death of a Salesman* was on an enormous face the height of the proscenium arch which would appear

and then open up, and we would see the inside of a man's head. In fact, *The Inside of His Head* was the first title. It was conceived half in laughter, for the inside of his head was a mass of contradictions … All I was doing was bringing things to mind. The assumption, also, was that everyone knew Willy Loman … Willy Loman does not merely suggest or hint that he is at the end of his strength and of his justifications, he is hardly on the stage for five minutes when he says so; he does not gradually imply a deadly conflict with his son, an implication dropped into the midst of serenity and surface calm, he is avowedly grappling with the conflict at the outset.

—Arthur Miller, Introduction to *Collected Plays* (1957)

Willy's conflict is not a result of the action within the play; it's there from the very start. Miller thrusts us smack dab in the middle of Willy's inner struggle, which tells us immediately that this is an intensely character-driven play.

Bookmarks

Miller's plays are slices of life and usually heavily character driven. If you haven't done so already, you may want to read *Death of a Salesman* (1949) and other Miller plays such as *A View from the Bridge* (1955), *All My Sons* (1947), or *Incident at Vichy* (1964). Miller's focus was on what was real and true in American society as he felt it at the time.

Nineteenth-century Norwegian playwright Henrik Ibsen's play *Hedda Gabler* is also mainly concerned with the exposition of character. Ibsen wants to make sure he gives us a good, clear picture of the character he intends to develop within his play. Here is how Ibsen's opening stage directions read:

Enter from the left Hedda Gabler. She is a woman of twenty-nine. Her face and figure show great refinement and distinction. Her complexion is pale and opaque. Her steel-gray eyes express an unruffled calm. Her hair is of an attractive medium brown, but is not particularly abundant; and she is dressed in a flowing loose-fitting morning gown.

A playwright doesn't always give us this much information about a character. Much of the time it is left to the reader's imagination. But this is a play in which Ibsen clearly wants us to know who Hedda Gabler is, so he doesn't leave it up for interpretation. By giving us this information, he is immediately inviting you into Hedda's house and her life, which is seemingly normal. You think you can see who this woman is and what she's about. (Eventually you learn that not all is what it seems on the surface. The play contains visceral moments of passion, jealousy, rage, sadness, murderous intentions, murder itself, and betrayal. Read those opening directions again, and ask yourself what the heck must happen to this serene character over the course of the play.)

The Power of Conversation

Playwrights are like any other type of fiction writer in that they want to take slices of life and have you make sense of them thematically on a larger scale. Where a playwright is different is that they hear dialogue in their minds that they then transfer to paper in order to tell a story.

Although there is dialogue in prose fiction, it can often be validated, explained, or evaluated by narrative text. Playwrights don't have that luxury unless they make one of the characters in the play a narrator—and even then that narrator will only pop up once in a while. Most of the time you're left to interpret the dialogue all by yourself.

Without narrative interjection, though, how does the playwright manage to hold to the structure of a complete story? How can conversations alone take us to the climax and finally to the conclusion in the same way a novel or short story might?

But isn't that just like real life? We don't have a constant narrator guiding us through the scenes of our lives—we do it ourselves both with our internal thought processes and through our conversations with other people. We may not live our lives like a complete arc of a story, but we have beginnings, middles, and ends—with many different scenes throughout. This is what the playwright is able to capture on paper and then portray to us through conversation.

One of the most powerful examples of the use of dialogue in recent theatrical history is demonstrated by twentieth-century playwright Edward Albee in his play *Who's Afraid of Virginia Woolf?* In this play, he has four characters who Albee describes as "Martha, a large boisterous woman, 52, looking somewhat younger, ample, but not fleshy; George, her husband, 46, thin, hair going gray; Honey, 26, a petite blond girl, rather plain; and Honey's husband, Nick, 30 … blond, well put-together, good looking."

The scene is set in "the living room of a house on the campus of a small New England college." Sounds nice, doesn't it? What on earth could go wrong there? Don't be fooled. That's exactly what Albee wants you to think. In actuality, this play is about the violent and destructive relationship of George and Martha.

Their dialogue is cruel and strikes you to the core with a sensation of disgust. You're in the middle of a battle of words that fly like missiles, and there's no way to duck them. Honey and Nick bear witness to it, too. So you not only feel the blows of the dialogue, you also feel that you are in the same boat with Honey and Nick. You're embarrassed for them in the same way that they are embarrassed to be a part of this madness.

Here's a sample of Martha speaking to George through Honey and Nick, after George tells her to stop her ranting:

> The hell I will! You see, George didn't have much push ... he wasn't particularly ... aggressive. In fact he was sort of a ... [spits the word at George's back] a FLOP! A great ... big ... fat ... FLOP!

There are pauses in the dialogue indicated by ellipses (...). This is the playwright's input as to where the actor needs to put emphasis within this piece of dialogue. He interjects his opinion with these ellipses and with his description of how Martha says the words to Honey and Nick—as though she is spitting them at George. All George keeps repeating after she hurls her anger at him is this:

> ... don't go on Martha ... don't Martha, don't ...

And all Honey can say is:

> I'm going to be sick ... I'm gong to be sick ... I'm going to vomit.

Honey is only saying what we all feel at this point in the play. We are all trapped within the scene as voyeurs—observers of a horror show.

As violent as this play may sound, all Albee is doing is showing us the psychological damage that words can cause. You don't need murder to kill someone emotionally—all you need are words.

The Least You Need to Know

- ◆ You will get different perspectives from reading a script versus seeing a play performed.
- ◆ Reading a play is a great way to get an idea of the playwright's intentions.
- ◆ The structure of a play depends greatly on the concept of expectation.

- Most plays are heavily character driven, with an emphasis on dialogue versus action.

- Plays are written in dialogue form to portray the relationships between characters; relationship dynamics are the substance of the writing and of the performances.

Part 3

Reading Nonfiction

As with fiction, nonfiction teaches us about ourselves, but it does so by using a different approach. Through essays, we learn about different schools of thought, and perhaps ideological movements in society. We read about the lives of people just like us and completely different from us through biographies and memoirs. We delve into philosophy, science, and history to learn about who we are as human beings—where we have been, and where we are headed.

In this part you learn the importance of nonfiction writing to understanding life as we know it in every dimension. You learn the essence of essay writing and the nature of an autobiography. You even learn how to relate nonfiction prose to fiction—how to use one type of literary genre to aid you in your understanding of another.

Reading Historical Books

In This Chapter

- ◆ Moving beyond date and place
- ◆ Old news, new theories
- ◆ Historical fiction as a learning tool
- ◆ The importance of a historian's research
- ◆ Understanding powers of persuasion

History, of course, is the study of human existence over the ages. It is the study of our ancestors, their acts, and their behaviors through time. It is one of the social sciences, like sociology and anthropology, which means it relies on facts, evidence, and interpretation to raise arguments and draw conclusions.

In this chapter, you learn what it means to investigate the past through the eyes of the specialists—the historians themselves. Learning history is not just about memorizing dates and places—it's about research, persuasion, storytelling, and theorizing—all for the sake of understanding who we are as human beings today.

The Need to Understand Historical Events

History is constantly in the making. What happened yesterday or five minutes ago may be a current event, but it may also take a spot in the history books. We talk about things that have happened in the past, whether they are global issues or events in our own little corners of the world.

In school, history was a lot of memorization of places and dates. Back then we learned what we really needed to know about past events: the dates, the people involved, and the places in which the events took place. Now, as an adult and as a critical reader, it's your job to understand how history affects the entire human race. It's time to move beyond dates and places (the bare minimum of facts concerning history) to ask questions such as these:

- ◆ Why did these events happen?

- ◆ What were the events that led to an historical turnabout?

- ◆ What did these events mean in their time, and subsequently in our time?

- ◆ Why is it important to know these things happened? How do we make use of them to change or improve human existence?

Knowing when something happened can never explain *why* it happened, or what good, if any, came from the event. You're ready to use your powers of analysis to understand the full impact of any historical happening.

History Is What You Make It

Try to put history in perspective by relating it to your own time. For example, how and why did the Vietnam War happen? Why did it last so long? Compare this to the current situation in Iraq. If we can understand why the Vietnam War lasted so long, maybe we can figure out how to avoid making the same mistakes today. The more we understand about past wars, the better our chances of avoiding war in the future.

Historians are life teachers—we need them to explain the past to us to help us understand what to do (and what not to do) in the future. The adage that history tends to repeat itself is true—and it's up to us to decide which events should and should not be repeated. We can't do that unless we're aware of all the details.

Historical Research

There are two sources of historical research: the events (the primary sources) and the written accounts of the facts (the secondary sources). The best way to describe this is to think of a crime scene. There are the eyewitness reports of the events, the police report of the events, and the accounts of anyone involved at the scene of the crime. The next day a news story will appear in the paper based on a journalist's account of the crime scene reports. But the journalist wasn't there, so he or she doesn't really know what happened. The journalist relies on what he is told and what he reads and researches. The facts are documented, but a journalist has to dig deeper to make sense of the big picture. What led up to the events? Why did they happen? What happens now?

Through the study of history, we will get differing viewpoints of an event. It's up to us to read as much as we can to form our own opinions of what really happened. Historians are just like that journalist, gathering the cold, hard facts from primary and secondary sources in order to interpret events and come to conclusions.

> **CAUTION**
>
> **Take Note!** _____
>
> Just as the journalist must be as accurate and factual as possible about current events, it's important that historians be as objective as possible in their historical narrative.

The Historian's Dilemma

Historians have a very difficult job. Whereas a journalist deals with events happening in the here and now, a historian is often dealing with events that happened a long time ago. The people who were involved may now be dead. The written accounts from the time (if written accounts exist) or another historian's research and narrative of events may be all the historian has to base his reporting on. He has to hope that past historians have done their research and have built their arguments as soundly as possible.

Interpretations through time vary and change because they include the perspective of a particular time upon an event. It is critical that we are able to identify not only the facts and evidence as collected, but how points of view about the event have changed over time. Someone writing history at the time of the Depression, for example, will have a very different outlook on the topic than a modern-day historian who is tackling the same issue. Those varying perspectives are vital in our understanding of how history is documented over time.

The Proof Is in the Pudding

The key for every historian is to find the most reliable historical sources and build new arguments from there. Whereas one historian might have a new idea about a past event and use other historians to back up the new idea, other historians may have been lucky enough to actually find a brand new source of information—a letter, a diary, an artifact—never before seen or written about.

> ### Between the Lines
>
> Letters are often invaluable primary sources of research. They show us what went on behind the scenes and can prove, disprove, or validate preconceived notions or studies. The historian who can get his or her hands on important letters or diaries is lucky indeed!

Verified evidence may be instrumental in affecting the rewriting of history by changing what was previously believed about a particular event. The onus is on the historian to present the new information so that other historians can have a look at it and perform their own assessments of it in order to understand how the historian formed his conclusions. The historian's reputation as a reliable researcher has much to do with acceptance of the evidence as well as the soundness of his or her interpretations of it.

It's New to You

Historians must be open to new discoveries and/or theories and try to remain as objective as possible. It takes courage to be this kind of historian and researcher— what he ultimately finds may go completely against what former mentors and scholars have assumed and accepted over the years.

As you read what the historians have to say and develop your own insights and conclusions from the experts and their painstaking research, you are able to form your own conclusions, making you a historian of sorts in your own right.

Let's discuss the true story of a groundbreaking historian. In his book *The Membership of the Massachusetts Bay General Court 1630–1686*, Amy's father, Dr. Robert E. Wall, made it his goal to advance knowledge of that period of history by shedding new light on the question of whether Massachusetts was a democratic, aristocratic deferential, or mixed society. He made it his mission to understand the political relationships based on what he found out about family and financial connections. Who was in charge, and why and how did people achieve leadership positions within the colony?

By taking this route in his research, Wall set a precedent for future generations of historians interested in the same subject matter. His research was new—it had never before been seen in his field of study.

The result of his hard work? Not only did he gather enough information to prove his theory, he also collected data for future historians to build upon.

Take Note!

Although new evidence or theories are a boon to the study of history, we must be very cautious as readers and as human beings when we talk about "rewriting" history. For example, there are "revisionists" who try to rewrite history through less-than-credible research methods. (For example, there are Holocaust revisionists who claim that the Holocaust never happened.) Be very wary of any historian whose theories negate every shred of evidence to the contrary.

One of the first challenges to any reader of nonfiction is to try to understand how historians think. Certain historians specialize in specific fields like Amy's father did. Some of these specialties include ancient history, medieval history, or Renaissance history; there are specialists in the history of specific regions of the world as well: African history, Asian history, or European history, for example.

Learning Through Historical Fiction

You'll recall we discussed *The Scarlet Letter* in Chapter 6, in terms of interpreting a novel written hundreds of years ago. In this section, we talk about how historical storytellers re-create the facts and blend them with fiction to teach us about the lives and times of those who went before us.

One of the ways Amy has always enjoyed learning about the past is through historical fiction. However, novelists are not required to be truthful about past events. They can take whatever *poetic license* they need to make their stories come alive. They can have the twentieth-century Queen Elizabeth II appear side by side with the sixteenth-century Queen Elizabeth I if they so choose.

Look It Up

Poetic license is a technique used by poets and prose writers that gives them the liberty to break conventional codes and rules of writing to produce a desired effect.

While that is an obvious manipulation of historical fact, sometimes an author will take liberties with history that are not quite so blatant. For example, an author may decide to make a real historical Native American princess a little bit older or younger if it makes the story move along more smoothly. If she was 12 years old in 1860, the author might choose to make her 30 years old instead.

It is always helpful for readers to know what facts the author has manipulated so that they are clear on fact versus fiction. Many authors will let you know where they have taken liberties for the sake of telling a good story versus whether or not they have stayed as close to the facts as possible. But that, too, is up to the author; if you want to be sure, you may have to do some fact checking on your own. It's important to do your own research either before or after you read the book—or at least read what the author has to say about his recounting of events—before drawing any conclusions as to its historical veracity.

A case in point exists in a novel called *The Sunne in Splendour* about the life of King Richard III of England, as told by historian and author Sharon Kay Penman. Here's what Penman had to say about her work in her Author's Note at the end of the book:

> It's never easy to piece together the past. That's even more true when history was rewritten by the victor. In attempting to distinguish between Tudor tradition and the truth, I gave greatest weight to those chronicles written during Richard's lifetime or immediately thereafter, relying as little as possible upon purely Tudor sources, for obvious reasons.

Between the Lines

Some societal-cultural writers are considered documentarians of history even though they write from a highly subjective point of view. Their work is read as a kind of social history of the times. Mark Twain is one such example. In *The Damned Human Race* and *The Diaries of Adam and Eve*, Twain plays the role of observer and record keeper of human behavior during the 1800s.

If you were to skip this explanation, you wouldn't know what the author's intentions were or what to believe or not to believe. Penman tells us herself that she tried to be as historically accurate as possible, and based on this information from her, we can decide how accurate we believe the story to be.

What we learn from Penman is that one of the points of writing this story was an effort to debunk what she believes to be a false interpretation of the life of Richard III as told through his enemies (the Tudors). Based on what we know of her and her work, we can trust that she has done the best she could to be accurate with her information. She is what historians would call "a reliable" reteller of history because she follows what the historians have been putting together for us for centuries.

The Problems with Historiography

One of the most important things a reader of history should know is that you can never rely on just one source of information. The whole point of recording history is to try to make sense of the "why" and the "how" of the events in addition to knowing the "who," "what," and "where." So in essence, you are not just reading history, you are analyzing the study of history, making you the *historiographer*.

Through time, and through certain historical writings, we have come to believe that what historians have told us is the undeniable truth. After all, they're the experts—they're dealing with the facts and theories. Who are we to question them?

> **Look It Up**
>
> **Historiography** is the analysis of how history is studied—meaning the principles behind the study and the means of research used.

This is one of the biggest errors that occurs in the study of history: The reader doesn't question the research and conclusions presented by the writer. Remember what Penman said in her Author's Note: History tends to be written by the winners. Ask yourself whether the defeated side would agree with the history books.

Taking (Many) Sides

Reading only one historian's perspective without looking at what others have to say on the matter is another common mistake readers make.

Consider the U.S. Civil War, for example, which lasted from 1861 to 1865. If you were to ask the average person what he or she thinks the war was about, some might say the issue of slavery caused the fighting, whereas others might say the war was fought to prevent the South from seceding from the Union. Both reasons are true, of course, but is that all? There were many other factors that played into the war, such as the economy, ideological differences, and even religion. But one particular historian may focus on one particular and limited aspect of the war and not necessarily the big picture, leaving you short on information.

Open for Discussion

The fact is that history is one form of expository writing, and it can be biased. It's written by human beings, after all, with all of their faults and prejudices. As in the case of Richard III, history can be written to distort the truth.

A historian's argument will be built on an idea through research. An historian interested in putting forth only one interpretation about a historical figure or event will attempt to prove it through rhetoric rather than research. It is important that you know the difference. (We discuss rhetoric a bit more in the next section. Think of it as tricky persuasion.)

To avoid falling prey to a less-than-credible historian, you need to question everything you read: the author, the research, and the conclusions. Read other sources, and compare one theory to another; then, and only then, should you consider drawing your own conclusions.

Here are some tips to help you to reach and trust your own conclusions in your reading:

+ Be skeptical.

+ Check (and recheck) the facts and sources.

+ Read as broadly on a topic as you can.

+ Be open-minded to all opinions.

Following these tips will ensure that you have taken the time to carefully consider the evidence presented to you and that you aren't accepting something as gospel truth just because some historian told you to.

The Importance of Source Material

The point of reading history, oddly enough, is to find out something new about something old. Through a methodology of truth-finding and objectivity, a whole new world of information can come to light, forcing us to rethink old truths. If historians can do that, they can change the world through perception and knowledge.

Bibliography

Isn't that the bit at the back that you always skip over? Don't! As you read in Chapter 4, the bibliography is invaluable to you as a reader of facts!

The bibliography is the culmination of the historian's work. It tells us so much about how he did his work and reached his conclusions. What is (or is not) in that bibliography matters more than you might have imagined.

If someone has written a history of science and has not included anything in the bibliography about Copernicus, Galileo, Newton, or Einstein, wouldn't we wonder whether the writer knows what he's talking about? Without knowing exactly what the writer has read of other experts' works, we have no way of knowing how he developed his perspectives.

The Introduction

Consider also what historians tell you in the introduction of their books. What are you told about the research methods? What about the thesis premise? What are the historian's thoughts and feelings about the topic? How does he or she plan to follow up this work? If you are to believe what the historian is telling you, you are entitled to this kind of clarity. Honesty of this nature is a testimony to the historian's truth-telling abilities.

Understanding Rhetoric

It's very important when you read history to be conscious of what *rhetoric* is. All historians, of course, want to persuade the reader to believe their thesis. And if you can't see the difference between a good snow job and genuine fact-finding, it's easy to be fooled.

The ancient Greek philosopher and teacher Aristotle defined rhetorical discourse as the art of discovering all of the available means of persuasion in any given case. Rhetoric is filled with invention—arguments (opinions) and proofs (evidence) shaded for a purpose. We are not looking at facts in the case of rhetoric at

Look It Up

Simply put, **rhetoric** is the ability to use any methods necessary to make people believe what you have to say.

all, but at style. Politicians spend years perfecting this craft. How they speak, stand, move their hands and head and eyes—it's all part of rhetorical persuasion.

Historians must be very careful when using rhetorical arguments in their writing. If a historian can prove to you that what he is saying is valid, he can use any art of persuasion he so chooses. But it's up to you to pay close attention to the details and determine whether the historian is presenting the truth or is using a lot of smoke and mirrors.

When you finished school, you probably had no idea there was so much involved with studying history. Through a general reading of history, you get the basic details: who did what to whom (and when it was done). Reading history critically, however, may change your mind about certain events, perhaps even altering everything you once believed. As long as your analytical reading gets you thinking about what may have really happened way back when, you can consider yourself enlightened.

Just remember, your mission is to move beyond the basics, and into the how and why of history—so choose your historians carefully.

The Least You Need to Know

- ◆ Historians have opinions, so you need to pay attention to matters of objectivity.
- ◆ Historical fiction can be accurate in some facts, but cannot be considered factual overall.
- ◆ Read more than one source of history before you draw your own conclusions.
- ◆ You should always pay attention to who the historian is and what kind of research she has done.
- ◆ It is the historian's job to prove his theory, but be aware of how he is doing that—is it by rhetoric or by research?

Chapter 14

Reading Science Books

In This Chapter

- ◆ Understanding scientific material
- ◆ Learning about the classical scientists
- ◆ Keeping an open mind to new ideas
- ◆ Where to find new scientific theories
- ◆ Science and ethics

Let's talk about science in a nutshell.

Ha! Tricked you. There is no way you can explain science briefly. Science is a subject so vast that it's almost impossible to fathom.

If you read science and you're not a scientist, it's because you are interested in what makes the world go around. Although most scientific books are written for people in the field, there is also a widening array of books written for the layperson. Scientists are always trying to include the public in the miracles taking place behind laboratory doors.

In Plain English

Scientists are always writing in ways that you can understand. If you're interested in weather patterns, in human anatomy, or in brain chemistry, there are books out there for you. Maybe you want to know why some trees live until they are 1,000 years old whereas others topple and die in a tenth the amount of time. Maybe you just want to know how to kill slugs in your backyard—why does salt act like acid on their bodies? What do trans-fatty acids do to our insides? How do we breathe? Why do we stand on two legs? What makes our planet what it is? What makes the universe what it is? How do we fit into the microcosm of existence?

Look It Up

The word **science** has its origins in the Latin word *scientia,* meaning "knowledge."

Phew ... this isn't even the tip of the iceberg. *Science* is obviously a complex and diverse field of study, and reading about it can be an amazing experience that will open all sorts of new doors for you.

Reading the Classics

When we talk about reading scientific books, we are actually talking about reading either the history of science or the conclusions of some form of scientific research. If you intend to read classical science, you need to familiarize yourself with the larger framework of science that spans many centuries and cultures. You should try to familiarize yourself with original discoveries and who made them. (This chapter covers a few of the classical scientists, but there is much more for you to learn on the topic.) This will help you to get the scope and depth required to understand how we got to where we are today in our scientific explorations and thinking.

When you do this research, you will find that there is more than just Western science to consider. (Western science is what we predominantly studied in school and is probably the most familiar to us now.)

As you read about other regions and the sciences upon which they focus, you will find things you probably never knew before, like the fact that an advanced Indian science was psychology, which made use of psychical and physiological techniques for the achievement of mastery over mind and body. You will find out that the sciences go back to many advance ancient cultures, including Chinese, Greek, Arab, and Persian civilizations.

An important thing to keep in mind is that most of the early scientists did not write in English, so if you go back to the "original" scientific texts, you will be reading a translated narrative. Be sure the person who did the translation is a reputable scholar.

Bookmarks

To figure out who all the classical scientists are, start by doing some research on the Internet or in an encyclopedia.

Different Scientific Perspectives

Although scientific books rely on facts, they can still contain different styles of narrative even if they are talking about the exact same scientific theory or discovery. If you don't get everything you need from one author's style, you can always turn to another source that might be easier to understand.

How something is explained makes all the difference in understanding difficult details. Points of view may be similar, but the emphasized elements may be very different. The reason is that science writers are all dipping into the same pool of information to explain the newest discoveries to the reader.

Science for the Masses

Before the nineteenth century, science was generally written for the layperson. Scientists who came up with a theory that was thought to be critical to humanity set out to put their discoveries in terminology that everyone could relate to. Sure, they had their experiments documented for the experts as well, but if they were to put those in a book, the collective eye of the general public would probably glaze over and turn to some other recognizable area of study.

For the average person to understand the significance of a scientific finding, the scientists had to spell it out in its most basic form. And it's a good thing they did because their theories tended to be so controversial they needed the support of other scientists, students, and those of the masses who could read to help support their ideas.

Some Basics of Scientific Discovery

Copernicus, Galileo, Newton, and Einstein—these names are probably familiar to you, not only because of their unequivocal contributions to scientific understanding, but because they were among the many scientists who explained their findings in simple language. There's another reason these scientists had to write out their experimental findings in narrative form—simply because the mass audience was their only audience. The fields in which they studied were brand new—there was no institutionalized specialization for the specific areas of science that they were studying.

We owe a great deal of modern understanding and technological growth to various scientists over the ages. They have taken us out of darkness and ignorance into understanding and advancement. Let's take a brief look at each of these four scientists and their major contributions to mankind.

Copernicus (1473–1543)

Nicolaus Copernicus was born Nicolaus Koppernik in Poland. He became a scientist and an astronomer and was the first to challenge Aristotle's theory that the sun revolved around the earth.

In about 1514, Copernicus distributed a pamphlet called the *Little Commentary*, which outlined, in simple language, his theory of the universe. He wrote it in this way so that he not only had a basic outline for himself but also he could state in layman terms what he was going to focus on in his scientific work.

Here is the outline from the *Little Commentary:*

- There is no one center in the universe.

- The earth's center is not the center of the universe.

- The center of the universe is near the sun.

- The distance from the earth to the sun is imperceptible compared with the distance to the stars.

- The rotation of the earth accounts for the apparent daily rotation of the stars.

- The apparent annual cycle of movements of the sun is caused by the earth revolving around it.

- The apparent retrograde motion of the planets is caused by the motion of the earth from which one observes.

> **Between the Lines**
>
> Copernicus's *Little Commentary* was not printed but handwritten. He distributed the pamphlet to a group of his friends who knew it was his even though he did not put his name anywhere on the cover or within the text. Copernicus would begin his major work on these theories the following year with the resulting publication of *De revolutionibus*.

Galileo (1564–1642)

Born in Italy, Galileo Galilei was one of the first scientists to use the telescope to uncover the truths about our solar system. He set forth to challenge the Christian belief of civilization by trying to convince the Roman Catholic Church of the validity of Nicolaus Copernicus's theory that the earth revolves around the sun, not the other way around. These were dangerous times to be questioning Church authority, what with the burning of heretics all over Europe going on at the time. So what he did was very brave, but he failed in his efforts and was forced to renounce what he knew to be the truth. In fact, legend has it that as he turned from his inquisitors, he muttered under his breath: "... nevertheless, it does move" (referring to the earth, of course).

If Galileo is famous for nothing else, he did shed light on Copernican discoveries, taking them away from the theoretical and making them reality.

Between the Lines
While studying in Pisa, Italy, Galileo disproved a commonly accepted Aristotelian theory that objects of different weights fall at different speeds. To disprove the theory, Galileo stood on top of the Tower of Pisa and dropped two objects. What he found is that no matter what their weight, they fell at the same rate, thus changing forever the theories of mass and velocity.

Newton (1642–1727)

You have probably heard the story of how scientist Sir Isaac Newton discovered the theory of gravity when an apple fell on his head as he rested under an apple tree. (Well, that's the version that makes people laugh, anyway.) Born in England, Sir Isaac Newton made significant contributions to the theories of motion, light, and gravity. When he saw the apple fall from the tree (it probably did not land on his head), he started to understand the underlying principles of gravity and built his theory on top of already existing theories, giving us the understanding of gravity as we know it today.

Einstein (1879–1955)

Born in Germany, Albert Einstein moved to the United States in the 1930s and became one of the leading scientific minds of the twentieth century. Einstein did not invent the atomic bomb as many people have come to believe, but his theory of relativity played a major part in its eventual construction. Einstein pointed out through his theory of relativity that a large amount of energy could be released from a small amount of matter (expressed in mathematical terms as $E = MC^2$ or Energy = Mass times the Speed of Light squared).

The invention of the atomic bomb would haunt Einstein for years to come because he was really a pacifist. Before he died, he had this to say:

> I made one great mistake in my life … when I signed the letter to President Roosevelt recommending that atom bombs be made; but there was some justification—the danger that the Germans would make them first.

The Scientists and You

We give you this information to show you not only how significant scientific research has been to our understanding of life on Earth and our place in the cosmos, but to demonstrate that all of this information is readable. Reading about the scientists themselves may be a good stepping-stone for delving deeper into some actual scientific theories. If you become interested in one of the scientists, perhaps you'd like to read more about his or her discoveries. In your reading you may find yourself building an awareness of scientific terminology and even certain methodologies that will inspire you to want to know even more. Scientific theory, study, and analysis is critically important to understanding who we are as human beings, how we got here, and where we might be headed.

Teeny Tiny Technology

Many authors of modern science have written books for you just like the scientists of old did for their mass audiences. For example, some recent books on nanotechnology will be of interest to anyone who dabbles with modern-day technology or who even has an interest in science fiction. Nanotechnology is far from fiction, however—it's a reality in development. This relatively new science involves the tiniest pieces of technological equipment that will one day change the course of human existence (yet again). For example, nanotechnology may give us tiny electronic devices that can be inserted into the bloodstream, find fatal tumors, and zap them into nonexistence. (Who wouldn't want to read about that?)

Once Upon a Theory

Scientists need to communicate their findings to the mass audience. If Copernicus had not published his findings, we might still think the sun revolved around the earth; if Galileo had not studied the heavens through a telescope and written down his findings in an effort to prove Copernicus right, perhaps Copernicus's theories would never have come to light, leaving us to struggle blindly in the darkness for answers.

All of these scientific discoveries influence our understanding of the world today, with all the good and the bad. We have built telescopes that can show us the movement of the planets, proving that we move around the sun and not the other way around. We have even seen, with telescopes that we have sent to space, what we believe to be the outer edges of the universe. As we learn, we build upon preexisting scientific discoveries.

Finding Popular Science

Countless magazines and newspapers nowadays tell you what is currently going on in scientific study and analyses. Magazines such as *Discover*, *National Geographic*, *Scientific American*, and *Popular Science* have very detailed articles about the latest scientific theories being tested today. You will also find that many of the national newspapers have "Science" sections that report, in lay terms, about what is going on in the realm of science.

You can also look at popular science magazines for information on new medical breakthroughs. Although most journalists specializing in science get their information from medical journals such as the British *Lancet* and the *Journal of American Medical Association* (*JAMA*), be aware that this material is written for the scientific community and not for laypeople like you and me.

Bookmarks

As you begin to read the sciences, you may want to pick up a copy of *The Essential Dictionary of Science* by John O. E. Clark. It covers every conceivable scientific term you may come across.

Dissecting New Ideas

So you're interested in reading more about scientific discoveries, either those taking place right now or those that took place hundreds of years ago. Where do you begin?

The first thing you need to do is find the areas of science that interest you. The second thing is find out who the major researchers are and what they have written that you might be able to understand.

If you are already a reader of science material, there are things you need to think about while you read, from how scientists think to why they need to let you know about their conclusions and, of course, what this means to human existence.

Let's say your interest is in black holes and you enjoy mathematics. You would want to look at *The Geometry of Kerr Black Holes*, by Burnett O'Neill. Or let's say you've been a little intrigued by the concepts of cosmology—try *The Book of Nothing*, about vacuums, voids, and the latest ideas about the origins of the universe, by John D. Barrow.

There are new ideas everywhere. The examination of new ideas is dependent on the layperson reading what researchers are doing. For example, scientists are starting to come up with brand-new conclusions about the causes and development of storms, about the nature of wild cats and gorillas, about butterflies, and about bird flight. Research into the natural world can tell us a great deal about our environment—how it works, for one thing, and the importance of its ecosystems, for another. We need to know about our own survival and/or potential demise; after all, many species vanish from the face of the planet every day.

Because scientists always lead us to the brink—to the edge of what we know—and dare us to leap along with them, we must remain open-minded to new ideas. Maybe what the scientists are saying is a little scary. (Will human beings really die off one day? Yikes! Or what about this controversial issue of cloning? Creepy or not?)

Whether science scares you or excites you, the research is underway and there are certain breakthroughs that we will have to face.

Thinking About Ethics

Scientific ethics is a field of study that is far too complex to broach here, but you should be aware as you read scientific books that scientists have to think about their discoveries in terms of societal responsibility. Although this will not stop research, it can slow certain scientific breakthroughs, for better or for worse.

Think of Einstein and the atomic bomb, for example. Einstein's guilt due to the fact that his theory led to the creation of the atom bomb was understandable—but his discoveries were nonetheless remarkable. It is what people did with his conclusions that created the danger—not the discoveries themselves.

It's important that scientists think about this while they work. People are flawed. They may not always use scientific discoveries responsibly. This always puts science in the hot seat and scientific work in jeopardy.

There are also religious and moral issues within our society that slow scientific outcomes. Although this can be frustrating to the scientific community and to the people anxiously awaiting certain health breakthroughs, for example, sometimes it doesn't hurt for us to stop and think about what we are doing and how we want to do it before moving too quickly.

There's a lot to think about here, and there is plenty to read on the subject of ethics and controversy in science. It's a controversial issue and says a lot about how human beings deal with current scientific matters. As you read, try to compare how society feels now about stem cell research, for example, to how the society, at that time, may have felt when they realized the earth is not flat. It shakes up the status quo and makes us rethink everything we knew—that's exciting and scary all at the same time.

What a Wonder-Filled World

Scientists are "our cosmic" eye on the world and the universe. We rely on them to explain things to us so that we can better understand the context in which we live on this planet, in this solar system, and in this universe. Their opinions are what feed our curiosity and our wonder.

The Least You Need to Know

- Scientific reading does not have to be complex. There are plenty of books for the layperson.
- Reading the classic scientists will help you understand where we are today, scientifically speaking.
- Keep an open mind to new ideas—you never know what will come of new discoveries.
- Scientific research is often challenged by the issue of ethics.

15

Reading Philosophy Books

In This Chapter

- ◆ Understanding the meaning of philosophy
- ◆ Pondering life's big questions
- ◆ Some famous "isms"
- ◆ The greatest philosophical minds
- ◆ How to approach complex philosophical reading

Philosophy is not only a field of study, it is a part of our daily existence. Everything you think and believe is philosophical. There are philosophers who have written books on some of the very things you ask yourself every day, from the seemingly smallest matters to ones that span the universe.

In this chapter, you learn what philosophy is, who the most renowned philosophers are (both past and present), some history of the study of philosophy, and, most importantly, how to read philosophy and incorporate philosophical thinking into your life.

The Study of Philosophy

Sometimes the word *philosophy* is used to mean any formulation of general basic principles for a practical activity such as politics or even gardening. You may hear people say "My philosophy about the environment is …" or "My philosophy on married life is …."

Needless to say, the actual *study* of philosophy goes a bit deeper than that. The most helpful place to start with the definition of philosophy is the meaning of the word itself: *Philosophy* is a word derived from the composite of two Greek words, *philo* and *sophia*, meaning the "pursuit" of "wisdom." What we think and what we do with our thoughts *is* philosophy.

What you think and how you put your thoughts and beliefs to work for yourself is your own philosophical life view, but philosophical thought in the larger sense is the pursuit of knowledge that pertains to all humankind. It is a cumulative building of ideas, thoughts, and beliefs that are shared with everyone so that we can understand why we think the way we do and do the things we do.

Of course, the best way to obtain knowledge and share knowledge is through books. The only way a philosopher can really share the complexity of his or her thought and the means by which that thought was developed is to write about it.

Look It Up

A **theologian** is someone who studies religion. Whereas some theologians specialize in one religion such as Judaism or Catholicism, other theologians study several different religions.

Spiritual and religious thinking is the earliest form of philosophical thought. It was a way of explaining the world and human existence in the world. It makes perfect sense that primitive human beings would think that a thunderstorm was an act of an angry higher power versus a natural weather episode. This is where some religious thinking begins. Although *theologians* would study the specifics of religion such as the nature of God and the human spirit, philosophers would study the nature of our belief systems by asking a question such as "Why do human beings need to believe in a god?"

So Many Questions

Although primitive human beings had to worry about the oncoming storm and flood and the possible anger of a higher power, as time went by the questions grew and became more complex. After the daily threats to their survival passed, people had the ability to start forming deeper thoughts. Questions such as "Why are we here?" "Why was I born a human being and my cat was born a cat?" "Why do we think the thoughts we think?" "How do we come to the conclusions we make?" "Are we right or wrong about what we think life is?"

Ah, the list goes on.

These are just a few of the questions the great thinkers through history have asked and attempted to answer.

Sometimes the philosopher simply asks the question. The question is enough to get people thinking. Other times the philosopher sets out on a course of finding answers. Questions such as "If a tree falls in the woods, and there's no one around to hear it, does it make a sound?" or "How many angels can dance on the head of a pin?" are riddles that have become part of our modern culture, but they have philosophical roots. They ask questions that we will not be able to answer, but they make us think about the answers. What is the sense of an event happening if there's no one around to observe and hear it, for example?

Great Minds Think Alike

Most of the questions you have asked about life, the universe, and our existence as we know it to this date have been asked before. (That should be a relief—you are not alone!) Great thinkers, educators, and leaders have asked these questions many times over and have tried to answer the questions for us all as well. Of course, there is no way to know whether any of their ideas are correct, but it's not about right or wrong—it's about processing the thinking of others and applying it to the way you see the world.

> ### Between the Lines
>
> Philosophers can work independently of one another, but the point is to build upon the thinking that has already been done or continues to be done. Philosophers will always look for new questions and new answers. They will even repeat old questions if they have come to new conclusions about them.

Thought Processing

Philosophical questions and ideas have been built over the years one on top of the other. You may already be familiar with some of the Western philosophers of ancient times and even more recent times—names such as Socrates, Plato, Aristotle, John Locke, Karl Marx, and Friedrich Nietzsche. You can be assured that each philosopher had read his predecessors' work. Although Locke may not have built his philosophical premises directly on Socrates's work, it is most likely that he had read his work and was well versed in Socratic thinking.

Philosophers and Their "isms"

Many of the philosophical movements through the ages have been given names, many of which end with three letters: *ism*. Ah, three little letters with so much meaning. Ism is used as a suffix for theories and dogmas. The dictionary gives a great definition of the suffix. For example, this is what the Random House dictionary has to say:

> Ism is a suffix meaning an action or a process, state or condition, doctrine of principle, usage or characteristic, devotion or adherence.

Let's look at the famous isms (philosophical movements) in Western history and what they represented at that time. (There are philosophical movements that happened in the Eastern portions of the world as well: Confucianism, Buddhism, Sufism, Hinduism, Shintoism. Many of the Eastern philosophical movements became religions that are practiced widely to this day in Japan, China, India, and several other Eastern civilizations.)

From 600 B.C.E. through 250 B.C.E.:

- **Naturalism, 600–350 B.C.E.** Everything can be explained by natural causes and laws.

- **Stoicism, 350–250 B.C.E.** To be truly happy one must be free of passion.

- **Skepticism, 350–250 B.C.E.** No knowledge is trustworthy.

- **Mysticism, 900–1000 C.E.** The direct union of the soul with God through love and contemplation.

- **Dialecticism, 1000–1400 C.E.** The art of logical argumentation to prove a theory.

- **Humanism, 1400–1600 C.E.** Human interests have primary importance in life.

The rest are 1600 to the present:

♦ **Empiricism.** Knowledge is derived from the senses.

♦ **Rationalism.** The human ability to "reason" or "to be rational" is the ultimate authority in matters of belief, opinion, and behavior.

♦ **Utilitarianism.** Emphasis on the practical and useful over the beautiful and ornamental.

♦ **Idealism.** The perception of how things should be versus how they are.

♦ **Pragmatism.** Truth is based on practical consequences of thought and action.

♦ **Existentialism.** People have ultimate free will in this absurd universe where nothing makes sense.

♦ **Evolutionism.** All living things exist in their current form due to the previous successive generations of development.

♦ **Intuitionism.** Truth and fact are based on anything but reason.

♦ **Deconstructionism.** Often used in reference to literature, it is the belief that contradictions exist beneath the surface and the way to find them is to look beyond preconceived ideas, beliefs, and practices.

As you read, think about what "ism" a particular philosopher may ascribe to. You may already know this before you begin to read, but keep in mind philosophers are not necessarily pigeonholed into one belief system. Sometimes they cross "isms." For example, *Marxism* (the belief that society is determined by the economic condition of the people) is derived from materialism, but does being a materialist make you a Marxist?

Look It Up

Marxism is the political, economic, and social doctrine of eighteenth-century German scholar Karl Marx and German socialist Friedrich Engels. Marxism calls for a classless society in which industry and production is commonly owned by the people within the society. Marx and Engels believed this kind of unity would bridge the divide between the capitalist and the worker. Communism is founded on this principle of thought.

Great Thinkers, Then and Now

Before we tell you how to read, we should first tell you either who to read or, at least, who to read *about!* To read philosophy well, you should have some idea what the philosophical movements are and who the key players were (and are, because their ideas are still with us and continue to be developed). We stick to Western philosophy only because it is probably more familiar to you through your education and because it may be more applicable to your understanding of life.

Here is a list of some of the most well-known philosophers (both Western and Eastern, but mostly Western):

- **Fifth century B.C.E.:** Buddha, Confucius, Socrates

- **Fourth century B.C.E.:** Plato, Aristotle

- **Thirteenth century C.E.:** St. Thomas Aquinas

- **Sixteenth century:** Thomas More

- **Seventeenth century:** Thomas Hobbes, René Descartes, John Locke

- **Eighteenth century:** Voltaire, Jean-Jacques Rousseau, Immanuel Kant

- **Nineteenth century:** Georg Wilhelm Hegel, Arthur Schopenhauer, Ralph Waldo Emerson, Frederick Douglass, Henry David Thoreau, Karl Marx, Friedrich Nietzsche

- **Twentieth century:** Ludwig Wittgenstein, Martin Heidegger, Jean-Paul Sartre, Albert Camus, Michel Foucault

> **Between the Lines**
>
> Despite the fact that people in the Western hemisphere are raised in Western philosophical thinking, there has been a strong movement toward Eastern philosophies and religions in the West, such as Buddhism, Hinduism, and Zen practices.

A first step in studying or reading philosophy is to understand some basic principles within the discipline. Philosophy involves interconnectedness between the various sciences. One of its objectives is to cultivate the ability to understand through the power of synopsis. In other words, philosophy bases itself, and builds itself, on specific outlines, summaries, and conclusions of general views.

To read philosophy well means you need to understand how connections are being made and what the conclusions are based on those connections.

The goal of the reader of philosophy begins with the understanding that philosophical thought strives to identify the relationships between physical, biological, and psychological sciences.

Specifically, you need to know that philosophical ideas and conclusions don't just have to be made by philosophers. Philosophical ideology has been discussed by modern physicists, biologists, economists, mathematicians, historians, and artists who may or may not incorporate the works of Plato or Aristotle in their thinking, but they, like the rest of Western civilization, have been influenced by many Western philosophers.

As a reader of philosophy it is important to recognize how one philosophical concept leads to another. It's also important to be able to see that what was once believed to be one mode of thinking changed and mutated to something else once the original concept was countered by another philosophical movement.

In the following sections, we take a look at some philosophical change and development.

Socratic Method

Socrates believed that the best way to learn is to ask questions. Without the question, there can be no answers. Sometimes a question will lead to another question, and then another, before an answer can be found. So essentially, you learn by conversation—whether it's a conversation inside your own mind or a conversation with one or more people. This teaching method, known today as the "Socratic method," is the basis of Western education to this day.

Between the Lines

Socrates claimed that he was an oracle of the gods because he knew how little he knew. Socrates had a large following of students and was criticized by the Greek authorities for denying the reality of the gods and corrupting the minds of the youth. He was tried and found guilty and was given the opportunity to choose his own punishment. But when he audaciously chose the highest honor of the republic, he was sentenced to death by poisoning (drinking hemlock).

Philosophy and Change

Natural philosophy was a term used to describe Aristotle's own view of "physics." But in the seventeenth century with the new natural science of Galileo and Newton, it becomes customary to use the phrase *moral philosophy* to cover not only the field of Aristotle's ethics and politics but also psychology and all the other traditional parts of philosophy (except logic).

Logic

To Aristotle an argument is actually dialectical, meaning that it originates from commonly held opinions, different from premises already known to be true. This concept of the "dialectic" was often used as a general name for logic.

When Hegel and Marx came on the scene in the nineteenth century, they applied the concept of logic to their philosophical principle of the development of the argument: thesis, antithesis, and synthesis (the idea, the counter-idea, and the final analysis). This is not so far from what Socrates was basically saying way back in his day in perhaps a more simple form: Draw conclusions based on questions.

Getting to Know You

Take some time to become familiar with the historical development of Western philosophy. Start with a book on the different schools of thought in ancient philosophy and work your way forward to modern Western philosophy. There are plenty of academic textbooks that will help you with this kind of research. It may be more interesting to look at books that specialize in certain eras of philosophical thinking. Once you are familiar with the chronology of Western thinking, delve a little deeper and try to understand some of the divisions in ancient philosophy. Examine pre-Socratic philosophy and then move forward from Socrates to Plato and then to Aristotle.

There is so much to learn that this reading could take you quite some time. And don't be surprised if reading about Western philosophy also spurs your interest to read more about Eastern philosophy. There's no telling what doors may open for you as you read about the world's great philosophers and philosophical movements. Your reading may take you into another genre altogether. Reading philosophy may inspire you to read more historical, scientific, or theological literature.

Eastern Philosophy

You may want to go even further afield, and leave Western philosophy behind. (After all, you are living it every day if you live in North America or Europe.) The oldest philosophies in the world come out of China and India, and are unfamiliar to many Western thinkers. You will find something new in Eastern ways of thinking; perhaps you will find yourself thinking things you never thought before and you will become a philosopher in your own right as you incorporate the West into the East in your own life.

Eastern philosophies cover every possible human concern for community; our ties as human beings to the natural world; ties to the ideals of order, justice, beauty, love, and spiritual and harmonious living. And perhaps Eastern philosophers are even more adept at demonstrating the interconnectedness we discussed earlier, which is the foundation of philosophical thinking. Don't forget that thousands of years of human existence passed before the advent of Western history and philosophy; philosophical thinking did not originate in Greece.

This is just a broad overview of how to connect the dots as you read philosophical works.

I Think Therefore I Am

Philosophers not only ask questions, they frame and reframe our world for us as a result of the questions they ask.

Philosophy can be complicated. The experts in the field are trying to answer questions that may seem to be impossible to answer. Although reading Aristotle's original work may be complicated, you are lucky that many others over the centuries have read his work, expounded on his work, and have written about his thinking in ways that may be more readable for the average person.

Don't let the issue of complex thinking frighten you away from any book, article, or journal. If it's something you want to know about, read it. The best way to approach complicated philosophical reading material is to read it once at a regular speed, then read it again, slowly, considering each sentence as you go along. Stop and think about what you've just read and then draw your own conclusions. Ask yourself whether you can believe this thesis and its conclusions. (Make Socrates proud!) If you don't understand it, there are many resources that

> **Between the Lines**
>
> *Cogito ergo sum,* Latin for "I think therefore I am," was coined by seventeenth-century French mathematician and philosopher René Descartes. Descartes studied Aristotelian philosophy and is most known for applying algebra to geometry giving us what we know now as Cartesian geometry.

can help you understand a particular philosophy or philosopher—you just have to do some extra reading to help you along.

There are philosophical questions, opinions, and perspectives that push the process of our thinking forward to examine our cherished premises and for that reason are worth some examination from the reader of philosophy—especially if you are interested in the evolution of thought.

Balderdash? Well, that's what contemporaries of Socrates may have said, too. Keep your eyes and ears open for modern ways of thinking.

The Least You Need to Know

- Philosophy is a methodological way of thinking that builds thought upon thought.

- Philosophy as a study relies on the interconnectedness of various sciences and arts to draw conclusions about human beings and life in general.

- Reading philosophy requires some study to familiarize yourself with names and philosophical eras.

- Reading philosophy can be complex, so read it once, then twice, then stop and ask yourself whether you understood it or whether you need to do more research.

- Socrates is one of the most well-known Western philosophers.

- Asking questions is the basis of learning; just ask Socrates!

Chapter 16

Essays and Memoirs

In This Chapter

♦ Similarities and differences between memoirs and essays

♦ How to understand and read an essay

♦ Putting the message to the test

♦ Understanding an essay's or memoir's point of view or perspective

♦ Essays are for everyone: the editorial pages

Essays and memoirs are forms of nonfiction writing that you'll want to explore at some point in your reading. Not only can they stand alone as reading material, they can often provide excellent backup for other books you have read or may be reading now.

In this chapter, you learn how to read these types of nonfiction material and incorporate them into your current knowledge base, as well as learn from the styles and perspectives used in each of these literary forms.

Similarities and Differences

Although both *essays* and *memoirs* are short pieces of nonfiction expository writing, they fall into separate literary genres. They are similar pieces of

Look It Up

The words *essay* and *memoir* come from French words *essayer* and *memoir,* meaning "to try" and "memory," respectively. An **essay** is an attempt to prove a point. A **memoir** is a life story, usually focusing on a particular period of time in a person's life. Both words have come to refer to literary genres in the English language.

writing in one way only—they each focus on a specific topic. An essay can focus on any subject, whether objective and academic or subjective and exploratory, whereas a memoir is a piece of subjective writing that focuses on a person's life memory or a series of memories that apply to one theme.

Understanding the Essay

To most of us, an essay has always been something we had to write in high school. We wrote essays because we had to, and we read essays because we had to—but have you ever tackled the essay on your own?

Essays are usually very specific to one topic and are written to make a point. At the college level, you'll find yourself predominantly reading essays during your research on any given topic. This is where the newest ideas can be found (and also the older ideas—when they were original to their time). Academicians specializing in specific areas of study are constantly trying to publish their ideas in order to maintain credibility in their respective fields, and to keep current with the thinking in their fields of expertise.

Scholarly Writing

A scholar of romantic poetry, for example, will not only read about new ideas and conclusions and research about Sir Alfred, Lord Tennyson's epic poem *Idylls of the King,* but will write about his own thoughts on that new idea. It's sort of a give-and-take between scholars within an academic field.

Perhaps one scholar discovers Tennyson's diaries, in which Tennyson gives some of his own insight as to his life and work. This new information could change the way we've always thought about this poem or about Tennyson in general. Let's say another scholar reads this essay and find errors in the thinking or has another perspective to add. That scholar will publish his ideas as well. Perhaps it's not as grand a discovery as a diary, but it's an opinion that has been developed by one scholar with a conclusion that contradicts previously conceived ideas. So the essays flow, building upon past ideas and uncovering new ones.

Where do you fit in? Well, if you're struggling to understand Tennyson's poems, reading these kinds of scholarly essays will help you tremendously. You'll be reading what the specialists have to say and from there you can draw your own conclusions.

Spelling It Out

In an effort to understand how one literary movement morphed into another, or how one literary concept can lead to new concepts, you can turn to the words of the writers themselves. Many poets, fiction writers, and playwrights were also essayists … and they had a lot to say!

T. S. Eliot, for example, is best known for his poetry, but he was also a playwright and an essayist. In his essays he discussed many aspects of writing. One of the ideas he focused on was the use of plain language in poetry and drama. He wanted to move past the flowery style of the romantic lyric (which used a lot of "thee's," "thou's," and "thus's") and find the beauty in the simplicity of language.

By reading Eliot's essays as well as his poetry and plays, you'll see how he applies his own theory of writing within his own creative work:

> The bad poet dwells partly in a world of objects and partly in a world of words, and he never can get them to fit. Only a man of genius could dwell so exclusively and consistently among words as Swinburne. His language is not, like the language of bad poetry, dead. It is very much alive, with this singular life of its own. But the language which is more important to us is that which is struggling to digest and express new objects, new groups of objects, new feelings, new aspects, as, for instance, the prose of Mr. James Joyce or the earlier Conrad.
>
> —T. S. Eliot, *The Sacred Wood: Essays on Criticism, Swinburne as a Poet* (1922)

Here, Eliot is not only acting as a critic of Swinburne; he's also promoting his own ideas about the use of language in poetry.

Here are the opening lines of Eliot's most famous poem, *The Waste Land*, from which you'll be able to get an idea of what Eliot is talking about when he refers to the use of plain language:

> April is the cruelest month, breeding
> Lilacs about of the dead land, mixing
> Memory and desire, stirring
> Dull roots with spring rain.

> Winter kept us warm, covering
> Earth in forgetful snow, feeding
> A little life with dried tubers.

And here is a sample of the late-nineteenth and early-twentieth-century poet Algernon Charles Swinburne's poetry, to give you an idea of what Eliot was talking about in his essay:

> I had grown pure as the dawn and the dew,
> You had grown strong as the sun or the sea.
> But none shall triumph a whole life through:
> For death is one, and fates are three.
> At the door of life, by the gate of breath,
> There are worse things waiting for men than death;
> Death could not sever my soul and you,
> As these have severed your soul from me.
>
> —Algernon Charles Swinburne, *The Triumph of Time*

If you've read nineteenth-century poets and then noticed a change in the twentieth century toward simpler language, you might wonder why. T. S. Eliot was one of the leaders of the modernist movement in poetry and he, along with another twentieth-century poet, Ezra Pound, changed the use of diction (word choice) in poetry, forever. You might only know this if you read about Eliot or read his own words on the subject.

 **Bookmarks**

Most often you'll have to do some digging for essays, unless you subscribe to a journal. There are science-based journals, history-based journals, literary journals, and more. Essays are also published in anthologies, which you can find in your local bookstore. If an essay is highly specialized, try looking around in the library.

Reading an Essay

Depending on the essayist, reading this type of literature can be complicated or very simple. Although the social commentary is easy to understand because its purpose is for you to be able to relate to the opinions it proposes, when you get to the academic essay you may have to spend a little more time analyzing the information.

Someone can write an academic essay about any topic such as art, literature, history, music, or science. You will also find essays in the form of social commentary, as you may have seen in the works of Mark Twain.

Here are the steps you should take when reading an essay containing complex writing style and/or content:

1. **Read the essay once.** Concentrate on the main idea and the author's point. Don't worry about details.

2. **Focus on key words and phrases.** If key words and phrases are used repeatedly, they are probably pertinent to the point the author is trying to make. Underline them and go back to them later if you don't understand them.

3. **Read the article again, slowly and carefully this time.** Find the thesis—the central ideas of the essay. Get a sense of structure of the essay and how it builds around the central theme. If you don't understand the thesis, the structure of the essay may lead you to its central idea. Sometimes it helps to look for key words such as *for example* or *for instance*—these will be terms used to back up the central idea. Follow the backup examples and you will locate the thesis.

4. **Ask yourself questions.** What is the author trying to prove? What does the author do to prove the thesis? Does he or she build an argument on the topic helping you see other sides? Does he or she disprove other theories to build his or her own? Is there one single statement that will qualify the entire essay? For example: "Creativity is not innate but environmental" or "Dogs are loyal but will attach to more than one master" or "If a tree fell in the woods and nobody heard it, it would still make a sound."

5. **Underline the main points.** Make notations in your own words as to what these main points are. Don't be surprised if there is more than one main point. They should all fit together to one main thesis (if it is a well-written essay).

When looking for structure in an essay, this is what you should find:

1. **The introduction.** If the thesis statement is not here, keep reading. Make a note where the introduction ends and the body of the argument within the text begins.

2. **The body of the essay.** Here you will see a series of paragraphs that will begin to explain the introduction by using various main ideas.

◆ Subdivisions: All these paragraphs should be subdivisions of the main topic. (This is especially true in longer essays.) If the essay is the concept of nature in romantic portraiture, for example, notice where the author talks about nature in general, nature as specific to the concept of romanticism, the general purpose of portraiture, and how landscape is used as a romantic ideal, etc. Notice where the essayist breaks up his points—label these points.

◆ Find the paragraphs that back up a point—these paragraphs will usually give examples and will fit into one of the subdivisions. Within each subdivision, find the author's central point. Find the "topic" sentence in each paragraph, where the author brings you back to the major issue.

3. **The conclusion.** Check again to see whether the thesis statement is made here for the first time, or whether it is reiterated to bring the essay full circle. Sometimes the thesis will not be stated at all, only implied.

When you're done with the final reading, ask yourself these questions, write them down, and then write down your answers so you are clear:

◆ What is the main thesis of this essay?

◆ Why did the author write this?

◆ Who did he or she write it for?

◆ What is the tone of the essay? Is it hostile or empathetic? Kind or indifferent?

◆ Did the writer convince me?

Finding an Essay's Theme

You will most often find the thesis stated in the beginning of the essay with the rest of the essay focusing on proving the point. Sometimes the essayist will build the case first and then clarify the thesis statement in the concluding paragraphs. But be prepared for the essayist who never states the thesis, but gives it to you in bits and pieces throughout the piece. That's a trickier read.

Between the Lines

Social and political commentaries in newspapers and magazines are found in a section usually referred to as the editorial pages. These pieces of writing are called "editorials," which differentiates them from the articles written by the journalists. A journalist's reporting is supposed to be objective and unbiased, whereas the editorials give readers and writers a place to say how they feel in the most subjective ways.

Make It Memorable

A memoir can be a short piece of prose in a sort of narrative essay style that stands on its own or a collection of short pieces that are specific to a given moment in a person's life. An entire book can be a memoir if it focuses on a particular theme in one's life. For example, Hillary Rodham Clinton's recent book, *Living History*, is an example of a memoir in a full-length book. Her book focuses not on her whole life (which would make it an autobiography), but on her years as first lady of the United States.

Putting Memories on Paper

A memoir, of course, must be written by the person who is sharing the memories. Memoirs are sometimes published posthumously, which means that a researcher would look through the writings of a deceased individual, find a central theme, and publish the collection as a single narrative manuscript. For example, if author Anaïs Nin kept diaries, a portion of which focused on her relationship with author Henry Miller, a researcher could isolate these pieces of writing and put them together in a nonfiction book and call it a memoir.

On the other hand, if Anaïs Nin's diaries were published without being set within the body of a narrative, they would simply be published diaries and would not necessarily be labeled in the genre of the memoir.

Not Just for the Famous

Memoirs can be based on a very broad reminiscence or something very simple and focused. For example, there's a young adult memoir called *My Thirteenth Winter: A Memoir*, by Samantha Abeel. This book focuses on one year in the life a girl who discovers while in the seventh grade that she has a learning disability. As an adult, Abeel is able to look back on how this one year shaped the rest of her life. The point of such a book is not just to appeal to other people who may have had similar learning challenges, but to reach all readers who ever had to struggle with a specific problem in their young lives.

A recently published memoir titled *Reading Lolita in Tehran: A Memoir in Books*, by Azar Nafisi, focuses on a book group a former Tehran professor organized in her living room in Iran. She and seven of her female friends began the group by reading banned pieces of literature by authors such as Vladimir Nabokov, Jane Austen, and F. Scott Fitzgerald. When the shyness wore off, these women let down their proverbial veils and opened the doors to discussion about everything, including the oppression of women under Islamic rule.

Neither of these authors are famous. The lure of their books is their interesting subject matters and the way they are written. Memoirs are, of course, about someone else's life; but in the lives of others not only do we find fascinating information about the world, we also find little details that we can all relate to.

> **Bookmarks**
>
> If you're interested in a particular historical or current figure, find out whether that person ever published his or her memoirs. It's one of the most interesting ways to learn about what other people thought and how they lived their lives.

Point of View and Perspective

You can expect to find a very strong point of view from an essay. Obviously it's written to persuade you to accept the author's thesis, so style and tone play a big part in the point of view of the essayist. Does the essayist use wit in a lighthearted way to help you see what he is saying? Does he use bitterness and sharp-edged sarcasm? Or is he simply formal, distant, and factual?

There are two kinds of essays when it comes to point of view: the formal essay and the informal essay. The formal essay is impersonal. The author writes as an authority, or at least as highly knowledgeable, on the subject and presents it in an orderly and thorough way. Informal essays are personal. The author assumes a tone of intimacy with the reader, and the subject matter is usually about everyday matters that affect everyday people.

A memoir, on the other hand, is an accounting of events as told by the person who witnessed or experienced them. The point of view, as in the case of the essay, can be found predominantly in the style or tone. Points of view and perspectives are developed by authors according to the kinds of subjects and topics they choose to write about.

The author of a memoir or an essay has something very specific to say about a particular situation, or about an idea, or even about a specific problem or question. In relation to the point of view, ask yourself what tone the author employs to keep you interested as an empathic observer, an angry respondent, or simply an interested thinker.

The essayist writes because he or she has something to say about a particular topic. You can agree or disagree with the thesis, the argument, and the conclusion. That's why essayists need to back up what they're saying. Their goal is to make you believe them—but, of course, you don't have to.

Take Note!

Depending on whether it's a formal or informal essay, you may have to check out facts and dig further. The one thing you have to trust in this process is yourself and the homework you are willing to do to find what you are looking for. That may mean investigating the work of more than one essayist.

What is the author trying to do in a memoir? Make you feel sorry for him? Make you feel angry at him? Make you cry or laugh? You can't be certain that the author is being truthful and honest, but you can trust your own gut reaction to the narrative voice within the story. Does the author sound whiney and irritating even though he might feel perfectly justified in what he has to say? Can you see through the narrative to a certain perspective—a place that the author seems to be coming from?

Ideas and Opinions

Let's take a look at another kind of essayist—the editorial writers for magazines and newspapers. They always have something new and different to say, which is why they're published to begin with, to give us a fresh idea or opinion about what's going on.

Letters to the Editor

Another kind of essay can be found in the section called "Letters to the Editor." This is a forum for anyone to express his or her feelings about anything that has been written about in that paper or magazine or about anything that is happening in the world today. If an article in the paper makes you angry or makes you think of something that might give the article more clarity, put pen to paper or fingers to keyboard and let your voice be heard.

Stand Up and Be Heard

Everyone has opinions about one thing or another, and some need to be heard more than others. The topics that can be found in the editorial pages of newspapers and magazines vary in opinions about religious, political, moral, and ethical issues. There are pros and cons about every conceivable human situation, thought, discovery, question, lifestyle, or point of view, and chances are good you'll will find them in print. So in reality, we all have an opportunity to be essayists of sorts.

The Least You Need to Know

- ◆ Essays and memoirs are subject-based pieces of nonfiction writing.

- ◆ Essays can be formal or informal, academic or social commentaries.

- ◆ To read a complicated essay you need to dissect it piece by piece to be sure you understand it.

- ◆ Memoirs are autobiographical accounts of a specific time or theme in a person's life.

- ◆ Memoirs can be published posthumously in narrative form using the actual writings of the person involved.

- ◆ Editorials and letters to the editor are essays that can be found in newspapers and magazines and can be written by famous and not-so-famous people alike.

Chapter 17

Newspapers and Magazines

In This Chapter

- ◆ An overview of journalism
- ◆ Your right to know the news
- ◆ Taking apart the newspaper
- ◆ How magazines are structured
- ◆ Evaluating current events

Newspapers and magazines are part of our everyday existence. Some people read bits and pieces of their favorite publications, whereas others read them cover to cover. There are good types of written media out there for everyone.

In this chapter, you learn to see newspapers and magazines as another form of written literature, adhering to certain structures and standards, all for the purpose of expanding your horizons.

Journalism in General

Journalism is a specialized field that serious and respected writers spend years perfecting as a craft. The object of American journalism is to report facts objectively as they occur in the world. The type of newspaper or magazine you choose to read will determine what kind of information you will be receiving.

Between the Lines

Although it has a local name, *The New York Times* is a national newspaper, as are *The Washington Post, The Wall Street Journal, The Los Angeles Times, The Chicago Tribune,* and *The Philadelphia Enquirer.* These papers contain a section that applies specifically to the city in which they are printed, but most of the content of these newspapers focuses on national and some international news.

The New York Times, The Wall Street Journal, The Washington Post, Time Magazine, and *Newsweek* are just a few of the most respected and well-read newspapers and magazines in the United States. This is because they hire talented writers, editors, researchers, photographers, and fact checkers who do their best to be objective and stick to the art of their craft as unbiased reporters of the world around us.

Of course, human beings have opinions, and it's easy to spot biases in even the most respected print media. This is where it is critical for you to be a good reader. The more you read, the more you develop your own opinions, which will allow you to spot poor journalism and draw your own conclusions about what is being reported as "fact."

Responsibility in Journalism

There is a doctrine in American journalism called the people's "right to know" as indicated in the first amendment of the United States Constitution:

> Congress shall make no law respecting an establishment of religion, or prohibiting the free exercise thereof; or abridging the freedom of speech, or of the press; or the right of the people peaceably to assemble, and to petition the government for a redress of grievances.

The press is protected under one of the primary laws set forth by this country— freedom of speech. The media is an important part of the checks and balances required to make sure our leaders are conducting business according to the standards of our Constitution and our laws.

Responsible Reporting

Although we need the media, it's important to remember that with all this freedom comes responsibility. Journalists who stand firm on the principles of journalistic integrity will always do their best to find you the truth, but there are so many journalists out there nowadays that there will be biases, prejudice, and political preferences, no matter how subtle or brazen. But if you familiarize yourself with the role of journalism in a democratic society, you will make yourself a more knowledgeable reader of print media and you will know how to spot the irresponsible or biased representation of the world around us.

Healthy Skepticism

Let's say a reporter's source of information is coming from an "anonymous source." You are now completely at the mercy of the journalist. Do you know this journalist? Is he credible? Do you trust what this writer has said in the past? Do you trust what she is telling you now? Maybe a quote about George W. Bush came from an army general. Was that general there with the president? Does he really know what was going on? Or did he merely hear about the events through others?

Just as it's important for you to pay attention to the sources a journalist uses, it's essential that a journalist pick his sources carefully. A journalist must ask himself the same questions you should be asking. Who is this person? Is he credible? Can I use what he is saying in a responsible way? A journalist must do a lot of background checking before using any source to back up an article.

CAUTION

Take Note!

Be wary of quotes in newspaper articles where the person speaking is labeled a "specialist" or "expert." What exactly makes that person a specialist? Look for the article to explain this to you. It's important that you know who this person is and what makes the person an "expert."

Extra! Extra!

Newspapers provide millions of people all over the country (and the world) with their daily dose of what's happening. How do you read the paper? Do you automatically reach for the Sports section, or does the front page grab your attention? (More importantly, especially if you live in a city with only one newspaper, do you ever question what you're being told in print?)

Section by Section

Like chapters in a book, newspapers are divided into sections. The average daily national newspaper will come in several sections, and these may change from day to day. One day you may have an "Arts" section, and the next day "Arts" won't be there, but you'll have a "Science" section instead.

The front section contains the main *headlines* and the current news. Other sections may be titled "Metro," "Business," "Arts," "Sports," or "Money." Obviously it's the front page parts of the business and sports sections that require writers and photographers to make tight deadlines with the news of the day.

Front-Page Headlines

The front page is the grabber. The most important events happening in the world should appear on the front page. Newspapers will also use a main headline to grab your attention. The physical size of the headline will depend on the magnitude of the event. For example, when we moved into the year 2000, *The New York Times* had a front page and headline big enough to show the significance of the event in our lives—the whole page!

On the front page of most newspapers you will also see a list of other highlights contained within the paper and the pages on which you can find the articles for quick and easy reference. This list usually runs down the left side of the front page of the paper.

The Inverted Pyramid

Newspapers have a structure. To understand the structure, think of an inverted pyramid (upside down with the peak at the bottom and the base at the top). The top of the inverted pyramid is wide and reduces down to the peak. Newspaper information starts big (with the major news) and winds its way down to the minor headlines and feature stories.

On a daily basis, the main headline will be at the top of the front page. It will appear in larger letters than other headlines and it should announce the major news story of the day, which is at the discretion of the editors. There will be smaller headlines throughout the paper that announce each story. These headlines are designed to give you an idea of what each article will be about.

For example, in the Sunday edition of a Wisconsin paper, *The Post-Crescent*, a newspaper focused on local Wisconsin news, the front-page headline reads: "State could aid in 911 safeguards," while a subheadline reads:

Take Note!

Newspapers are supported financially by advertisements as well as subscription and newsstand revenue, so don't be surprised if you are bombarded with advertising on various pages of the newspaper—depending on the newspaper, of course. Newspapers prefer subscribers to newsstand buyers because they can count on the income.

"Winnebago [County] acts to assure accuracy of phone database." The newspapers editors obviously felt this would be of top importance to its Wisconsin readers, so they chose to make this their top news story. The national newspapers were focused on the troubled elections in Afghanistan.

Smaller headlines on the front page of this same Wisconsin paper read: "Survey: Health costs top concerns: State residents look to candidates for a solution." Finally at the bottom of the front page: "Afghanistan presidential election thrown into chaos." Although the Afghanistan news may have made the top story in national and international newspapers, residents of Wisconsin who read this paper are most concerned with issues that directly affect their lives within the state. They can get other major news stories in this paper, too, they will just not have the strongest focus.

Feature Story

Accompanying an article about Wisconsin health concerns may be a feature story about a family dealing directly with the issue. Newspaper editors do this to give the story a more human angle, taking it out of the realm of politics and putting names and faces to it so that you can better relate to what the issue means for everyday people.

So the news that you are interested in will appear in different newspapers. For news about the 2004 elections or the latest rulings of the U.S. Supreme Court, you will want to read a national newspaper. For information pertaining to your state, such as environmental cleanup or specifics about the state governor's recent activities, you will want to read a local paper that reports news of the state. There are also local papers that will tell you what is going on in your own city, county, or region.

The Five W's (and One H)

The five W's are the general rule when writing a newspaper article. You got it: who, what, where, why, and when. Add an H for how. You want to get the who, the what, the where, and the when in the opening paragraph. This is called "the lead." The why and the how can be investigated in the conclusion of the article or in a follow-up article depending on how much the reporter knows.

There are good newspaper articles and bad ones. Bad ones consist of biases and/or what is known as "burying the lead." Readers want to know what happened, so tell them up front. The rest should be the explanation—as much of an explanation as the reporter is able to give based on the facts he or she has.

Magazine Structure and Subject Matter

There are hundreds of magazines all over the world on every imaginable subject: babies, health food, fashion, gardening, arts and crafts, race cars, tools … you name it. Find your passion and there will be a magazine that focuses on it—we can almost guarantee it! Magazines tell you about specialized subjects and topics, teach you how to do something, or tell you about the latest happenings in your area of interest. There are weekly, bi-weekly, monthly, and bi-monthly magazines.

> **Between the Lines**
>
> Before books were inexpensive and readily available to all, many fiction writers were published in newspapers and magazines. Each time a new edition of a newspaper would come out, readers would be treated to the next chapter of the latest Thomas Hardy or Charles Dickens novel.

Newsmagazines have the same responsibility to journalistic integrity that newspapers have. Magazines such as *Time*, *Newsweek*, and *U.S. News and World Report* are weekly newsmagazines that summarize world events for you, giving them some additional perspective. Specialty magazines such as *Discover*, *National Geographic*, and *The Economist* adhere to these same rules with regard to your right to know what is going on in the world of science, nature, and the economy.

It's important to know where to find responsible articles, and a good place to start is with some of these magazines.

Other kinds of magazines have absolutely no real obligation to objectivity. Several pop culture magazines focus on the current movie trends or on the celebrity industry of movie and television stars. They write about entertainment as a means of entertainment.

Pretty Pictures!

A magazine will contain, more than anything else, hundreds of advertisements. In fact, you may find yourself digging through advertisements to get to the articles you want to read. Magazines are expensive to make. They contain glossy, high-color pages, so in order for magazine publishers to make any money, they need to charge hefty ad prices. Like newspapers, magazine publishers depend on subscriptions to keep track of revenue, but even more than newspapers, they depend on advertisers.

Cover Story

The cover of the magazine is extremely important to a magazine in the same way a newspaper headline might be. Magazine publishers pick their covers carefully, paying attention to what image will sell the magazine. Famous people have a huge impact on sales, as do interesting subject matters. *Time*, for example, is well known for the faces it puts on its magazines, and *People Magazine* thrives on its front-page lure. *Sports Illustrated* magazine has made many a model world-renowned just by putting her on the front cover of their annual swimsuit edition.

The cover of the magazine will reflect the magazine's featured article. For example, if *Vanity Fair* puts a photograph of actresses over the age of 40 on its cover, its feature story might be the increase in movie parts for actresses in that age range. Inside the magazine will be several other articles on many different topics, but the lure of the front cover will draw you to the cover story, usually found somewhere in the middle or near the end of the magazine.

Flipping Pages

Most magazine readers skim first and read later. This is a very good way to get a handle on what this type of magazine or this particular edition of the magazine has to offer. You'll likely be looking for photographs that draw your attention to an article. Other magazines such as the *New Yorker* contain very few articles and have to lure you in with article headings and placement of stories within the magazine.

After you have skimmed your magazine, go through it more slowly, absorbing the style of the magazine and getting a feel for the articles contained within. Fold down pages of articles you want to read as you turn the pages and go back to them and read them thoroughly when you have the opportunity.

Read the articles the way you would any piece of journalism. Look for the point of view, the style, the tone, and the aspect of persuasion: Are the five W's there? Is the H there, too? Ask yourself the same kinds of questions you might when you read an essay, keeping in mind that some articles are written more for entertainment than for information.

Tabloids

The meaning of *tabloid* actually did not have any negative connotations at one point in time. The tabloid was introduced in the late nineteenth century as a small-format newspaper—small and compact, almost like a writing "tablet." That's where the word *tabloid* comes from. Now, however, the word *tabloid* immediately conjures images of scandal, gossip, and even lies.

The faster the tabloids are cranked off the presses, the less time there is for accuracy—but that hardly seems to be the concern of these publications. The articles may contain information that is accurate in the most basic ways—the who, what, where, and when of the event will be clear, but don't look for too much depth or insight as to why and how. Because of this "gossip" aspect of the tabloid, they have come to lack a certain amount of journalistic prestige and credibility.

It's often hard to tell the difference between truth and fantasy in tabloids, so it's best to stick with the newspapers and magazines that hold some sort of journalistic standards. If you are going to read the "scandal sheets," as they are also called, do some research. Is any other news organization saying these things? If not, chances are good it was all made up and is nothing more than gossip.

There's an old reporter expression that goes like this: "Tell 'em what you're going to tell 'em. Tell 'em. Tell 'em what you told 'em." In other words, tell them what happened, back it up, and then repeat it with a conclusion. That is the essence of any newspaper article—and the trick to never "burying the lead."

Current Events and You

Magazines and newspapers focus mainly on current events. Don't accept any one report of what's happening in the world. Read broadly on a subject. Take your time and be patient. Be aware of your feelings about current events and how they have shaped, grown, and sprouted new roots over the years and what this has done to the way you think about the world now. New discoveries, new technologies, and new perspectives all have an effect on our lives and our thinking, and we have to reexamine our opinions and conclusions constantly in a variety of areas.

Reading newspapers and magazines will not only help you understand the world, but your place in the world, too, as well as your beliefs, ideologies, skepticisms, and hopes. Articles are written about the world around you, to help you understand life. It is your job to do the reading and find the truths that apply to you.

The Least You Need to Know

- Journalists are held to a high standard of integrity.
- Newspapers follow an inverted pyramid structure, in which the major news is presented first, winding down to the less-important news.
- Magazines are largely for entertainment and may be less objective than newspapers.
- Current events happening throughout the world are reported in newspapers and magazines as well as on television, radio, and the Internet.

Part 4

The Final Analysis

Finally, we pull it all together for you in this last part. You've done so much reading already and you understand so much; but now, what do you do with all of this new information?

In this part, we show you how everything you've read correlates to each other. Fiction is not isolated from nonfiction and vice versa. Thoughts build upon thoughts, ideas upon ideas, fiction upon nonfiction. What do we need to do to see these connections? Well, we show you. We have a bit of a surprise for you in this part, so keep reading. There *will* be a test on this! But don't worry; there are no set-in-stone "correct" answers. The questions are here as a guideline to help show you how to read various literary works, how you should be connecting them to each other, and how to question them as individual pieces. This part may be the most valuable to you because it allows you to put your newfound knowledge to work for you.

Chapter 18

Exploration and Research

In This Chapter

- ◆ Your growth as a reader and individual
- ◆ Challenging yourself for fun
- ◆ Understanding library search systems
- ◆ The construction of a research paper
- ◆ Tips for keeping track of references

You've heard it many times before: "No pain, no gain." Reading is by no means painful—it's a pleasurable experience that will only make you a better person in the long run, but there is work involved. In this case, work means you have to pick up the books that will challenge your mind, open your eyes, and teach you something.

In this chapter, we show you some more useful ways to get the most out of your reading. If you're in school, this information will be invaluable to you as you begin a research paper. If you're finished with school and working on your reading abilities by yourself, these are hints that will not only make you more knowledgeable, but will also provide you with all the background you need to become a better reader.

New Avenues of Exploration

When you're ready, plunge in deeper and start doing some of your own research to back up your knowledge and expand your thoughts and ideas even further. This really is the fun part, we promise.

Here's an example of a novel that will challenge your preconceived ideas and may make you look at things from a new perspective: Try reading Dan Brown's best-selling novel *The Da Vinci Code*. It's a mystery that involves art, history, myth, religion, and folklore. Brown takes us on a wild adventure that begins with a murder at The Louvre Museum in Paris and ends where we least expect it to end. But it's the information in the middle that has people scurrying to the Internet and the library for more information.

In *The Da Vinci Code*, Brown challenges the reader in many ways. Everything you ever believed to be true, everything you never noticed about art, things you never knew about religion, and what you thought you knew about myth and folklore—all are put to the test.

For example, take a look at the *Mona Lisa*. What is she smiling about? Brown suggests that the painting is actually a testament to the divine feminine (goddess worship) in its style, framing, and setting, and, as a result, bears an innate negation of Christianity.

So is the Mona Lisa smiling because she knows Da Vinci's secret? Has Da Vinci hidden something in the painting that we can't see or understand, and is the Mona Lisa amused by this inside joke? We may never know, but it's interesting—and just plain fun—to challenge ourselves to think about it. Although you most likely won't have to write a research paper on *The Da Vinci Code*, a book like this will open your mind to new ideas and possibilities—plus, you'll be able to hold your own during those water-cooler conversations.

All-You-Can-Read Buffet

You can find almost any book in a local library. It's a book lover's paradise. If they don't have it, they will often order it for you. A library offers even more than just books, though. It offers people, trained in library science, to help you by giving you personalized assistance that you can't get on the Internet and cannot necessarily do by yourself.

Where to Start

Some people prefer to do their own research, whereas others prefer the assistance of the librarian. Librarians may have many people to help at any one time, so they most likely will not have time to do your research for you, but they will help you find your way around the stacks.

Bookmarks

Some libraries will supply researchers to help you, but most of the time you will walk in and find the librarians showing people how to do their own research.

Keeping Order

Although most libraries use a computerized research system, some still use the old-fashioned card catalogue. You will find the card catalogue in the reading areas or by the library desk, and you can search under either author name (last name first), title of the book, or subject matter (in the case of nonfiction). The card catalogues are usually small, wooden file-cabinet drawers that pull out by a small handle. When you find what you want in the card catalogue, look at the number on the card. This number refers to what is known as the Dewey Decimal System of Classification. The number is the reference number that allocates a spot for the book on the library shelf. This system of numbers and letters keep the books in order. The Dewey Decimal number is located on the base of the spine of every book and is referred to as the call number.

Imagine you worked in a room full of books and didn't know where each one went when they were returned. It would take a long time for anyone to find any given book. Using the Dewey Decimal System, the librarian always knows where to find a particular book.

Here is a sample of how the Dewey Decimal System works. All books are broken up in main categories with reference numbers ranging from 000 through 999:

- 000 Generalities
- 100 Philosophy and Psychology
- 200 Religion
- 300 Social Science

- ◆ 400 Language

- ◆ 500 Natural Science and Mathematics

- ◆ 600 Technology

- ◆ 700 Arts

- ◆ 800 Language

- ◆ 900 Geography and History

These categories are then subdivided. Suppose you were researching the silkworm. Well, silkworms would fall under the Natural Science category, so it would be under the 500s. Here are the divisions of the 500 classification:

- ◆ 510 Mathematics

- ◆ 520 Astronomy

- ◆ 530 Physics

- ◆ 540 Chemistry

- ◆ 550 Earth Sciences

- ◆ 560 Paleontology

- ◆ 570 Life Sciences

- ◆ 580 Botanical Sciences

- ◆ 590 Zoological Sciences

> **Between the Lines**
>
> The Dewey Decimal System was created by Melvil Dewey in 1876, and is still used in libraries today. Another major system of book classification was devised by the Library of Congress. The main difference in the systems is that the Library of Congress uses broader subject categories.

The silkworm would be a zoological science, which also has more subdivisions. And the breakdown continues until you find all the books on silkworms located in one spot on the stacks (or library shelves).

Three Little Search Words: *and, or, not*

Most libraries, if they use card catalogues at all anymore, use them only for backup reference. Libraries, like the rest of the world, have gone high tech and have filed all their books in a library database that uses the Boolean search method; and believe it or not, if you're an Internet user, you use Boolean logic every day.

Boolean logic, which most database search engines use today, was devised by George Boole, an Irish-born mathematician. It's a system of logic that is used in mathematics and consists of three logical concepts based on the ideas of *and*, *or*, and *not*.

When you do your research on the Internet, you often just type in a series of words connected by the word *and*. This way of searching is based on Boolean logic. Internet search engines are databases of information and derive their searches from what you feed them. Libraries are using the same type of system—it's just a little bit more involved.

> **Between the Lines**
>
> In 1854, George Boole published his most well-known work, *An investigation into the Laws of Thought, on Which are founded the Mathematical Theories of Logic and Probabilities*. Boole applied logic to mathematics, which has since been applied to computer construction and other modern scientific techniques.

Library searches are designed for you to find books and documents on your topic and not just general information as you might need from the Internet, so the library search is a little more detailed.

For example, let's say you want to research the resistance of religious educators to teaching Darwin's theory of evolution in schools as a topic for a research paper or simply for your own understanding. How would you search this either in a library database or on the Internet? You would probably want to type in the following words:

- Education
- Darwin
- Religion

But if you wanted *all* of those topics to come up in a library search, you would type in "Education *and* Darwin *and* religion." This search will bring up everything it can find on all three topics.

First the search engine will show you how many "hits" (or responses) the database comes up with in relation to each word:

- Education: 72,260 hits
- Religion: 98,302 hits
- Darwin: 33,980 hits
- Education and Religion and Darwin: 312 hits

Wow … do you really want to search through 312 hits? Maybe you want to narrow it down, because it simply brought up too much information about colleges and not enough about the lower levels of education. You can do a new search and type in "High school *or* elementary school *and* Darwin *and* religion." This way you will be given information on high school or elementary school education in relation to Darwin and religion.

Now you encounter a new dilemma in the search. You might have way too much information on this topic and you might now want to do a subsearch that excludes, rather than includes, certain subject matters within this area. Let's say you want to know only about the elementary school level and not Christian schools. You can type in another search that will exclude certain topics or words: "Elementary *and* education *and* Darwin *and* religion but *not* Christian schools."

 **Bookmarks**

The Boolean system enables you to subsearch any of your search results by using the same words: *and, but,* and *or.* Check with your librarian for shortcuts in your searches such as using the plus sign (+) for *and* and the minus sign (–) for *but* and *or.* The more you practice using this kind of search tool, the easier it will be and the more invaluable it will become in your research.

Reading, Writing, and Understanding

The first thing you need to do when developing your own ideas about what you have read is to focus on your opinions. While you were reading, what struck you as interesting? What struck you as biased? What angered you or simply made you think? Did you have any of your own epiphanies while you read that led you to draw certain conclusions?

Now, why not try to put your thoughts on paper? Sometimes it's the best and easiest way to see whether your argument can hold up either within a discussion or within education. It's not necessary to write in order to read well, but it may help you put a thesis together and build your argument. You'll have to do this when you write a research paper. The best place to start is with reading. The next place to move to is research.

Head to the Stacks

To develop your ideas, you can head for the primary research material, by attempting to find original records, letters, or documentation to back up the information you have absorbed by reading or conclusions you have drawn. Or you can turn to secondary sources by reading what others thought about the same subject matters. To do that, you'll need to find books that other people have written and do some extra reading.

If you do this kind of research, whether you put your thoughts on paper or not, you'll be able to build your argument and back it up with additional information and documentation.

Here's how to begin building your thesis:

♦ Think about the ideas you have had while you were reading.

♦ Go to the library and do a Boolean search on the subject matter that relates to your idea.

♦ Check to see whether other authors have already come up with the same idea, and if so, think about other perspectives in relation to your idea to keep your thoughts new and fresh.

♦ If you can't find another angle, try thinking of comparisons between different literary texts. For example, what are the similarities between Nathaniel Hawthorne's *The Scarlet Letter* and Margaret Atwood's *A Handmaid's Tale?*

> **CAUTION**
>
> **Take Note!**
>
> If you're writing your ideas down either for yourself or in the form of a research paper, you should have someone else read it. If your reader doesn't understand it or finds holes in your argument, you may have to do some rethinking and further research.

Getting a Grip

Throughout this book, you have been provided with the meanings of certain terminology so that you know what meter is when you read poetry, or the role point of view plays in literature, what character development means to a story, and how to identify theme when you read fiction.

For improved reading comprehension, make use of the extras provided for you and think about them. Check out for yourself how these features work in a piece of writing and keep all of this information close at hand as you read. Consciously think about the things you've learned while you read. Eventually you will learn to spot them automatically without having to think quite so hard every time.

Bookmarks

Keep a dictionary handy when you read and write. After all, if you're reading an eighteenth-century novel, you may not understand a particular word and/or how it's being used. Perhaps that same word isn't used today as frequently or with the same meaning. Don't let any word you don't understand pass you by. Be an active reader—look it up! (Flip to the back of this book to find a glossary that defines the terms we use to help you understand how to improve your reading skills.)

Writing a Research Paper

Research paper: two little words that send shivers down the spines of students everywhere. Relax. It's really not so hard to wow your teachers with a clear, concise, well-written discussion of any given topic. This section breaks down the parts of the clear, to-the-point research paper.

But wait, there's more! If you're writing a research paper, you'll need to construct a bibliography and footnotes—alphabetical lists of all the sources you have used to make your thesis argument. Just as you have used the bibliographies of other people to look deeper into a subject, people reading what you wrote are going to want to check out the kinds of resources you relied on in your work.

Before you find yourself in a jam and making excuses with a teacher or professor about why you couldn't submit your assignment, be sure you know what you're doing. There are guidebooks that can help you, like the *MLA Handbook* (Modern Language Association), which is a standard book used in American educational institutions.

A research paper should consist of the following:

- ◆ **Introduction.** State your thesis and how you intend to prove it.

- ◆ **The text.** Restate the argument within the introduction of the text itself and build the argument from there.

- **Conclusion.** Based on the body of the text, state the final outcome of your argument directly.

- **Footnotes and endnotes.** Quotations and references used within the body of the text. Footnote references are made at the bottom of each page and endnote references are made in the body of the text with a list of sources indicated in a separate section at the end of the paper. The way these are sourced depends on the style you are requested to use.

- **Bibliography.** An alphabetic list by author of the sources you used to write your paper.

Put your research to good use. Follow through with logical writing so that the reader stays with you. Most of all, you want your style to be understandable so the reader can absorb your message.

Take Note!

Be sure that you know what the teacher or professor expects of you and in what style he or she wants the bibliography, footnotes, and/or endnotes. There are several different ways to list your references. Your teacher or professor should be clear about which method your school prefers. Most often in American education it is the Modern Language Association (MLA) standard—but double check!

Building a Bibliography

Make sure you document every source you have taken information from, whether it's a quote from a book or from an article, or just something you read that helped you develop your ideas. Keep a notebook handy at all times and jot down the following information about your source:

- Title

- Author (or editors)

- Publishing information (who published it, where it was published, and the year it was published, and the edition number of the book)

- Page numbers

If you have taken information from the Internet, be sure to note the website and the date you visited it.

Footnotes and Endnotes

Make sure you use footnotes if you're quoting another source or speaking about someone else's argument or point of view. Give them credit for it in a footnote. (Neglecting to do so is considered plagiarism, which can spell big trouble for you and your academic career.) Footnotes are numbered in your text. You may also use endnotes and put these at the end of your work.

The biggest mistake you can make when writing a research paper is not to keep a running list of footnotes for yourself. A hint: Number each footnote in the text and on a separate piece of paper, jot down that same number with its reference information and page number!

A Few Words About Plagiarism

"Plagiarism" is a word you may have heard over the course of your education. At different points in time, you were probably told never to copy anything from another book and claim it as your own. While this is true for taking someone else's exact words and transferring them to your own piece of writing, it can also be true for using someone else's ideas and claiming them as your own. Even if you paraphrase someone else's writing, you are walking a dangerous line of plagiarizing.

If you're writing a college paper, you are going to be doing a lot of research. You might come across something that someone else has written that sounds so good you can't imagine being able to say it in your own words. If this happens, the best advice we can give is walk away from it for a minute and think about it, see if you understand it, and then put it in your own words. If it is someone else's idea, introduce your own thoughts on the idea by starting with something like "According to Darwin's theory of evolution ..." then add your own ideas to the original idea.

When you research, it's important to document every source that helps you in your work and never copy anything from another source. You can do this by keeping a notebook with you and jotting down reference information for quotes and ideas that you want to use in your own work. There are both ethical and legal reasons for this. Ethically, it's wrong to claim that something is yours when it's not, and legally there are copyright laws, which means someone actually owns the writing. Taking it without permission, or without crediting the original source, is considered stealing and may be punishable by law. This holds true for all pieces of writing, whether published and sold in the mainstream marketplace or written within an educational setting.

All About You

At the end of all this hard work, ask yourself this: Have you learned more? Have you been able to think more clearly? See more deeply into an area? If your answer is yes, then you have, without doubt, grown as a reader and a thinker. Ultimately what you get out of your reading and research is personal. The answers are not in a book, but inside your head.

The Least You Need to Know

- ◆ A best-selling paperback can be as challenging a read as anything else.

- ◆ Smaller libraries use the Dewey Decimal System of book classification, whereas larger libraries use a more expanded system of reference and locating books in the stacks.

- ◆ A good way to be sure whether your thesis and conclusions are clear is to write it down and let someone else read it.

- ◆ It's important to document your sources while writing a research paper and not after the fact.

Chapter 19

Connecting the Dots

In This Chapter

♦ What it means to think progressively

♦ Reading at an advanced level

♦ Reading more than one book at a time for optimal understanding

♦ Making connections between different texts

By this point you understand what it takes to be a better reader. Take a step back now and ask what it is that you've actually learned. Do you know everything you need to know about critical reading? Are you prepared to go out and learn even more?

In this chapter, you learn how to read at an even more advanced level by connecting the dots of your knowledge. As you've read, you can do this by exploring your ideas through research, but you can also do this by reading more than one book on the same subject. This is how you learn to put the pieces of your reading experiences together. You will realize that this is what makes all the difference between being well read and being a good reader.

Progressive Thinking

What makes someone a progressive thinker is the ability to connect bits of information that one acquires in life. For example, if you can see that life can be a chain reaction of events, you will be able to relate one aspect of our existence to another.

Think about the philosophers we discussed in Chapter 15. Each of these men took one existing theory and expanded upon it by either adding their own new ideas to the old or by discovering new ideas altogether. For example, at one point in time it was an extremely progressive idea that the earth is round. After all, we can walk forever and not fall off, right? Wouldn't logic tell you that if the land goes on forever it must be flat? Well, sure, until the next thinker comes along to take one piece of knowledge, connect it to another, and challenge everything that was ever thought to be true.

So we know one thought leads to another. Philosophers read the scientists, scientists read the philosophers, artists and poets read the philosophers and the scientists, and so on. If everyone is reading about each other's thoughts and ideas, it's inevitable that certain conclusions will be made—some will be right and some will be wrong, but it's the thinking process that's important.

You are no different from the scientists or the philosophers. You are in fact, by the very essence of the questions you ask, one of them. As a reader, it's your task to put the pieces together and grow along with them to benefit yourself and possibly the rest of the world.

Syntopical Reading

In the well-known book (and one of the earliest of its kind on the topic) first published in 1940 titled *How to Read a Book* by Mortimer J. Adler and Charles Van Doren, the authors refer to *syntopical reading* as the process of reading more than one book on the same subject matter. The effects of syntopical reading are significant—there are no boundaries to the ideas you might develop when you read this way.

Look It Up

Syntopical reading is the ability to read more than one book at a time about a specific subject in order to get different perspectives.

Take the legend of King Arthur, for example. (The existence of King Arthur has never been proven. His legacy exists in the legend alone.) What do you know about this story right now? Do you know that Arthur had a teacher named Merlin? Do you know that he built an ideal society of knights and ladies? He created a utopian society—Camelot—where honor was a way of life and chivalry was anything but dead. Arthur set forth a code of ethics based on chivalric standards in order to create a contented kingdom.

So what you have to begin with are, perhaps, some preconceived ideas about the story of King Arthur. Did King Arthur's wife, Guinevere, have an affair with Arthur's favorite knight of the Round Table, Sir Lancelot? Is that what brought down Camelot, and is that what crushed King Arthur's dream in the end?

Twists in a Tale

If you were to read Sir Thomas Malory's account of the legend in *Le Morte D'Arthur: King Arthur and the Legend of the Round Table* (1470), you would go with the theory of Guinevere and Lancelot's guilt. The same would be true for Alfred, Lord Tennyson in his *Idylls of the King* (1859).

But several years ago, another writer named Marion Zimmer Bradley wrote a book called *The Mists of Avalon* in which she made an attempt to completely retell the story of King Arthur—this time from a female perspective.

Zimmer Bradley left in all of the details of the original story, but she told it from the point of view of Arthur's half-sister, Morgaine. In Zimmer Bradley's account of the story, she takes accountability away from Guinevere and puts it on Morgaine, her bitter son, Mordrid, and even on Christianity itself. She attributes the fall of Camelot to many other mistakes—not only those made by Guinevere and Lancelot.

Although King Arthur's story is legendary and not factual, in order to draw any of your own conclusions about why so many authors were so fascinated with these times, you must expand your range of vision to include other factors.

Lessons Learned

If Malory and Tennyson took so much time to re-create the tale of King Arthur, Zimmer Bradley, in effect, turned their theories upside down. If you were to read all three accounts, you may find yourself trying to find the truth to the Arthurian legend itself by plunging into some research on the Internet or at the library.

But why not take it even a step further? Take a deeper look at the works of these writers, the times in which they lived, as well as their personal motivations.

Let's start with Malory. Why did he write the book when he was imprisoned? What was his inspiration? Was there something that inspired him from his own life? Or was there some motivating factor in the times in which he lived that led him to want to write about this legend?

Malory's Motives

Information about the life of Sir Thomas Malory is scanty at best. As you read about him, you will discover that he lived a life that was a far cry from the chivalrous world of knights and ladies that he is famous for writing about so beautifully in *Le Morte D'Arthur*. Yes, he was a knight, but he also earned himself the reputation of being a thief, rapist, and murderer. He spent a great deal of time in prison, which is where he is believed to have written his version of the legend of King Arthur.

This is what we know about Malory:

◆ He lived from 1420 to 1471 in England.

◆ He was educated, but not a professional writer.

◆ He was a knight and a politician.

◆ He was repeatedly imprisoned for involvement in conspiracies and most likely died in Newgate Prison in England.

Not knowing a great deal about Malory makes it difficult to figure out his motivations in writing his version of the King Arthur legend. So the next step would be to turn to the times in which he lived. What was going on in the fifteenth century that would make such a man think back 9 or 10 centuries to the time of a legendary king?

Tumultuous Times

Malory was born during the 100 Years' War between England and France. King Henry V died shortly after Malory was born and Joan of Arc fought against the English and was burned at the stake. The Black Plague rampaged across the land and the War of the Roses began. So here we have an idea of what Malory's surroundings may have been like at the time he wrote about King Arthur.

Do we know enough about Malory at this point to understand why he may have dreamt of chivalry and a utopian society? What was Malory trying to tell his readers through his version of the story of Arthur?

The biggest question of all is why is there such a huge discrepancy between the Malory who wrote of chivalry, heroic knights, and virtuous ladies and the murdering, treacherous, robbing villain he is purported to have been?

You would have to do a lot more reading to answer these questions. But you may have already started developing ideas. Maybe you're thinking, "Okay, Malory was a politician and a knight. What can I deduce from those two careers in relation to what kind of man he was? Maybe he was a rebel with a cause rather than the villain he was portrayed to be. Maybe he wanted his society, which was on the brink of the Renaissance, to move back to the days of medieval chivalry and dreams of Christian purity."

What you are doing now is developing a thesis. But to back it up you would need to prove your ideas by providing solid information and documentation, which would require a great deal more research on your part.

> **Bookmarks** _____
>
> Malory was quite an enigmatic historical figure. While he had all the makings of any common English landholder with a wife and children, history documents that there was a sharp downturn in his life in which he became a rebel, thief, and rapist. If you did want to take up Malory as a thesis topic, you might want to delve into what made his life take such a turn.

Other Authors' Take on the King

Well, you've plunged into Malory and done your research, which means you had to read more information to get a broader perspective of the man, his work, the times in which he lived, and the times of which he wrote. You may even have done enough reading to formulate a thesis idea about who Malory really was. But now it's time to think about what all this fuss over King Arthur is really about. So you move forward with your reading material—keeping in pace with King Arthur.

Alfred, Lord Tennyson

So why, four centuries later, did Tennyson feel the need to revisit this early king? What is the fascination with Arthur?

To understand what would inspire Tennyson to rewrite the legend of King Arthur in _Idylls of the King_, you would have to take a closer look at Tennyson himself and the times in which he lived, just as you did with Malory. This time, your goal is not so much to understand who Tennyson is but why he wrote what he did.

Here is what we know about Tennyson:

◆ He lived from 1809 to 1892 in England.

◆ He wrote several other Arthurian tales in addition to *Idylls*.

◆ He was a poet of the Victorian era who lived during the time of Arthurian revival in literature and art.

When Tennyson wrote his story, England was undergoing great change as it headed into the industrial revolution. Perhaps society seemed like it was headed in the wrong way to this poet of such epic and romantic sentiments. Maybe there was a longing for an England that once thrived on romantic idealism of utopia and honor. As Tennyson's world slipped into factories and smokestacks, is it so unimaginable that he would dream of more delicate times? The Pre-Raphaelites of the nineteenth century were painting images of Guinevere and Persephone and the Lady of Shallot. Tennyson was a product of his times and his work reflects that.

Ah, you've come up with another thesis now. But where to go from here?

Revisiting King Arthur in the Twentieth Century

Let's jump ahead now to the twentieth century, when Marion Zimmer Bradley wrote *The Mists of Avalon*. What was going on at this point in time? Why are we revisiting such an old story? Haven't we moved beyond yearning for knights and long-haired damsels?

Zimmer Bradley was writing in modern times, which include the era of the rise in feminism—women making more demands on society for better jobs, better pay, better daycare, and overall better lives with an equality that parallels the men of their society. Women in this age are willing and able to fight for what they want.

What an opportune time for Zimmer Bradley to revisit the legend of King Arthur yet again. It's understandable that in this day and age, someone would write the story of Arthur from a female perspective. If you think about it, the story of King Arthur can be considered quite misogynistic in many ways.

Why, for example, have all the women in the story of Arthur traditionally taken on the persona of either good or evil (or at the very least corruptible)? Why is Guinevere deemed the destroyer of utopia when Sir Lancelot, the knight sworn to the code of chivalry, is just as guilty? Why is maintaining the essence of purity placed solely on the shoulders of the idealized image of woman?

In the days Zimmer Bradley writes about, women were revered (not so in Mallory's and Tennyson's tales). Camelot, to Zimmer Bradley, depicts the new Christian (pro-man, and, sadly, anti-woman) world while Avalon reflects the pagan rite of goddess worship and female strength. In *The Mists of Avalon*, Camelot is not a utopia—it represents the end of any kind of female power within society.

Will the Real King Arthur Please Stand Up?

Only a few hundred years before Arthur was supposed to have ruled, paganism dominated the land and Christianity was a relatively newfound faith that was just beginning to grow its roots in Western society.

During Arthur's life, the code of chivalry had not yet been established, so both Malory and Tennyson were idealizing an era that never even existed when Arthur was believed to have been alive. It almost seems as though there is a wistful longing for an era that they wished they lived in or wished they could revive in their own times.

What about Zimmer Bradley's motives for writing her story? Is she trying to make any kind of statement about her own society? Is her tale a study of the denial of a woman's place in society? A condemnation of a woman's obligation to manage everything at once, while she should have the freedom to reclaim what is now and was once rightfully hers as a member of society (namely, the matriarchal position of power)?

Between the Lines
While Tennyson and Malory may have dreamed of the ideal that chivalry represented for them, in reality the Middle Ages were far from ideal times. It was a time of chastity belts and the crusades—a far cry from the courtly love and bravery and honor conjured by the romantic writers over the eras.

Which take on King Arthur is right? Might they all be right in one way or another? The only way to answer that is to research the stories and their authors—and then decide for yourself.

The Art of Reading Well

What you have done by reading three different authors on one subject is to help yourself draw conclusions about the authors, their societies, and their works. To be able to make connections between three different books, written in three different eras, by three different perspectives is quite remarkable.

Check out these three scenes that occur after the fall of Camelot. See whether you can sense not only the different styles, but the different message each author is trying to convey to the reader:

From Malory's *Le Morte D'Arthur:*

> My most redoubted king, ye shall understand, by the Pope's commandment and yours, I have brought to you my lady the queen, as right requireth; and if there be any knight, of whatsomever degree that he be, except your person, that will say, or dare say, but that she is true and clean to you, I here myself, Sir Launcelot du Lake, will make it good upon his body, that she is a true lady unto you; but liars ye have listened, and that hath caused debate betwixt you and me. For time hath been, my lord Arthur, that ye have been greatly pleased with me when I did battle for my lady, your queen; and full well ye know, my most noble king, that she hath been put to great wrong ere this time; and sithen it pleased you at many times that I should fight for her, meseemeth, my good lord, I had more cause to rescue her from the fire, insomuch she should been brent for my sake.

> —Lancelot to Arthur after saving Guinevere from being executed by fire for the crime of adultery

From Tennyson's *Idylls of the King:*

> … Is there none
> Will tell the King I love him though so late?
> Now—ere he goes to the great Battle? None:
> Myself must tell him in that purer life,
> But now it were too daring. Ah my God,
> What might I not have made of thy fair world,
> Had I but loved thy highest creature here?
> It was my duty to have loved the highest:
> It surely was my profit had I known:
> It would have been my pleasure had I seen.

We need must love the highest when we see it,
Not Lancelot, nor another.

—Guinevere to herself after King Arthur visits her in the nunnery

From Zimmer Bradley's *The Mists of Avalon:*

In the spring of the year after this, Morgaine had a curious dream … She dreamed that she was in the ancient Christian chapel upon Avalon, built in the old times by that Joseph of Arimathea who had come here from the Holy Land. And there, before that altar where Galahad had died, Lancelet stood in the robes of a priest, and his face was solemn and shining. In her dream she went, as she had never done in any Christian church, to the alter rail for the sharing of their bread and wine, and Lancelet bent and set the cup to her lips and she drank. And then it seemed to her that he knelt in his turn, and he said to her, "Take this cup, you who have served the Goddess. For all the Gods are one God, and we are all One, who serve the One." And she took the cup in her hands to set it to his lips in her turn, priestess to priest, he was young and beautiful as he had been years ago. And she saw that the cup in her hands was the Grail.

—Morgaine after the fall of Camelot

Now it's time to connect the dots. Find the differences and the similarities in the message; identify the tone and the author's message. Most importantly, trust your intuition, your own interpretation, and your newfound strength as a well-rounded reader.

The Least You Need to Know

- It's important to identify progressive thinking as you learn and grow into your progressive reading skills.

- Reading more than one book on the same subject matter will help you grow as a reader.

- It's necessary to identify the messages and the moods that different authors try to convey in an effort to better understand the subject and develop your own conclusions.

- After you learn to connect the dots in your reading experiences and trust your judgment, you will have achieved a higher reading-skill level.

Chapter 20

Testing Your Knowledge of Fiction

In This Chapter

◆ Testing your newfound reading abilities

◆ Getting the most from character descriptions

◆ Understanding the relationship between narrative voice and point of view

◆ The importance of literary devices to accentuate meaning

◆ Being an independent thinker by finding your own way through literature

It's time to put your newfound knowledge to the test. If you've absorbed the material you've read in this book up to this point, you should be able to move easily through these next test chapters. If you don't feel like you've absorbed enough, go back and reread some of the chapters you think you need to brush up on. Remember, this is a test for you—about *your* understanding—and not about what anyone else thinks about what you know.

In this chapter, you have to put your thinking cap on, grab a pencil and paper, and start to examine what you already knew and what you have learned from this book. Even if you choose not to test yourself, reading this chapter will help you put the last pieces of all this information together.

Bookmarks

We know that a test often means an evaluation of your work, but in this case, you need to evaluate yourself. If you feel confident about your responses, you are on the right track in your thinking process, analysis, and understanding. If you feel that you are missing information or cannot give complete answers, you need to do some further reading and research.

The Final Exam

With this new knowledge of critical reading you now have, there's only one thing left to do—practice. Although it's an excellent start to read a book such as this one, without practice (which of course means more reading), what can you do with all of this information?

For the most part, you're on your own now. It's your turn to determine how much you know and in which areas you need further growth and understanding. Your answers will be subjective in relation to most of these questions. There is no right or wrong, just your interpretation.

For the questions that do have correct answers, we provide them at the end of the chapter—so no peeking! Take your time, relax, think about what is being asked of you, and enjoy this new leg of the journey.

Character and Mood

In Chapter 7 you read a great deal about character analysis. And although you need to read any given book in its entirety to fully understand a character, you can also get a strong sense of a character by reading some relatively brief descriptions—as long as you know what to look for.

The following is an excerpt from *The Scarlet Letter*, by Nathaniel Hawthorne, which gives a very good description of Hester Prynne, the heroine of the book. Keep in mind that she has already been branded with the scarlet *A* at this point in the novel. Everyone in the town knows she has sinned and she is, therefore, an outcast.

To begin with, just read the excerpt—don't read too much into it, just get a sense of the tone and style. Then go back and read it again, this time looking for descriptions of Hester, whether they're subtle or direct.

The questions will follow. After you have read the questions, go back and try to identify what is requested of you, jotting down your impressions on the lines provided.

> It was not an age of delicacy; and her position, although she understood it well, and was in little danger of forgetting it, was often brought before her vivid self-perception, like a new anguish, by the rudest touch upon the tenderest spot. The poor, as we have already said, whom she sought out to be the objects of her bounty, often reviled the hand that was stretched forth to succor them. Dames of elevated rank, likewise, whose doors she entered in the way of her occupation, were accustomed to distil drops of bitterness into her heart; sometimes through that alchemy of quiet malice, by which women can concoct a subtile poison from ordinary trifles; and sometimes, also, by a coarser expression, that fell upon the sufferer's defenceless breast like a rough blow upon an ulcerated wound. Hester had schooled herself long and well; she never responded to these attacks, save by a flush of crimson that rose irrepressibly over her pale cheek, and again subsided into the depths of her bosom. She was patient,—a martyr, indeed,—but she forebore to pray for enemies; lest, in spite of her forgiving aspirations, the words of the blessing should stubbornly twist themselves into a curse.

Questions About Characterization

The narrator in this excerpt is giving you a look inside the mind of Hester Prynne, allowing you the reader to understand her in ways that other characters in the book cannot. Knowing this, and knowing that an author uses characters to clarify the themes contained in the novel, consider the following:

How does Hester respond to the way she is treated by all that shun her?

_____

_____

_____

_____

What brings Hester to life for you?

_____

_____

_____

_____

In what ways can you relate to Hester? Or in what way is she different than you or other women of your times?

_____

_____

_____

_____

Identify words and phrases that show how the author uses descriptive language in reference to the characterization of Hester.

_____

_____

_____

_____

What do you know about Hester based on this excerpt?

_____

_____

_____

_____

Questions About Mood

For this next excerpt, consider the following questions as you read—then go back and answer them:

How does Hawthorne make you feel as the reader?

_____

_____

_____

_____

What mood has he set in his description of his protagonist?

_____

_____

_____

_____

What words or phrases does Hawthorne use to create the mood in this excerpt?

_____

_____

_____

_____

In this manner, Hester Prynne came to have a part to perform in the world. With her native energy of character and rare capacity, it could not entirely cast her off, although it had set a mark upon her, more intolerable to a woman's heart than that which branded the brow of Cain. In all her intercourse with society, however, there was nothing that made her feel as if she belonged to it. Every gesture, every word, and even the silence of those with whom she came in contact, implied, and often expressed, that she was banished, and as much alone as if she inhabited another sphere, or communicated with the common nature by other organs and senses than the rest of human kind. She stood apart from mortal interests, yet close beside them, like a ghost that revisits the familiar fireside, and can no longer make itself seen or felt; no more smile with the household joy, nor mourn with the kindred sorrow; or, should it succeed in manifesting its forbidden sympathy, awakening only terror and horrible repugnance. These emotions, in fact, and its bitterest scorn besides, seemed to be the sole portion that she retained in the universal heart.

Identifying Figurative Language

With Chapter 9 as your resource for these next questions, think of what you learned about the tools an author uses so that you can better visualize a scene. Remember metaphor, symbolism, and hyperbole? Refresh your memory or even make yourself a list and keep it handy as you go through this next excerpt from Edith Wharton's *The Age of Innocence*. This is a novel about New York society and the dangers and consequences of breaking its severe ethical and moral codes of behavior and decorum.

> The immense accretion of flesh which had descended on her in middle life like a flood of lava on a doomed city had changed her from a plump active little woman with a neatly-turned foot and ankle into something as vast and august as a natural phenomenon. She had accepted this submergence as philosophically as all her other trials, and now, in extreme old age, was rewarded by presenting to her mirror an almost unwrinkled expanse of firm pink and white flesh, in the centre of which the traces of a small face survived as if awaiting excavation. A flight of smooth double chins led down to the dizzy depths of a still-snowy bosom veiled in snowy muslins that were held in place by a miniature portrait of the late Mr. Mingott; and around and below, wave after wave of black silk surged away over the edges of a capacious armchair, with two tiny white hands poised like gulls on the surface of the billows.

Do you see any examples of hyperbole in this excerpt? If so, what are they? And why do you think the author uses them here?

_____

_____

_____

_____

Wharton compares Mrs. Mingott's looks to a natural phenomenon and then proceeds to describe her as one. List some examples of how she does this.

_____

_____

_____

_____

Scrutinizing Poetry

Let's revisit the concept of poetic structure, which we discussed in Chapter 10. When you read poetry, it's important to know what kind of poem you're looking at, for several reasons:

- ◆ To know how the poem sounds and should be read

- ◆ To understand the rhythm of the poem, which reflects the poet's intention, especially in terms of style

- ◆ To know what to look for in order to develop a complete understanding of the meaning of the poem

We'll take a look at two poems. Read them once, then twice, and even a third time if necessary, to get a feeling for rhythm, style, structure, and meaning.

Questions on Reading Poetry: Identifying Poetic Type

Poem 1:

> Life is a stream
> On which we strew
> Petal by petal the flower of our heart;
> The end lost in dream,
> They float past our view,
> We only watch their glad, early start.
> Freighted with hope,
> Crimsoned with joy,
> We scatter the leaves of our opening rose;
> Their widening scope,
> Their distant employ,
> We never shall know. And the stream as it flows
> Sweeps them away,
> Each one is gone
> Ever beyond into infinite ways.
> We alone stay
> While years hurry on,
> The flower fared forth, though its fragrance still stays.

> —*Petals*, Amy Lowell

What kind of poem is this?

_____

_____

What is the poet trying to say to you about life? What are the petals? What happens to them? The poem is metaphorical, but what does it mean?

_____

_____

_____

_____

Poem 2:

> Being your slave, what should I do but tend
> Upon the hours and times of your desire?
> I have no precious time at all to spend,
> Nor services to do, till you require
> Nor dare I chide the world-without-end hour
> Whilst I, my sovereign, watch the clock for you,
> Nor think the bitterness of absence sour
> When you have bid your servant once adieu;
> Nor dare I question with my jealous thought
> Where you may be, or your affairs suppose,
> But, like a sad slave, stay and think of nought
> Save, where you are how happy you make those.
> So true a fool is love that in your will,
> Though you do anything, he thinks no ill.
>
> —William Shakespeare, _Sonnet 57_

What type of poem is this?

_____

_____

What is the author saying about love?

_____

_____

_____

_____

What is the mood of the poem? Is the narrator happy? Sad? Frustrated?

_____

_____

_____

_____

What words or phrases does Shakespeare use to accentuate the mood of the poem?

_____

_____

_____

_____

Find the Narrative Voice

In the next few excerpts from different novels, think about who is telling the story and from what point of view. Review Chapter 8 if you don't remember the specifics about narrative voice and point of view. As you read, think about why the author chose this narrator, and be sure to identify the point of view used by the author in the excerpts:

From _The Adventures of Huckleberry Finn_, by Mark Twain:

> You don't know about me without you have read a book by the name of _The Adventures of Tom Sawyer_; but that ain't no matter. That book was made by Mr. Mark Twain, and he told the truth, mainly. There was things which he stretched, but mainly he told the truth. That is nothing. I never seen anybody but lied one time or another, without it was Aunt Polly, or the widow, or maybe

Mary. Aunt Polly—Tom's Aunt Polly, she is—and Mary, and the Widow Douglas is all told about in that book, which is mostly a true book, with some stretchers, as I said before.

From *Anne of Green Gables*, by Lucy Maude Montgomery:

With a sigh of rapture she relapsed into silence. Matthew stirred uneasily. He felt glad that it would be Marilla and not he who would have to tell this waif of the world that the home she longed for was not to be hers after all. They drove over Lynde's Hollow, where it was already quite dark, but not so dark that Mrs. Rachel could not see them from her window vantage, and up the hill and into the long lane of Green Gables. By the time they arrived at the house Matthew was shrinking from the approaching revelation with an energy he did not understand. It was not of Marilla or himself he was thinking of the trouble this mistake was probably going to make for them, but of the child's disappointment. When he thought of that rapt light being quenched in her eyes he had an uncomfortable feeling that he was going to assist at murdering something—much the same feeling that came over him when he had to kill a lamb or calf or any other innocent little creature.

Questions on Narrative Voice and Point of View

Think for a moment what these two books are about. *The Adventures of Huckleberry Finn* is a coming-of-age story—a boy learning about life as he travels down the Mississippi River with an escaped slave. *Anne of Green Gables* is another coming-of-age story, but Anne doesn't change as much as the people around her do as a result of her presence in their town. Knowing this, consider these questions about narrative voice:

In the excerpt from *The Adventures of Huckleberry Finn*, who is speaking? And who is the narrator speaking to?

_____

_____

_____

_____

From what you know about Huckleberry Finn and from this excerpt, why does Twain choose to tell this story from Huck's point of view?

_____

_____

_____

_____

In the excerpt from *Anne of Green Gables*, what is the point of view?

_____

_____

_____

_____

In the excerpt from *Anne of Green Gables*, do you sense the narrator's feelings? Can you see how the narrative voice can affect your own feelings?

_____

_____

_____

_____

Bookmarks

In *Anne of Green Gables*, Lucy Maude Montgomery tells the story in third person omniscient. Sometimes we are inside Anne's mind understanding her feelings and sometimes we are closer to Matthew and/or Marilla. The previous excerpt regarding Matthew's feelings, however, uses the third person limited. You can tell because we are learning *only* how Matthew feels at this point and not how Anne or Marilla might feel.

Identifying Humor

Think of the excerpt in this chapter from Edith Wharton's *The Age of Innocence*. There was a great amount of humor in her description of Mrs. Mingott:

> The immense accretion of flesh which had descended on her in middle life like a flood of lava on a doomed city …

That's quite a way to describe the size and appearance of somebody's face. Despite the harsh description, though, the narrator seems to be taking a playful look at the character. The tone is light and engaging despite the descriptive language.

Mark Twain does the same thing in his use of humor. There's always a bittersweet aftertaste to many of his scenes. Although they can be interpreted as harsh, they can also be viewed with a certain amount of tenderness. Consider the following excerpt from *The Adventures of Huckleberry Finn*, for example:

> Then Miss Watson she took me in the closet and prayed, but nothing come of it. She told me to pray every day, and whatever I asked for I would get it. But it warn't so. I tried it. Once I got a fish-line, but no hooks. It warn't any good to me without hooks. I tried for the hooks three or four times, but somehow I couldn't make it work. By and by, one day, I asked Miss Watson to try for me, but she said I was a fool. She never told me why, and I couldn't make it out no way.

What does this excerpt say about Huck? Does it denote a certain amount of innocence?

_____

_____

_____

_____

Is Huck Finn at all aware of the society he is trying to become a part of?

_____

_____

_____

_____

What about Huck's way of thinking makes us smile? How do you relate to what Huck says in this excerpt? Is Twain making any kind of universal statement about human behavior to his readers?

_____

_____

_____

_____

Fable and the Art of the Allegory

Finally, take a look at this last excerpt. You probably haven't read any of these since elementary school.

> An astronomer used to go out at night to observe the stars. One evening, as he wandered through the suburbs with his whole attention fixed on the sky, he fell accidentally into a deep well. While he lamented and bewailed his sores and bruises, and cried loudly for help, a neighbor ran to the well, and learning what had happened said: "Hark ye, old fellow, why, in striving to pry into what is in heaven, do you not manage to see what is on earth?"
>
> —From _The Astronomer_, a fable

This is a fable—one of Aesop's, no less. After you've read the fable, briefly state the theme and/or lesson that you learned from this tale.

There you have it. Everything you've read about fiction in this book should help you to answer all of the questions here. We are confident that you are doing just fine!

The Least You Need to Know

◆ Identifying how an author uses devices to perpetuate meaning is important to being a good reader.

◆ Although there are rules for narrative point of view, the author also has the creative license to break the rules and switch perspectives.

◆ Poetry relies on words to give a poem a powerful message, but a poet is also reliant on other devices such as rhythmic pattern and rhyme.

◆ Authors use humor to either lighten a mood or to identify the narrator's tone or a character's voice.

Chapter 21

Testing Your Knowledge of Nonfiction

In This Chapter

- Essays from the great thinkers
- Connecting philosophy, nonfiction, and fiction writing
- Looking at journalism objectively
- Continuing the critical reading adventure on your own

You must admit it's hard work, but it's also a lot of fun, to challenge your mind. What we'd like to see is your eyes pop open wide as you say, "I get it!"—kind of your own little "Eureka!" If that happens to you during these test chapters, you're there. You're a critical reader. Way to go!

In this chapter, you learn how to connect various pieces of nonfiction writing to each other. You also learn to see pieces of writing as unique unto themselves. Mostly, though, we want you to understand how important nonfiction is to your understanding of people, places, events, and ideas. Use the spaces provided in this chapter to jot down your answers and impressions.

Following the Thinkers

It is as important to understand how thoughts connect to each other as it is to understand each individual thought. And that's exactly where we are going to start—with the essay.

You've read about "isms" and grand ideas in Chapter 15 and elsewhere in this book. But how did certain schools of thought emerge, and how did the thinkers unify as one group or as various different groups? Simple. They unified through their writing. One person read someone else's philosophy and then came up with his or her own ideas and then another person did the same, and so on, and so on … That's how movements gain momentum and thoughts expand.

Look It Up

Transcendentalism originated in the early nineteenth century as a movement away from traditional Christian doctrine of reason being the path to divine wisdom. It was a more emotional way of looking at faith that extended to the literary and philosophical world.

Let's start by looking at a movement that has its roots in American ideology: *transcendentalism.*

To understand transcendentalism, the first thing you have to do is understand the Unitarians. The Unitarians are a liberal branch of Christianity, who don't believe you have to deprive yourself of earthly pleasures in order to get to heaven, nor do they ascribe to the overly emotional enthusiasm of some Christian services.

They arose from the Age of Enlightenment, when intellect and reason came to be accepted as the driving forces behind all aspects of life, including spirituality.

Well, if you can get more liberal than the liberals, the Transcendentalists pulled it off. The Transcendentalists wanted to rise above (transcend) the idea that spirituality is based on reason. The transcendentalists believed that intuition was as viable a source of the human thought process as reason.

The literary movement of transcendentalism took the concept even further by asking people to see objects in the world as smaller pieces of the bigger universe. They took their inspiration from English and German Romanticism—from the literature of Coleridge and Wordsworth and the idealism of the thinkers of the era such as Thomas Carlyle.

Now let's take a look at a piece of writing from one of the most prominent members of the literary movement, Ralph Waldo Emerson:

> ... To believe your own thought, to believe that what is true for you in your private heart is true for all men, ... that is genius. Speak your latent conviction, and it shall be the universal sense; for the inmost in due time becomes the outmost,—and our first thought is rendered back to us by the trumpets of the Last Judgment. Familiar as the voice of the mind is to each, the highest merit we ascribe to Moses, Plato, and Milton is, that they set at naught books and traditions, and spoke not what men but what they thought. A man should learn to detect and watch that gleam of light which flashes across his mind from within, more than the lustre of the firmament of bards and sages. Yet he dismisses without notice his thought, because it is his. In every work of genius we recognize our own rejected thoughts: they come back to us with a certain alienated majesty. Great works of art have no more affecting lesson for us than this. They teach us to abide by our spontaneous impression with good-humored inflexibility then most when the whole cry of voices is on the other side. Else, to-morrow a stranger will say with masterly good sense precisely what we have thought and felt all the time, and we shall be forced to take with shame our own opinion from another.
>
> —Essay II, *Self-Reliance*

Questions About Transcendentalism and the Essay

Before you answer the following questions, be sure you understand the definition of transcendentalism and what that means as a literary movement. Also, think about how you feel about transcendentalism. Can you relate to this philosophy based on your own personal philosophies? Once you are clear on this, try answering these questions:

Based on what you know about transcendentalism, what is Emerson saying about thought versus intuitive feeling?

_____

_____

_____

_____

What metaphor does Emerson use to describe your intuition—that inner knowledge that transcends through all other rational thinking?

_____

_____

_____

_____

Emerson is issuing a warning at the end of the essay. What is it? Can you relate to it? Has this ever happened to you?

_____

_____

_____

_____

Between the Lines

Ralph Waldo Emerson (1803–1882) derived some of his philosophical thinking on transcendentalism from Asian mysticism. Emerson believed that God exists within every human being. Intuition is what connects human beings to the universe with the individual being the spiritual core of the world. This is why it's so important to know yourself. To know yourself is to know the world and God.

Questions About Transcendentalism and the Individual

In 1845, philosopher and essayist Henry David Thoreau built himself a small cabin on the shore of Walden Pond just outside Concord, Massachusetts, and went there to think and learn. He wanted to live beyond the world of materialism and get back to nature. While he was there, he thought, explored nature, read about life, and wrote his own thoughts down for us in a journal, which is now a book titled _Walden_.

Here is an excerpt—and of course, questions to follow:

> Early in the morning, while all things are crisp with frost, men come with fishing-reels and slender lunch, and let down their fine lines through the snowy field to take pickerel and perch; wild men, who instinctively follow other

fashions and trust other authorities than their townsmen, and by their goings and comings stitch towns together in parts where else they would be ripped. They sit and eat their luncheon in stout fear-naughts on the dry oak leaves on the shore, as wise in natural lore as the citizen is in artificial. They never consulted with books, and know and can tell much less than they have done. The things which they practice are said not yet to be known. Here is one fishing for pickerel with grown perch for bait. You look into his pail with wonder as into a summer pond, as if he kept summer locked up at home, or knew where she had retreated. How, pray, did he get these in midwinter? Oh, he got worms out of rotten logs since the ground froze, and so he caught them. His life itself passes deeper in nature than the studies of the naturalist penetrate; himself a subject for the naturalist. The latter raises the moss and bark gently with his knife in search of insects; the former lays open logs to their core with his axe, and moss and bark fly far and wide. He gets his living by barking trees. Such a man has some right to fish, and I love to see nature carried out in him. The perch swallows the grub-worm, the pickerel swallows the perch, and the fisher-man swallows the pickerel; and so all the chinks in the scale of being are filled.

The very essence of what Thoreau did in giving up the material world for solitude in nature is transcendental in the act alone. How so?

_____

_____

_____

_____

What is Thoreau saying about the fishermen? How does the idea of living on intuition apply to Thoreau's observations on these men?

_____

_____

_____

_____

If transcendentalists believe that God is inside us and we are one with the universe, how does Thoreau's experiment at Walden reflect this concept?

_____

_____

_____

_____

Cross-Connections

This is a chapter on nonfiction, but it's important to note that fiction writers were also record keepers of ideological movements. American poet Emily Dickinson, for example, showed evidence of transcendental thinking in her work.

Now, it's interesting to note here that there has been a great deal of discussion about where to place Emily Dickinson in terms of philosophical literary movements. Whereas some label her writing as being in the transcendental school of thought, others consider her more of an existentialist—albeit before the existential movement really began with writers like Jean-Paul Sartre and Albert Camus.

Consider this definition of existentialism, and then read the two poems by Emily Dickinson that follow.

> **Between the Lines**
>
> Emily Dickinson (1830–1886) was born in Massachusetts. She published just seven poems in her lifetime; the rest were published posthumously.

Existentialism is a philosophical and literary movement that opposes naturalist thought. It emphasizes free will, whereas naturalists deny the existence of free will. So to the existentialist, human beings are completely free to do as they wish and are therefore entirely responsible for themselves. With this kind of responsibility there is always the quality of fear or dread, which is often reflected in the existential works of literature.

Here is a poem by Emily Dickinson:

> Split the Lark—and you'll find the Music—
> Bulb after Bulb, in Silver rolled—
> Scantily dealt to the Summer Morning
> Saved for your Ear when Lutes be old.

Loose the Flood—you shall find it patent—
Gush after Gush, reserved for you—
Scarlet Experiment! Sceptic Thomas!
Now, do you doubt that your Bird was true?

—Poem 352, year 1864

Here is another poem by Emily Dickinson:

Our journey had advanced—
Our feet were almost come
To that odd Fork in Being's Road—
Eternity—by Term—

Our pace took sudden awe—
Our feet—reluctant—led—
Before—were Cities—but Between—
The Forest of the Dead—

Retreat—was out of Hope—
Behind—a Sealed Route—
Eternity's White Flag—Before—
And God—at every Gate—

—Poem 255, year 1862

What is the first poem about? Is it a complete concept or does it simply give you a glance at an idea?

_____

_____

_____

_____

Are there any surprises in either poem? Were you expecting it to take you where it did in terms of its meaning?

_____

_____

_____

_____

Like a good transcendentalist (which you may or may not be), what does your intuition tell you about the first poem as you read it? What brought up emotion for you and at which point in the poem?

_____

_____

_____

_____

Keeping in mind that the transcendentalist movement was a reaction against traditional spirituality as adopted by the Unitarians, how does the second poem reflect transcendental thought?

_____

_____

_____

_____

Where do you fit in? Do you think you're an existentialist or a transcendentalist?

_____

_____

_____

_____

 Bookmarks _____

Knowing that there has been some debate about which school Emily Dickinson fits into, read more of her poems and try to identify for yourself what school of thought she leans toward.

Objectifying Journalism

Let's take a look at journalism in three different ways: historically, subjectively, and objectively.

To begin with, take a look at this article that was printed in the *London Gazette* in 1666, just one week after the Great Fire of London:

> The ordinary course of this paper having been interrupted by a sad and lamentable accident of Fire lately happened in the City of London: it hath been thought fit for satisfying the minds of so many of His Majesties good Subjects who must need be concerned for the Issue of so great an accident, to give this short, but true Accompt of it.
>
> On the second instant, at one of the clock in the Morning, there hapned to break out, a sad in deplorable Fire in Pudding-lane, neer New Fishstreet, which falling out at that hour of the night, and in a quarter of the Town so close built with wooden pitched houses spread itself so far before day, and with such distraction to the inhabitants and Neighbours that care was not taken for the timely preventing the further diffusion of it, by pulling down houses, as ought to have been; so that this lamentable Fire in a short time became too big to be mastred by any Engines or working neer it. It fell out most unhappily too, That a violent Easterly wind fomented it, and kept it burning all that day, and the night following spreading itself up to Grace-church-street and downward from Cannon-street on the Water-side, as far as the Three Cranes in the Vintrey.

As wordy as this article may seem, it actually does give a very good accounting of the events and in many ways is true to the modern journalistic form. Although today an article such as this one would not make so many interjections of words such as *lamentable*, it would tell you basically the same information: There was a fire, it's out now, and this is what it did to the city.

This article was written only seven days after the start of the fire, and it is clear that the writer of the article was emotional over the ordeal. This is an example of subjective journalism—a style that is avoided as much as possible today. The power of journalism lies in its ability to maintain objectivity. (After the 9/11 terrorist attacks in 2001, however, there were elements of this style in many news reports of the events. It just goes to show that journalists are people, and they can be horrified like anyone else.)

Reread the previous excerpt from the journalist's account of the Great Fire of London and then rewrite it in your own words. Try to write it without feeling, giving only the facts.

_____

_____

_____

_____

_____

_____

_____

_____

Does the journalist bury any information? Is there something you want to know right away that he is not telling you?

_____

_____

_____

If you were researching the Great Fire of London, would this article be a primary or secondary resource of information?

_____

_____

_____

Your Right to Know

Now consider this article from the Associated Press published on October 23, 2004—but before you do, think about this: There was an earthquake in Japan. That is the fact. What do you want to know about the earthquake? The questions that would come to us right away upon hearing such news would be in this order:

◆ Where in Japan?

◆ Did anyone die?

◆ If so, who were they and how did they die?

◆ What was the extent of the damage?

- How strong did it register on the Richter scale?

- What did people have to say about it? What did they see and feel?

- How often do earthquakes strike Japan?

- What was the strongest one ever?

As you read, ask yourself this: Does this article answer the questions that the reader wants to know?

OJIYA, Japan - A series of powerful earthquakes and aftershocks rattled northern Japan on Saturday, killing at least 15 people and injuring more than 700 as buildings crumbled, a bullet train derailed and roadways were torn apart.

At least 10 people were missing Saturday night. Throughout the region, electric, gas and telephone services were knocked out and water and sewage mains burst.

The quakes—the most powerful recorded as magnitude-6.8—were spread over several hours and centered on Ojiya, about 160 miles northwest of Tokyo. Still, buildings swayed in the Japanese capital.

"I've never felt anything like it before," said Yoichi Kato, the owner of a 7-11 store in Kashiwazaki, about 12 miles west of the epicenter. "It was so strong, I was too surprised to be scared."

The quake knocked bottles and food off the convenience store's shelves, but otherwise caused his shop limited damage, Kato said.

The first quake hit at 5:56 p.m. and was centered about 12 miles beneath the surface, the Meteorological Agency said. At least six more tremors hit over the following hours, including quakes of magnitude 6.2 and 5.9, the agency said.

The second floor of a Jusco nationwide supermarket chain store was smashed.

There were 300 customers inside when the earthquake hit, and everyone tried to grab something nearby to keep from being knocked off their feet," said Reiko Takahashi, the store's manager, as she stood guard to prevent looting or possible injuries. "Several people were hurt by glass shards and falling debris."

Teams were dispatched to assess damage and aid residents but darkness and buckled roads hampered their efforts, officials said. Eleven military helicopters fanned out to check the damage and help with rescue operations, the agency said.

The quakes were centered in relatively rural areas. The government has estimated that some 7,000 people would die if such a powerful quake hit the Tokyo area.

The victims included a 34-year-old man who was struck by a falling wall as he fled his home in Tokamachi and a 55-year-old man buried by his concrete garage wall.

Takejiro Hoshino, 75, lost his 12-year-old grandson when their house collapsed. "I got out and then we all went back to try to save the others, but it was too late," Hoshino said.

Two others were stuck in a house buried by a landslide in Ojiya, and four people were missing in Nagaoka city after two homes collapsed, NHK said. Telephone service to the area was cut and the deaths could not be confirmed with local officials.

Nearly 50 people were injured by flying glass or items that fell from shelves in Tokamachi and Ojiya cities, according to media reports.

Questions About Good Reporting

Think of all the general questions you know a news article should answer. Remember, they all start with *who, what, where, why, when,* and if possible, *how.* Now try to answer the following questions:

Does this article tell you everything you want to know about the earthquake? Does it answer all the questions you had upon hearing the news?

_____

_____

_____

_____

Is this article well written or poorly written? Does the reporter bury the lead or is it clear right away?

_____

_____

_____

_____

If you could talk to the reporter, what questions would you ask him or her about the incident?

_____

_____

_____

_____

Consider the concept of objectivity in journalism. What key words does the reporter use to stay as objective as possible? Go through the article with a pencil and underline words and/or phrases the reporter uses in an attempt to maintain objectivity.

Think about objectivity versus subjectivity when reading this article. If the reporter concentrated on his or her opinion about why there was so much devastation (poor construction, for example) and the emotional impact the earthquake had on the people, would you feel you had all the information you needed about the event? On a separate piece of paper, try rewriting the article to reflect a subjective versus objective point of view.

_____

_____

_____

_____

_____

_____

_____

_____

To say "At least 10 people were missing last night" is telling you that there could be more, but then again that might be all. The reporter will give you the number of _confirmed_ missing so as not to lead you astray on whether or not there will be more. One other hint: A reporter will use eyewitness accounts because he or she was not there and the reporter wants to be as accurate as possible in the information he or she is giving you.

Bookmarks

The best way to deal with the lack of information from a journalist is, of course, to read more articles about the incident. If that doesn't help, look up earthquakes in Japan and inform yourself. You are never at the mercy of just one writer.

One Journey Ends, Another Begins!

In the previous excerpts, you may have noticed how philosophy, science, theology, and ethics all connect to each other. One question leads to another and another and the speculations move across disciplines.

We've taken you through several examples of major ideas that are now part of our cumulative understanding. These are the issues we think about as citizens of the twenty-first century—we think about them, we battle with them, we come to terms with them, and we even ignore them.

In this chapter, you have seen a small overview of a very big picture. It's your job now to become an explorer and adventurer, and to get out there and learn even more. Stack up your books, dive in, and read—all the while keeping in mind what you've learned from this book.

The greatest adventure of all is the discovery of a thought, idea, pattern, and connection. Greater understanding and ever-deepening awareness depends on your ability to venture out and discover all of this for yourself.

Keep asking questions such as the ones you've asked yourself throughout this book and especially along the lines of those asked in these last two chapters. Asking questions will allow you to journey into deeper awareness and understanding of yourself, your fellow human beings, your planet, and—let us not forget—the stars.

Good luck! You're on your way!

The Least You Need to Know

- Being aware of an author's philosophical perspective gives you a better handle on understanding his or her writing.

- Knowing how you fit into a philosophical perspective allows you to build your own theories and present arguments either for or against an author's work.

◆ To get the most information from a news article, it's important to understand the concept of objectivity in journalism.

◆ Building your understanding and acquiring cumulative knowledge will help you become the best reader you can possibly be (and maybe even a scholar!)

Appendix A

Recommended Reading List

There are countless reading lists on the Internet that will advise you as to what you should read to be considered well read. When we embarked upon the twenty-first century, many people and organizations compiled lists of what they considered to be the best books of the last century. While we have made every attempt to include some of the best examples of reading material in this book, there are so many more that we couldn't possibly fit in.

Some lists of books will give you the most difficult, complex, and scholarly works out there as a basis for understanding all other reading material, even if it is far too difficult for most people to understand. It's a good idea to check out other lists and certainly to attempt to read difficult works of literature, but keep in mind that reading should not just be a challenge, it should be fun.

Must-Read Novels

Regina and Amy chose this particular list of books for the following reasons: They are written by some of the Western world's greatest authors; they are classic pieces of writing with references that, to this day, may appear in your everyday world; they are excellent examples of certain literary movements and philosophies; and in some cases, they are just plain fun to read.

Sherwood Anderson: *Winesburg, Ohio*

Maya Angelou: *I Know Why the Caged Bird Sings*

Margaret Atwood: *The Handmaid's Tale*

Jane Austen: *Pride and Prejudice; Sense and Sensibility; Emma*

James Baldwin: *Go Tell It on the Mountain*

Saul Bellow: *Henderson the Rain King; The Adventures of Augie March*

Elizabeth Bowen: *The Death of the Heart*

Charlotte Brontë: *Jane Eyre*

Emily Brontë: *Wuthering Heights*

Anthony Burgess: *A Clockwork Orange*

Erskine Caldwell: *Tobacco Road*

Lewis Carroll: *Alice's Adventures in Wonderland; Through the Looking Glass*

Willa Cather: *My Antonia; Death Comes to the Archbishop*

John Cheever: *The Wapshot Chronicles*

Joseph Conrad: *Heart of Darkness; Lord Jim; Nostromo; The Secret Agent*

Charles Dickens: *David Copperfield; A Tale of Two Cities; Oliver Twist; A Christmas Carol; Great Expectations*

E. L. Doctorow: *Ragtime*

John Dos Passos: *USA* (trilogy)

Theodore Dreiser: *An American Tragedy; Sister Carrie*

Ralph Ellison: *Invisible Man*

James T. Farrell: *The Studs Lonigan Trilogy*

Ford Maddox Ford: *The Good Soldier*

William Faulkner: *The Sound and the Fury; As I Lay Dying; Absalom, Absalom!*

E. M. Forster: *A Passage to India; Howards End; A Room with a View*

F. Scott Fitzgerald: *The Great Gatsby; Tender Is the Night*

William Golding: *Lord of the Flies*

Robert Graves: *I, Claudius*

Graham Greene: *The Heart of the Matter; Travels with My Aunt; The Quiet American*

Nathaniel Hawthorne: *The Scarlet Letter*

Thomas Hardy: *Tess of the D'Urbervilles; Far from the Madding Crowd*

Robert Heinlein: *The Moon Is a Harsh Mistress; Stranger in a Strange Land*

Joseph Heller: *Catch-22*

Ernest Hemingway: *The Sun Also Rises; A Farewell to Arms; For Whom the Bell Tolls; The Old Man and the Sea*

Frank Herbert: *Dune*

Aldous Huxley: *Brave New World*

John Irving: *A Prayer for Owen Meany; Cider House Rules; The World According to Garp*

Washington Irving: *Rip Van Winkle; Legend of Sleepy Hollow*

Henry James: *The Wings of the Dove; The Ambassadors; The Golden Bowl; The Portrait of a Lady; The Turn of the Screw*

James Joyce: *Ulysses; Finnegan's Wake; A Portrait of the Artist as a Young Man*

Jack Kerouac: *On the Road*

Harper Lee: *To Kill a Mockingbird*

D. H. Lawrence: *Sons and Lovers*

C. S. Lewis: *The Chronicles of Narnia*

Sinclair Lewis: *Main Street; Babbitt*

Somerset Maugham: *Of Human Bondage*

Carson McCullers: *The Heart Is a Lonely Hunter*

Herman Melville: *Moby-Dick*

Margaret Mitchell: *Gone with the Wind*

Toni Morrison: *Beloved*

Iris Murdoch: *Under the Net*

Vladimir Nabokov: *Lolita*

V. S. Naipaul: *A Bend in the River; A House for Mr. Biswas*

Flannery O'Connor: *Wise Blood*

George Orwell: *1984; Animal Farm*

Robert Pirsig: *Zen and the Art of Motorcycle Maintenance*

Sylvia Plath: *The Bell Jar*

Ayn Rand: *Atlas Shrugged; The Fountainhead; Anthem; We the Living*

Jean Rhys: *Wide Sargasso Sea*

Salman Rushdie: *The Satanic Verses; Midnight's Children*

J. D. Salinger: *The Catcher in the Rye*

Mary Wollstonecraft Shelley: *Frankenstein*

Muriel Spark: *The Prime of Miss Jean Brodie*

John Steinbeck: *The Grapes of Wrath*

William Styron: *Sophie's Choice*

Jonathan Swift: *Gulliver's Travels*

J. R. R. Tolkein: *The Hobbit; The Lord of the Rings*

Mark Twain: *Tom Sawyer; The Adventures of Huckleberry Finn*

Kurt Vonnegut: *Slaughterhouse Five*

Alice Walker: *The Color Purple*

Evelyn Waugh: *A Handful of Dust*

Edith Wharton: *The Age of Innocence; Ethan Frome; The House of Mirth*

Oscar Wilde: *The Picture of Dorian Gray*

Thornton Wilder: *The Bridge of San Luis Rey*

Virginia Woolf: *To the Lighthouse*

Richard Wright: *Native Son*

Must-Read Nonfiction

You will most likely choose to read nonfiction subjects that interest you, but here is a list of writers whom many other people have read as well. If you choose to read any of these books, you will definitely become a more well-rounded reader.

Meyer Howard Abrams: *The Mirror and the Lamp*

Stephen E. Ambrose: *Undaunted Courage: Meriwether Lewis, Thomas Jefferson and the Opening of the American West*

Henry Adams: *The Education of Henry Adams*

James Baldwin: *Notes of a Native Son*

Isaiah Berlin: *The Proper Study of Mankind*

John Berger: *Ways of Seeing*

Rachel Carson: *Silent Spring*

Kenneth Clark: *Civilisation: A Personal View*

Robert Coles: *Children of Crisis*

John Dewey: *Philosophy and Civilization*

Isak Dinesen: *Out of Africa*

W. E. B. Du Bois: *The Souls of Black Folk*

Albert Einstein: *Relativity; Ideas and Opinions*

T. S. Eliot: *Selected Essays, 1917–1932*

Richard Phillips Feynman: *Six Easy Pieces*

Shelby Foote: *The Civil War*

E. M. Forster: *Aspects of the Novel*

Anne Frank: *The Diary of a Young Girl*

James Frazer: *The Golden Bough*

Sigmund Freud: *The Interpretation of Dreams*

Northrop Frye: *Anatomy of Criticism*

John Kenneth Galbraith: *The Affluent Society*

Peter Gay: *Freud, A Life for Our Time*

Brian Greene: *The Fabric of the Cosmos: Space, Time, and the Texture of Reality; The Elegant Universe: Superstrings, Hidden Dimensions, and the Quest for the Ultimate Theory*

Stephen J. Gould: *The Mismeasure of Man*

Robert Graves: *The White Goddess; Goodbye to All That*

Ernest H. Gombrich: *Art and Illusion*

Alex Haley and Malcolm X: *The Autobiography of Malcolm X*

Stephen Hawking: *A Brief History of Time*

Bert Hoelldobler and Edward O. Wilson: *The Ants*

Martin Luther King, Jr.: *Why We Can't Wait*

William James: *The Varieties of Religious Experience*

John Maynard Keynes: *The General Theory of Employment, Interest, and Money*

Anne Lamott: *Operating Instructions*

Tibor Machan: Classical Individualism: *The Supreme Importance of Each Human Being*

James M. McPherson: *Battle Cry of Freedom*

Peter B. Medawar: *The Art of the Soluble*

H. L. Mencken: *The American Language*

G. E. Moore: *Principia Ethica*

Gunnar Myrdal: *An American Dilemma*

Vladimir Nabokov: *Speak Memory*

Joseph Needham: *Science and Civilization in China*

Reinhold Niebuhr: *The Nature and Destiny of Man*

George Orwell: *Homage to Catalonia*

Elaine Pagels: *The Gnostic Gospels*

Vernon Louis Parrington: *Main Currents in American Thought*

Milman Parry: *The Making of Homeric Verse*

Leonard Peikoff: *Objectivism: The Philosophy of Ayn Rand*

Richard Pipes: *The Russian Revolution*

Ayn Rand: *The Virtue of Selfishness*

John Rawls: *A Theory of Justice*

Richard Rhodes: *The Making of the Atomic Bomb*

Arthur Schlesinger, Jr.: *The Age of Jackson*

Dava Sobel: *Longitude*

Aleksandr I. Solzhenitsyn: *The Gulag Archipelago*

Gertrude Stein: *The Autobiography of Alice B. Toklas*

Lytton Strachey: *Eminent Victorians*

William Styron: *Darkness Visible*

Lewis Thomas: *The Lives of a Cell*

D'Arcy Thompson: *On Growth and Form*

E. P. Thompson: *The Making of the English Working Class*

Arnold J. Toynbee: *A Study of History*

Lionel Trilling: *The Liberal Imagination*

Barbara Tuchman: *The Guns of August*

Frederick Jackson Turner: *The Frontier in American History*

Mark Twain: *The Autobiography of Mark Twain*

Paul Twitchell: *The Flute of God*

Jude Wanniski: *The Way the World Works*

Booker T. Washington: *Up from Slavery*

James D. Watson: *The Double Helix*

Alfred North Whitehead and Bertrand Russell: *Principia Mathematica*

William Carlos Williams: *In the American Grain*

Edmund Wilson: *To the Finland Station*

Tobias Wolff: *This Boy's Life*

Virginia Woolf: *A Room of One's Own*

Richard Wright: *Black Boy*

Francis A. Yates: *The Art of Memory*

W. B. Yeats: *Autobiographies*

Short Stories

This list contains some of the greatest shortest stories of all time and some that are just beautifully written and well worth reading—even if only for pleasure.

Sherwood Anderson: *The Other Woman; Hands; The Man in the Brown Coat*

Honore de Balzac: *The Brothers-in-Arms; The False Courtesan*

Saul Bellow: *Seize the Day; A Silver Dish*

Truman Capote: *Miriam*

Willa Cather: *Double Birthday*

Anton Chekhov: *The Lady with the Dog; The Kiss; About Love*

John Cheever: *The Country Husband*

Kate Chopin: *A Respectable Woman*

Joseph Conrad: *The Secret Sharer; The Lagoon*

William Faulkner: *That Evening Sun*

Edna Ferber: *What She Wore; The Kitchen Side of the Door*

F. Scott Fitzgerald: *Crazy Sunday*

Susan Glaspell: *A Jury of Her Peers*

Maxim Gorky: *The Birth of a Man; The Dead Man*

Ernest Hemingway: *The Killers*

Nathaniel Hawthorne: *Rappaccini's Daughter; Young Goodman Brown*

O. Henry (William Sydney Porter): *The Gift of the Magi; The World and the Door; The Ransom of Red Chief*

Henry James: *Daisy Miller: A Study; The Real Thing*

Franz Kafka: *The Metamorphosis; A Hunger Artist*

Rudyard Kipling: *Beyond the Pale; Cupid's Arrows*

D. H. Lawrence: *The Fox*

Mary Lerner: *Little Selves*

Thomas Mann: *Tonio Kröger*

Carson McCullers: *The Ballad of the Sad Café*

Herman Melville: *Bartleby the Scrivener*

Joyce Carol Oates: *Where Are You Going, Where Have You Been?*

Flannery O'Connor: *Greenleaf*

Dorothy Parker: *You Were Perfectly Fine; Here We Are*

Edgar Allan Poe: *Ligeia; The Fall of the House of Usher; The Tell-Tale Heart; The Pit and the Pendulum*

Katherine Anne Porter: *Pale Horse, Pale Rider; Theft*

Annie Proulx: *The Skinned Steer*

Benjamin Rosenblatt: *Zelig*

Philip Roth: *Defender of the Faith*

Susan Sontag: *The Way We Live Now*

James Thurber: *The Secret Life of Walter Mitty*

Mark Twain: *The Notorious Jumping Frog of Calaveras County; The Mysterious Stranger*

John Updike: *Gesturing*

Robert Penn Warren: *Christmas Gift*

Eudora Welty: *The Hitch-Hikers*

Edith Wharton: *The Descent of Man; The Letter*

E. B. White: *The Second Tree From the Corner*

Tennessee Williams: *The Resemblance Between a Violin Case and a Coffin*

Richard Wright: *The Man Who Lived Underground*

Poets

It is hard to pinpoint what poems you should read on this list of poets because there are so many poems that are wonderful. It's a good idea to pick up a book containing a collection of poems and decide for yourself. You can be sure that the most notable works of these poets will be contained in any anthology or collection of their poems.

Maya Angelou

W. H. Auden

William Blake

Robert Browning

Elizabeth Barrett Browning

Joseph Brodsky

Gwendolyn Brooks

Robert Burns

Lord Byron

Samuel Taylor Coleridge

e. e. cummings

James Dickey

Emily Dickinson

John Donne

Rita Dove

T. S. Eliot

Robert Frost

Allen Ginsberg

Thomas Hardy

Langston Hughes

James Joyce

John Keats

Philip Larkin

Henry Wadsworth Longfellow

Amy Lowell

Robert Lowell

Christopher Marlowe

Marianne Moore

Thomas Moore

Pablo Neruda

Mary Oliver

Sir Walter Raleigh

Rainer Maria Rilke

Christina Rossetti

Carl Sandburg

Sappho

Sir Walter Scott

Anne Sexton

William Shakespeare

Percy Bysshe Shelley

Edna St. Vincent Millay

Gertrude Stein

Robert Louis Stevenson

Mark Strand

Alfred, Lord Tennyson

Dylan Thomas

Robert Penn Warren

Walt Whitman

Oscar Wilde

William Carlos Williams

William Wordsworth

William Butler Yeats

Plays

From ancient Greek dramatists to modern-day playwrights, here's a list of some classic plays—and some that are just plain fun.

Aeschylus: *Agamemnon; Prometheus Bound*

Aristophanes: *The Birds; The Clouds; The Wasps; Lysistrata*

Edward Albee: *Who's Afraid of Virginia Woolf?*

Samuel Beckett: *Waiting for Godot*

Albert Camus: *Caligula*

Anton Chekhov: *The Cherry Orchard; The Three Sisters; Uncle Vanya; The Seagull*

Noel Coward: *Blithe Spirit; Hay Fever; Private Lives*

Margaret Edson: *Wit*

Eve Ensler: *The Vagina Monologues*

Euripides: *The Cyclops; Medea; Electra*

Johann Wolfgang von Goethe: *Faust: A Tragedy*

Lillian Hellman: *The Little Foxes; The Children's Hour*

Henrik Ibsen: *Peer Gynt; A Doll's House; Hedda Gabler*

William Inge: *Picnic; Bus Stop*

Eugene Ionesco: *The Bald Prima Donna; The Lesson; Rhinoceros*

Ben Johnson: *The Alchemist; Bartholomew Fair*

D. H. Lawrence: *The Daughter-in-Law; David*

David Mamet: *Glengarry Glen Ross; Speed the Plow; Oleanna; American Buffalo*

Christopher Marlowe: *Tamburlaine; The Jew of Malta; Doctor Faustus*

Arthur Miller: *The Crucible; All My Sons; Death of a Salesman; A View from the Bridge; After the Fall*

Molière: *The Misanthrope; Tartuffe*

Joyce Carol Oates: *Friday Night; Greensleeves*

Eugene O'Neill: *The Iceman Cometh; Long Day's Journey into Night; Desire Under the Elms; Mourning Becomes Electra*

Harold Pinter: *The Room; A Slight Ache; The Birthday Party*

Willy Russell: *Educating Rita; Shirley Valentine*

Jean Paul Sartre: *No Exit*

William Shakespeare: *Macbeth; A Midsummer Night's Dream; Hamlet; Romeo and Juliet; King Lear; Henry V; Othello; Richard III; The Merchant of Venice; Twelfth Night*

George Bernard Shaw: *Arms and the Man; Mrs. Warren's Profession; Man and Superman; Pygmalion; Heartbreak House; Saint Joan; Major Barbar*a

Sam Shepard: *Fool for Love; Buried Child; La Turista; True West*

Neil Simon: *Barefoot in the Park; The Odd Couple; Sweet Charity; The Sunshine Boys; California Suite; Lost in Yonkers*

Sophocles: *Antigone; Oedipus Trilogy; Electra*

Tom Stoppard: *Aracadia; The Real Thing; Night & Day; Indian Ink; Hapgood*

August Strindberg: *Miss Julie; A Dream Play; The Father*

Wendy Wasserstein: *The Heidi Chronicles; Uncommon Women and Others*

Oscar Wilde: *An Ideal Husband; A Woman of No Importance; The Importance of Being Earnest*

Thornton Wilder: *Our Town*

Lanford Wilson: *Balm in Gilead*

Tennessee Williams: *Cat on a Hot Tin Roof; The Glass Menagerie; A Streetcar Named Desire*

Herman Wouk: *The Caine Mutiny Court-Martial*

Gore Vidal: *The Best Man*

Modern Fiction Favorites

Many of the books on this list (and the following nonfiction list) are popular books you may see on current book club lists and on bestseller lists in the newspapers or at bookstores. Whether or not these books attain the kind of fame that makes classic literature remains to be seen, but these books will likely remain imprinted on the minds of readers for years to come.

Mitch Albom: *The Five People You Meet in Heaven*

Isabelle Allende: *Daughter of Fortune*

Margaret Atwood: *Cat's Eye; Alias Grace*

Dan Brown: *The Da Vinci Code*

Douglas Coupland: *Generation X*

Jeffrey Eugenides: *Middlesex; The Virgin Suicides*

Helen Fielding: *Bridget Jones's Diary: A Novel*

Janet Fitch: *White Oleander*

Joy Fowler: *The Jane Austen Book Club*

Jonathan Franzen: *The Corrections*

Ernest J. Gaines: *A Lesson Before Dying*

Arthur Golden: *Memoirs of a Geisha*

David Guterson: *Snow Falling on Cedars*

Mark Haddon: *The Curious Incident of the Dog in the Night-Time*

Jane Hamilton: *The Book of Ruth*

Ursula Hegi: *Stones from the River; Visions of Emma Blau; Floating in My Mother's Palm*

John Irving: *The Fourth Hand*

Susan Kaysen: *Girl, Interrupted*

Sue Monk Kidd: *The Secret Life of Bees*

Barbara Kingsolver: *The Poisonwood Bible*

Wally Lamb: *She's Come Undone; I Know This Much Is True*

Yan Martel: *Life of Pi*

Toni Morrison: *Sula; Paradise; The Bluest Eye; Song of Solomon*

Ann-Marie MacDonald: *Fall on Your Knees*

Alice Munro: *Runaway (Stories)*

Joyce Carol Oates: *The Falls; We Were the Mulvaneys*

Alan Paton: *Cry, the Beloved Country*

Annie Proulx: *The Shipping News*

Philip Roth: *The Plot Against America*

J. K. Rowling: The *Harry Potter* series

Bernhard Schlink: *The Reader*

Alice Sebold: *The Lovely Bones*

Carol Shields: *The Stone Diaries*

Anita Shreve: *The Pilot's Wife*

Tom Wolfe: *I Am Charlotte Simmons*

Modern Nonfiction Favorites

Mitch Albom: *Tuesdays with Morrie: An Old Man, a Young Man, and Life's Greatest Lesson*

Lance Armstrong and Sally Jenkins: *It's Not About the Bike: My Journey Back to Life*

Harold Bloom: *Shakespeare: The Invention of the Human; The Best Poems of the English Language: From Chaucer Through Frost; Genius: A Mosaic of One Hundred Exemplary Creative Minds*

Augustine Burroughs: *Running with Scissors: A Memoir*

Bill Clinton: *My Life*

Hillary Rodham Clinton: *Living History*

Katie Couric: *Tales from the Bed: On Living, Dying, and Having it All*

Dave Eggers: *A Heartbreaking Work of Staggering Genius: A Memoir on a True Story*

Joseph Ellis: *His Excellency: George Washington; Founding Brothers: The Revolutionary Generation*

Harold Evans: *They Made America: Two Centuries of Innovators from the Steam Engine to the Search Engine*

Gabriel García Márquez: *Living to Tell the Tale*

Barbara Goldsmith: *Obsessive Genius: The Inner World of Marie Curie (Great Discoveries)*

Katharine Graham: *Personal History*

Temple Grandin: *Thinking in Pictures: and Other Reports from My Life with Austism*

Stephen Greenblatt: *Will in the World: How Shakespeare Became Shakespeare*

Ernesto Che Guevara: *The Motorcycle Diaries: A Latin Journey*

Kay Bailey Hutchison: *American Heroines: The Spirited Women Who Shaped Our Country*

Walter Isaacson: *Benjamin Franklin: An American Life*

Robert T. Kiyosaki and Sharon L. Lechter: *Rich Dad, Poor Dad: What the Rich Teach Their Kids About Money—That the Poor and Middle Class Do Not!*

Frank McCourt: *Angela's Ashes; 'Tis*

Azar Nafisi: *Reading Lolita in Tehran: A Memoir in Books*

Barack Obama: *Dreams from My Father: A Story of Race and Inheritance*

Robert Pirsig: *Zen and the Art of Motorcycle Maintenance: An Inquiry into Values*

Cokie Roberts: *Founding Mothers: The Women Who Raised Our Nation*

Dava Sobel: *Galileo's Daughter: A Historical Memoir of Science, Faith, and Love*

Donald Trump: *The Art of the Deal*

Lynne Truss: *Eats, Shoots & Leaves: The Zero Tolerance Approach to Punctuation*

Gloria Vanderbilt: *It Seemed Important at the Time: A Romance Memoir*

Glossary

active reading   Reading with the intention of analyzing the text. Having an awareness of the material that allows you to make connections both to your own ideas and feelings and to other works of literature.

allegory   An extended narrative in prose or verse in which characters, events, and settings represent abstract qualities and in which the writer intends a second meaning to read beneath the surface story. The underlying meaning may be moral, religious, political, social, or satiric. The characters are usually personifications of such abstractions as greed, envy, fortitude, and courage.

alliteration   Repetition of consonant sounds for rhythmic effect (most often used in poetry).

analogy   A comparison of similar ideas, often for the purpose of using something familiar to explain something unfamiliar

analytical reading   The ability to read beneath the surface of the text while making connections between thoughts, concepts, and ideas.

antagonist   A prominent character that opposes the protagonist or hero or heroine in a dramatic or narrative work.

anthology   A book containing either various works of literature or specifically chosen literature of a given literary era or genre.

antithesis   A contrast or opposition in meaning, emphasized by a parallel in grammatical structure.

archetype   Elemental patterns of myth and ritual that recur in legends and ceremonials of the most diverse cultures.

argument   In the specialized literary sense, a brief summary of the plot or subject matter of a long poem or other work. In the case of a thesis, it is the discussion within the text that backs up the idea.

argumentation   A mode of writing, the purpose of which is to prove a point or to persuade the reader to accept a point of view.

assonance   The repetition of vowel sounds for rhythmic effect (most often used in poetry).

atmosphere   The tonality pervading a literary work, which sets expectations in the reader as to the course of events.

autobiography   A life story written by the subject about him- or herself.

ballad   A story told in verse form with a consistent rhyming pattern.

ballade   A narrative poem consisting of three eight-line stanzas with a specific rhyming pattern.

Bildungsroman   A German term signifying a coming-of-age story or story of growth.

biography   A relatively full account of a person's life, involving the attempt to establish the person's character, temperament, place, time situations, experiences, and activities.

blank verse   Consists of lines of iambic pentameter that do not rhyme.

caricature   Descriptive writing that exaggerates specific features of appearance or personality, usually for comic effect.

character   A person in a narrative or dramatic work.

characterization   Representation of persons in narrative and dramatic works or a prose sketch briefly describing a recognizable type of person.

cinquain   A poem that adheres to a rhythm involving a certain number of syllables per line.

closed couplet   A pair of rhymed lines of poetry in which thought and grammatical structure are complete.

closed form Poetry that adheres to a specific poetic structure.

comedy Any literary work that aims to amuse by dealing with humorous, familiar situations involving ordinary people speaking everyday language.

comic relief The use of humor to break the tension within the text. Used most often in plays and prose fiction.

concrete and **abstract** In traditional philosophy a *concrete term* is defined as a word that denotes a particular person or thing; and an *abstract term* is defined as a word, such as *brightness, beauty, evil, despair,* which denotes qualities that do not exist except as attributes of particular persons or things.

conflict The struggle between opposing forces that determines the action in drama and most narrative fiction.

content Refers to what is said in a literary work, as opposed to how it is said.

context Parts of a text preceding and following any particular passage.

couplet Rhyming verse lines, usually of the same length.

critical reading The ability to read analytically, examining literature by looking beneath the surface of the text. The ability to make connections between thoughts, concepts, ideas, and emotions, and in some cases applying them to yourself or the world around you.

criticism The reasoned discussion of literary works; also a branch of study concerned with defining, classifying, expounding, and evaluating works of literature.

critique A considered assessment of a literary work, usually in the form of an essay or review. In philosophy, politics, and the social sciences, a critique is a systematic inquiry into the nature of some principle, idea institution, or ideology, usually devoted to revealing any kinds of limits or self-contradictions.

description The picturing in words of people, places, and activities through detailed observations of color, sound, smell, touch, and motion.

deus ex machina Any forced or artificial device introduced by an author to solve some difficult problem.

dialect The version of a language spoken by people of a particular region or social group.

dialogue The conversation of two or more people as represented in writing, especially in plays, novels, short stories, and narrative poems.

diary (or **journal**)   An autobiographical day-to-day account of a person's life.

diction   Word choice.

discourse   Spoken or written language.

drama   A literary work written in dialogue to be performed before an audience by actors on a stage.

effect   The impression made by a work of literature.

elegy   A poem of mourning written in memory of one who has died.

emphasis   The stress placed on words or passages by highlighting their importance in some manner.

endnote   An explanation of a reference found within the text of the book and listed at the end of the book.

epic   A long narrative poem on a great and serious subject, related in an elevated style and centered on a heroic or quasi-divine figure on whose actions depends the fate of a tribe, a nation, or the human race.

essay   A brief composition in prose that undertakes to discuss a matter, express a point of view, or persuade us to accept a thesis on any subject.

exposition   The immediate or gradual revelation to the audience of the setting, relationship between characters, and other background information needed for understanding the plot. A systematic explanation of or argument about any subject; the opening part of a play or story.

fable   A short and fairly simple story designed to illustrate a moral lesson.

fantasy   A work that is set in an imaginary, unreal, or utopian world. Often referred to as imaginative literature.

farce   A type of comedy, primarily visual, that depends for laughs on outlandish situations, stereotyped characters, and exaggerated, sometimes abusive, physical action.

fiction   Any narrative that is feigned or invented rather than historically or factually true.

figurative language   Techniques used by the author to give the text more meaning and emotional impact.

figure of speech   Expressions such as metaphors, similes, and personifications that make comparisons or associations; meant to be taken imaginatively rather than actually.

first person point of view   The perspective assumed by a writer from which an "I" narrator experiences, sees, hears, and understands the story he or she is telling.

foot   A measured and patterned poetic rhythm involving accented and unaccented syllables.

footnote   An explanation of something (an idea, definition, or reference) found within the text, denoted by a number, asterisk, or other symbol and listed at the bottom of the page.

free verse   Poetry that does not follow any particular poetic structure, including the use of rhyme.

genre   A term taken from the French, used in literary criticism to signify a literary species, a literary form.

haiku   A poem originating in Japan that captures the essence of a moment in a simple image. A haiku is governed by a specific pattern of words and syllable use.

hero/heroine   The central character in a literary work.

historian   A person who studies historical people, places, and events.

historiography   The analysis of how history is researched and studied.

hyperbole   An exaggeration used to evoke strong emotion or opinion.

iamb   A specific poetic meter where a short syllable is followed by a long syllable.

iambic pentameter   A specific poetic meter where there are five groups of two syllables each per line (with the second syllable being stressed more than the first syllable).

imagery   Used to signify all the objects and qualities of sense perception referred to in a poem or other work of literature. A picture made out of words that can incorporate touch, smell, taste, and sensations of movement.

irony   The difference between what is asserted and what is true. Verbal irony is a statement in which implicit meaning intended by the speaker differs from that which is being asserted. Dramatic irony involves a situation in a play or a narrative in which the audience shares with the author knowledge of which a character is ignorant. There is also cosmic irony, romantic irony.

light verse   The use of ordinary speaking voice and a relaxed manner to treat its subjects in amusing ways, comically or whimsically or with good-natured satire.

limerick   A five-line poem with a rhyming pattern where the first, second, and fifth lines rhyme (this is referred to as trimeter) and the third and fourth lines rhyme (dimeter).

literary criticism   The practice of describing, interpreting, and evaluating literature.

literary devices   Techniques such as symbolism, metaphor, simile, hyperbole, and humor that are used by an author to help the reader discover deeper meanings.

lyric   A non-narrative poem presenting a single speaker who expresses a state of mind or a process of thought and feeling.

memoir   An autobiographical detailed accounting of a specific time in a person's life.

meter   The rhythm of a poem. A recognizable variable pattern. The beat of the stresses in the stream of sound.

metaphor   A figure of speech, an implied analog in which one thing is imaginatively compared to or identified with another, dissimilar idea or thought.

monologue   A theatrical device in which one character in a play speaks aloud for a relatively long period of time without interruption. This speech is addressed to either the audience or to other characters in the play.

narrator   The teller of a story or other narrative.

naturalism   A philosophical era and literary term that identifies the mind, body, and spirit as having material origins. For example, the idea that love is caused by a chemical reaction in the brain would be considered a naturalist approach to the understanding of an emotion.

nonfiction   Literature based on fact, not fiction.

nonsense verse   Silly poems using real or nonsense words, usually in a particular rhyming pattern and usually written for children.

novel   Refers to a variety of writings that are extended works of prose fiction. There are sociological, historical, and regional novels.

novella   A short prose narrative or tale, about the length of a long short story, that usually presents a single, major incident rather than a series of events as in the novel.

objectivity   The detached, impersonal presentation of situations and of characters and their thoughts and feelings.

ode   A long lyric poem written in an elevated style with an elaborate stanzaic structure.

omniscient point of view   The point of view from an author who in a godlike way reveals all.

parable   A short tale illustrating a moral lesson.

passive reading   The act of reading without absorbing the text. Skimming is a form of passive reading, as is reading without analytical interpretation.

perspective   Looking at people, places, and/or events from different angles, allowing you to consider different interpretations or points of view.

philosophy   Ideas that take on a greater worldview. There are personal philosophies and philosophies that grow into larger and more global movements of thought.

play   A literary work written in dialogue and intended to be performed.

playwright   A person who writes scripts for the theater.

plot   The careful arrangement by an author of incidents in a narrative to achieve a desired effect.

poetic license   Writing that strays from a specific conventional style or structure.

poetry   Literature in its most intense, imaginative, and rhythmic form. It is intended to be a speaking picture that teaches and delights.

point of view   The vantage point, or stance, from which a story is told.

prose   All forms of ordinary writing and speech.

protagonist   The main character who experiences change as the result of a resolved conflict in the plot.

quatrain   One stanza of verse containing four lines that either may or may not rhyme.

realism   Accuracy in the portrayal of life or reality. Also the name of a literary movement.

rhetoric   A fictional representation of human beings thinking, feeling, acting, interacting.

rhyme   The similarity of sound between two words.

rhythm   The patterned flow of sound in poetry and prose.

rondeau   Poetry divided into stanzas: the first containing five lines, followed by three lines, then another five lines. The poem is structured around 2 main rhymes and consists of 13 lines of 8 or 10 syllables each.

sarcasm   A harsh and sometimes humorous commentary about someone or something.

satire   Blends ironic humor and wit with criticism, ridiculing something, usually the whole range of human frailties in individuals and institutions. Satire differs from comedy in that satire seeks to correct, improve, or reform through ridicule, whereas comedy aims to amuse.

science fiction   Futuristic literature. The settings, plots, characters, and themes are usually based on some kind of scientific or technological developments, actual or that are in the works or imagined.

second person point of view   When the author directs the narrative as though speaking to a person using "you" instead of he, she, it, or I.

setting   The setting of a narrative or dramatic work in a general locale and in a historical time in which its action occurs.

short story   A short work of prose fiction containing as few as 500 words and as many as 20,000 words.

simile   A figure of speech that uses *like*, *as*, or *as if* to compare two essentially different objects, actions, or attributes that share some common aspects.

sonnet   A 14-line lyric poem in iambic pentameter. Often a love poem.

stanza   Italian for "stopping place." Refers to a grouping of verse lines in a poem.

stereotype   A character who represents a trait generally attributed to a social or racial group and lacks credibility because the character lacks the reality of individualized qualities.

style   A writer's characteristic way of saying things, based on his or her arrangement of ideas, word choice, imagery, sentence structure, variety, rhythm, repetition, coherence, emphasis, unity, and tone.

subjectivity   Emphasis in writing on the expression of the writer's feelings and personal opinions. Also the way you emotionally relate to a piece of writing.

symbol   Anything that signifies something else. For example, a storm may signify anger, a tree may signify life, autumn may signify aging, and so on.

syntopical reading   Reading two or more pieces of literature based on the same subject in order to gain perspective.

theme   The underlying meaning of a story. A novel can consist of several different themes, while a short story focuses on one central theme.

third person point of view   Telling the story from the point of view of a character that exists outside the action of the story as the narrator of events.

tragedy   A serious work of fiction that presents the downfall of its protagonist.

transcendentalism   A philosophical and literary movement flourishing between 1835 and 1860 in New England. The idealistic philosophy of human nature stood in opposition to the pessimism of Puritan Calvinism.

verse   A synonym for poetry.

Taking Notes on Reading Material

Use the following templates to take notes for each work of fiction or non-fiction you read. Make several copies of both of these templates so that you always have a supply as you read new books.

Fiction

Name of Book: _____

Author: _____

Date Read: _____

Major Theme: _____

_____

Minor Themes: _____

_____

Major Characters and Their Relationships: _____

_____

_____

Protagonist: _____

Antagonist: _____

Conflict: _____

_____

_____

Climax: _____

_____

_____

Summary of Plot: _____

_____

_____

Summary of Subplots: _____

_____

_____

Major Metaphors: _____

_____

_____

Significant Symbols: _____

_____

_____

Favorite Lines from the Work: _____

_____

_____

_____

_____

_____

Personal Reflections: _____

_____

_____

_____

_____

_____

_____

_____

_____

_____

Nonfiction

Name of Book: _____

Author: _____

Date Read: _____

Type of Nonfiction Literature (essay, biography, journalism, etc.) _____

Major Theme: _____

_____

Minor Themes: _____

_____

Subjective References: _____

_____

_____

Objective References: _____

_____

_____

Theory: _____

_____

_____

Argument: _____

_____

_____

Conclusion: _____

_____

_____

_____

Personal Reflections: _____

_____

_____

_____

_____

_____

_____

_____

_____

_____

Index

G

H

literary tools, 82
Little Commentary, 178
logical philosophy, 192
lyric poetry, 23, 127

M

magazines, 38-39, 210
  advertisements, 211
  cover stories, 211
  current events, 213
  editorial pages, 204
  Letters to the Editor, 203
  reading, 212
  responsibility, 210
  skimming, 211
  tabloids, 212
magical realism, 112
main characters, 142
Malory, Sir Thomas, 232-233
Marxism, 189, 192
meanings of writings, 64
Melville, Herman, 80
The Membership of the Massachusetts Bay General Court 1630–1686, 168
memoirs, 201
  author's purpose, 203
  compared to
    autobiographies, 36
    essays, 195
  defined, 35
  nonfamous, 201
  point of view, 202
  putting on paper, 201
messages of authors, 236-237
metaphor, 9, 110
  allegories, 80
  defined, 83, 108
  The Scarlet Letter, 70
  superstition as, 114-115
meter, 121

Miller, Arthur, 157
Moby-Dick, 80
Mommie Dearest, 56
monologue, 152
mood, 240, 243
moral philosophy, 192
motives of authors
  Bradley, 234
  Malory, 232
  Tennyson, 233
movements of philosophy, 188-189
Mrs. Dalloway, 83
multiple authors on subjects, 236-237
My Thirteenth Winter: A Memoir, 201
mysticism, 188
mythical references, 113-114

N

names of characters, 110
nanotechnology, 180
narrators
  as characters, 96
  reliability, 96-99
  tense/tone, 99-100
  voice, 16, 247-249
naturalism, 188, 191
newspapers, 38-39, 207
  current events, 213
  editorial pages, 204
  feature stories, 209
  five W's, 210
  front pages, 208
  leads, 210
  Letters to the Editor, 203
  sections, 208
  structures, 208-209
Newton, Sir Isaac, 179

nonfiction
  asking questions, 58-60
  editorial pages, 204
  essays, 196
    author's purpose, 203
    compared to memoirs, 195
    diction, 197-198
    editorial pages, 204
    Letters to the Editor, 203
    point of view, 202
    reading, 198-200
    scholarly, 196-197
    themes, 200
  fact versus fiction, 59-60
  genres, 20-21, 32
    autobiographies, 21
    biographies, 21
    essays, 21
    practical, 32
    theoretical. *See* theoretical nonfiction
  inspecting, 46-48
  journalism, 38
    current events, 213
    editorial pages, 204
    good reporting, 264-265
    healthy skepticism, 207
    Internet, 39
    Letters to the Editor, 203
    objectivity, 261-262
    people's right to know, 206, 262-264
    responsibility, 206
    sources, 207
  Letters to the Editor, 203
  magazines
    advertisements, 211
    cover stories, 211

plot, 8, 102
  action, 103
  background, 103
  climax, 104
  conclusion, 104
  conflict, 104
  dénouement, 104
  movement, 103
Poe, Edgar Allan, 144-146
The Poet, 132
poetic license, 169
poetry, 20, 120-121
  forms, 130
  free verse, 132-135
  perfect fit, 136-137
  poet's purpose, 131-132
  rhythms, 122-123
  structures, 130
  terminology, 121-122
  twists, 135-136
  types, 123
    ballad, 123
    cinquain, 124
    elegy, 124
    epic, 125
    haiku, 125-126
    identifying, 245-247
    limerick, 126
    lyric, 127
    nonsense verse, 127
    ode, 128
    quatrain, 129
    rondeau, 129
    sonnet, 130
point of view
  essays, 202
  memoirs, 202
  narrative voice identification, 247-249
  novels, 92-93
    dialogue, 94-95
    exceptions, 93
    narrators, 96

popular science, 181
practical nonfiction, 32
pragmatism, 189
preferred readings for plays, 153
primary research materials, 223
progressive thinking, 230-231
prose, 20
protagonist, 94

Q-R

quatrain, 129
questions
  asking, 58-60
  philosophical, 186-188

rationalism, 189
readers
  grabbing their attention, 48
  relationships with authors, 17
  responses, 65-66
    emotional, 67
    gray areas, 69
    intellectual, 68-69
    personal beliefs/ experiences, 69
    subjective, 67
reading comprehension, 223
references
  myths/religion, 113-114
  nonfiction, 47-48
regional themes, 88
relationships between authors and readers, 17
religious references, 113-114
reporting in journalism, 264-265

research papers
  researching, 223
  writing, 224-225
    bibliographies, 225
    conclusions, 225
    footnotes/endnotes, 225-226
    introductions, 224
    plagiarism, 226
    text, 224
research systems of libraries
  card catalogue system, 219
  Dewey Decimal System of Classification, 219-220
  Internet database, 220-222
  librarians, 219
researching history, 167
resolutions, 104
responses of readers, 65-66
  emotional, 67
  gray areas, 69
  intellectual, 68-69
  personal beliefs/ experiences, 69
  subjective, 67
responsibility
  journalism, 206
  magazines, 210
rhetoric in historical books, 173-174
rhythms in poetry, 122-123
right to know, 262-264
rising action, 8
rondeau, 129

S

The Scarlet Letter, 43
  character analysis, 240-241
  mood, 240-243
scholarly essays, 196-197

Check Out These
Best-Selling
COMPLETE IDIOT'S GUIDES®

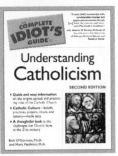

Understanding Catholicism
SECOND EDITION

Bob O'Gorman, Ph.D. and Mary Faulkner, M.A.

1-59257-085-2
$18.95

Learning Spanish
THIRD EDITION

Gail Stein

0-02-864451-4
$18.95

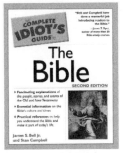

The Bible
SECOND EDITION

James S. Bell Jr. and Sean Campbell

0-02-864382-8
$18.95

Being a Groom
SECOND EDITION

Jennifer Lata Rung and Mark Rung

0-02-864456-5
$9.95

Grammar and Style
SECOND EDITION

Laurie E. Rozakis, Ph.D.

1-59257-115-8
$16.95

Playing the Guitar
SECOND EDITION

Frederick Noad

0-02-864244-9
$21.95 w/CD

Personal Finance in Your 20s & 30s
SECOND EDITION

Sarah Young Fisher and Susan Shelly

0-02-864374-7
$19.95

Knitting and Crocheting
SECOND EDITION
Illustrated

Barbara Breiter and Gail Diven

1-59257-089-5
$16.95

The Perfect Resume
THIRD EDITION

Susan Ireland

0-02-864440-9
$14.95

Buying and Selling a Home
FOURTH EDITION

Shelley O'Hara and Nancy D. Lewis

1-59257-120-4
$18.95

Low-Carb Meals

Lucy Beale and Sandy G. Couvillon, M.S., L.D.N., R.D.

1-59257-180-8
$18.95

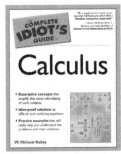

Calculus

W. Michael Kelley

0-02-864365-8
$18.95

More than *450 titles* in *30 different categories*
Available at booksellers everywhere

ALPHA